*T*he *S*overeign *D*emocratic *M*ajority

Reconquering the American Frontier

CP McCollum

—

Dedication

This book is dedicated to my 23 year old son Michael. He and his generation are just beginning their lives. They will either suffer by the events that unfold over the next several years to decades, or they will determine to become the architects of their own future, and so undertake the necessary steps to reclaim their lives, their rights, and their nation. The people of his generation are not deserving of the current state of the nation, and the world they stand to inherit. Like it or not, they will inherit the mess; the absolute disaster that America has become, to make of it what they will. It is my sincere hope that the philosophy presented here can impart to him and his generation insight for moving their world back onto the course of liberty, which respects the sovereign rights of the common people, and away from the current course, which left unchecked leads to profound oppression and economic disaster.

— CP McCollum

CHAPTER ONE
Introduction

About Me

My name is CP McCollum. I have a background in Engineering and technology, having practiced electrical engineering (electronic design) for about 2 decades. I have discovered I have competency in inventing, originating more than 100 different inventions which have resulted in 8 patents to date. For the vast number of these inventions I have yet to file patents for lack of time and money. Recently I did considerable soul searching and decided to write down many of my thoughts; compiling an extensive series of observations, views, conjectures, notes, intuition, etc., finally culminating in several books spanning a number of genres and subjects of interest to me involving mostly technology, politics, economics, and history; boring subjects indeed. However, as I have discovered, the reason for my interest is that these *'boring subjects'* greatly affect me, my family and most everybody I know. So this is about me, what I am about, and what I believe.

I mention the engineering and inventing to make the point that what I really do best can be summed up as problem-solving. That is important because what I have observed in this time of trouble is that we as a nation and a people have grown to become exceptional among all nations and people, but like with the decline of an empire we are encountering serious problems and facing complete failure. It is my view that problems are really opportunities in their distressed state. In other words we have angst and distress but these are really growing pains and like any organism as it grows from infancy to adulthood, it metamorphoses but not without significant pain. The trick is to understand the process and plan for a desirable outcome. This is where I think that I can help because I realized I have a unique ability to make observations that others do not, and improvise sound solutions others do not see, thus my talent for invention.

Why I wrote this book! It is the culmination of thought and frustration over what I have seen approaching for many years. In 1992 I joined the John Birch Society which significantly changed my view of the world. Up until then I considered myself very right-wing and conservative politically but found the messages from the republican party significantly duplicitous, and being a seeker of truth, I wearied of making excuses for their failures. The Birch society gave me a view that filled-in many of the inconsistencies in the picture and I learned that the reality I was led to believe in, is not reality but something false and scripted, put before me and everyone else to shape our view of the world. The real world is quite different. I came to realize that most everything that we are told by the sources of information and instruction is false and designed to shape our thoughts and views to fit what someone else defines. I realized that the American public is not told much of the truth about anything. This idea is similar to the message in the movie '*The Matrix*', where reality for virtually everyone is computer generated and piped into our heads. It is not exactly like that, but in many ways the world we know is one which has been programmed.

The Christian Church, despite its own foibles and idiosyncrasies has been a considerable source of truth and vital instruction for successful civilization for two millennia, but it is increasingly being marginalized and pushed out of our lives and culture. The question is why? The answer is, the message of Christianity conflicts with the agenda of a small cabal of powerful people that believe they have the right and substance to usurp and define for the rest of us what truth is. They have emerged from the dark crevices they inhabit into the dominant mainstream of our culture due to apathy and our lack of understanding of what they represent. The good news is, the small group can really only do what they will to the extent that the rest of us do not object, or even approve of their actions. Simply put, this limits their power. If they had the power to enact on the balance of civilization, the schemes their sages and planners have concocted, they would already have done so. Since they have not, although they are patient and persistent, it does mean they are limited and it means we have considerably more power than we even know. I have witnessed a considerable move down the road toward their intrigue, but I am now sensing resistance by the masses and a considerable disgust with their prescribed course.

I am convinced that much of our ever accelerating, compounding, cascade of mounting problems stem from the lack of knowledge for dealing with the path on which we are being taken as we proceed into a new century in which we will need new ideas and new tools to manage new problems in the advance of our civilization. The churning of old knowledge will not get us very far, as old ways are not always useful with new problems. Some principles are universal and will always serve us, however, in the abstract the churning of old knowledge, meaning that we continue to hash over old ideas while looking for solutions to new problems in the process, is futile, it will not produce them, much as the churning of money does not create much in the way of new wealth or growth.

Throughout history, new solutions and new ways have always emerged to deal with new problems associated with advances in civilization. These often come by thinking, as they say, 'outside the box.' We have had to abandon those things we thought to be bedrock principles and ideals, and embrace the new and unfamiliar, however, what seems to be new may just be the rediscovery or new application of the old. Much of this comes by-way of thesis. Thesis is the putting forward of new ideas and proposals that have yet to be proven.

Much of what I have to say is thesis, and much is a return to the old time tested principles that are universal. Because of the nature of thesis, I have not taken the time to attempt to formally prove by conventional means much of what I have put forward. I have also not attempted to document or cite precedent. I instead rely on the intelligence and judgement of the reader to determine whether the ideas make sense and merit consideration. It is my intention to support the thesis as time permits, with the hope that some of it will have been deemed worthy of consideration.

About the Book

One or more definitions of groups referred to in the following and their names, needs to be created in order to make clear sense of the book; who is being talked about, or referred to and so forth. The first of these can be summed up and called by several names such as **'American v1.0'**, **'Original-American'**, **'Natural-American'**, etc.; all representing the people that founded the nation, who ventured into our land from Europe between about the early 17th century up until about the middle of the 19th century, and the first group to call themselves by the moniker, ***Americans***. These are the people that founded and built the nation. It is from these that ***Original-Americans*** descend. These should be distinguished from the similar sounding **'Native Americans'**, who are also called by the misnomer, 'Indians', and also founders of the nation from a much earlier time.

The next group we will call European Immigrants, or Euro-Americans, coming from about the mid 1800s to the 1920s. These are immigrants, but have been adopted into the pool of

Original Americans because they are basically the same group of people; they just arrived late.

Then there is a crossover group consisting of Euro-American immigrants that landed in established ports and cities but ventured into the hostile interior to carve it out. These were both founders and immigrants. We call them pioneers, frontiersmen, explorers, and so forth. They were key to founding and building the two thirds of the nation from the Appalachian mountains to the west coast.

There are other groups of various ethnic identity that I have chosen to leave out of this discussion because they played very minor roles in the founding and building of the nation. One group that I will mention are *Native-Americans* who are very much founders, just as much as anyone of European extraction. Indeed, they are the very reason that europeans were able to establish a foothold, although they also constituted a significant threat to the early prospects of foothold. They provided the Europeans significantly with the knowledge for survival in the land. They provided the native foods and taught the Europeans how to cultivate native crops to sustain themselves, and today the same foods developed by these people feed the entire world. They gave many names to places and the features of our nation, and they were treacherously treated, exploited, and cheated by the established republic. They deserve better and so do we.

Addressing a glaring misconception that has been pushed by narrow-interests through the mainstream media into the popular culture, the nation was not founded by immigrants but was founded by *founders*; the 2 groups are not the same. Founders ventured over with trepidation, having left everything and faced a very uncertain future. Upon arriving, they were faced with creating everything needed for survival and comfort from scratch. They had to adapt to survive. The had to hew shelter from the forest, cultivate and harvest crops for food, construct fortresses for protection against hostile tribes, fight-off the ravages of nature and many never knew if they would survive or ever see their families again. Many did not survive but succumbed to the hardship.

The earliest immigrants faced some of the same hardships, but for the most part, the bulk of what were later immigrants landed at various already established ports of entry and checked into a hotel with little lost sleep. During some periods they were offered employment as they left the boat and were welcomed into a growing nation that needed them to bring their talent and labor to help build it. While it may not seem like much of a distinction, there is a huge difference in terms of the status of these people and their offspring in the makeup and definition of the nation.

What does all this have to do with anything? There are founders and there are those that have realized the benefit of what the founders who went before them put together before they entered the land. It greatly distinguishes one set of attitudes, values, and views from a much different set, and it makes a great difference in the idea of 'rights.' I will discuss where we have gone off track based on the purposed misdirection and immense misconceptions about 'rights'; what they are and who has them, inorder to hopefully correct the perspective in the minds of those that are wondering what went wrong. These are powerful ideas and there is considerable power for change in correctly understanding them. Some will take great exception to what I have to say but that is ok. Even though those persons would benefit greatly by digesting the message, it is not for everyone.

The message of the book is primarily written to 3 distinct groups:

1) Anti New-World-Order / Anti-Globalists

2) Conservatives

3) Everyone else

The Anti-NWO movement is somewhat new but significant. It is growing faster than any other ideology due to the rapid move the nation has experienced going down the path of globalism. When I was growing up in the 1960s and '70s, and during the '80s as a young adult, the concept that we would be globally connected or dependent on foreign nations, or ruled by a global cabal of bureaucrats was nowhere on my radar, nor anyone that I knew. It was only in the '90s when I learned about it and what it meant; how it would affect our American lives in very negative ways, when I started to take notice and realize that there were not enough folks concerned enough to do anything about it.

Most did not want to hear about such things, I am guessing due to their skepticism that something like the *'New World Order'*, whatever that is, could ever happen here in *'A-Merca'*, and their perceived lack of ability to do anything about it. Now that we have made considerable moves down the road toward whatever the ultimate globalist role for America is, I am sensing a great deal of the necessary concern, but still have not seen much in the way of effective resistance or solution. The advent of the Tea Party is a great indicator of that concern, and a great hope, although in my view they are chasing up the wrong trees. There is considerable smoke and heat from the Tea Party crowd, but very little light.

Conservatives have traditionally appealed to a broad spectrum of people on principle and on an idealogical basis. They are the people who have traditionally been the guardians of the civilization for several generations, but like the Tea Party, they are blind to the actual cause and effect for what is moving the nation and the world down the dark path we are on. Conservatives have lost their way and are not able to persuade enough people of the virtue of their ideas, so they are a fading influence.

That is not to say that the Liberals or the Democrat Party are faring any better. In my view they are even more short-sighted than the conservatives, only really appealing to those who stand to personally benefit by the reckless initiatives of the party, driven by their equally reckless ideology. This book should appeal to conservatives because the message is a natural extension of what drives the conservative sentiment and thought, although it repudiates much of what is thought of as conservative virtue, but is really dead-ended and wishful thinking.

Others not yet having been trapped into subscribing to either of these ostensibly *'polar opposite'* aligned camps, or not wanting to commit to any particular political ideology can also benefit from the message of the book. The book does not have an ideological pitch, and does not attempt to persuade anyone that they should or should not adopt any particular view; it is more a practical invitation to learn about who we are and where we are going, describing an alternative destination to where the current path leads.

As for me, I was a conservative who went in the direction of the Anti-NWO, which only laid a foundation for my perspective. I do not subscribe to any particular ideology other than my own.

CHAPTER TWO
Something is Wrong

From Japan With Love

I grew up knowing the phrase *"We the people"*, and I had an idea what that meant, however, it really never seemed to live up to it or to fit what I thought it meant. I have since come to realize that when it was written into the constitution, it meant what I thought it did, but over time it has lost that meaning.

I mentioned my earlier days as a young engineer. What partially led me to pursue that field was the fact that as a young boy I was very curious about electronic components; I would collect them. I had drawers full of parts and pieces of old televisions, motors, electrical cords, and assorted junk, which I would experiment with by randomly wiring together large assemblies from many scavenged parts. To see what would happen, I would plug the creation into an electrical outlet to the chagrin of my parents. I grew up being affectionately called a 'wire-twister' by my father and older brother.

The advent of the electronics industry took place in the US and Europe, but mostly the US. I remember growing up with and seeing my first televisions, and transistor radios. As a career minded young man, I remember investigating the electronics industry as a possible college and career path, even though I really wanted to be a musician. I chose the

9

electronics and electrical engineering field because I thought it would probably provide a stable future for employment. With the advent of the microprocessor,[1] I remember dreaming about all the products to be invented and I was knowledgeable about the workings of digital and analog electronic components and the standards used for product development. In the mid to late '80s I went through a series of design engineering jobs, layoffs, and job hunting, as I realized that there were more of these jobs being sent overseas than were being retained or created here. This did not sit well with me. I saw my chosen and trained-for field being sent abroad wholesale. Something was wrong and it stunk.

I knew we had invented and developed virtually every aspect of modern scientific inquiry, laying the foundations for modern industry from the inception, going back for at least 500 years and accelerating with the invention of calculus[2] by Isaac Newton forward, to the entire world of technological development. I shrugged it off and made excuses figuring there must be enough to go around. Although, I began to see industries that I thought we would always lead in, being moved wholesale overseas. We, the European descended Americans along with Europe, having created the entire techno-industrial world in the last 500 years, are now witnessing what we created being taken away from us and sent to others. What the heck is going on? I began to notice the trend starting with the transistor radio imported from japan. The radio[3] and the transistor[4] were European and American inventions and the industry was well developed and

---

[1] Garrett AiResearch, MP944, 1968
Pico, Glenrothes Scotland, GI250, 1971
Texas Instrument, TMS 1000, 1971
[2] Isaac Newton, 1666
Gottfried Wilhelm Leibniz, 1675
[3] Guglielmo Marconi, 1897
Lee De Forest, 1906
Edwin Howard Armstrong, 1922, 1933
[4] John Bardeen, Walter Brattain, William Shockley, 1947

established here, yet the Japanese were soon outproducing us in our own field and selling them in our backyard.

Then I noticed the trend affecting the television industry, from American brand names like General Electric, Motorola (remember the Quasar Works in a Drawer), Magnavox, GE, Sylvania, Westinghouse, Philco, Packard Bell, Zenith and so on; all of those brands of televisions manufactured in America were suddenly no longer the brands carried in the stores. Instead it was strange foreign names like Panasonic, Sanyo, Sony, Matsushita, etc.; most were companies started in Japan after the second world war, courtesy of, and with the help of American business and Uncle Sam. Then it happened with automobiles; Ford/Mercury, General Motors along with Chevrolet and apple-pie, Oldsmobile, Pontiac, Buick, Cadillac, and Chrysler, Dodge, Plymouth; these were suddenly horrible junk, and we needed to start buying Datsun, Honda, Toyota, and Subaru. Even though I, and as far as I know, millions of other Americans were satisfied with their American 'junk', we were nevertheless admonished to do the right thing, shun American and buy the Japanese labels. We were supposed to punish our own bad selves, ostensibly for being lazy and cheap and cutting corners.

I remember in the 1980s always having had a preference for American made anything. I grew up in the 60s and 70s with virtually every manufactured product being made by Americans and was satisfied with quality and workmanship, but in the '80s I started hearing through saturation media campaigns how crappy American products were. Cars and so forth were junk while the japanese made perfect quality products. This did not compute for me because I had owned some Japanese made motorcycles as a kid in the '70s and my experience was they really were junk and did not compare with the stout American products. The same applied to the Japanese cars and anything that came from Japan. It was all common knowledge and considered junk.

In the late 70s and early 80s, the media started to beat the drum that we needed to be schooled on the quality of Japanese products versus American products. Clearly the Japanese products were 'superior.' I never bought into that subtle lie because my experience told me otherwise. Nonetheless, the media campaigns were successful and Americans tossed aside American 'junk' for the smarter, better designed, and sleeker, more fuel efficient Japanese products. The problem was that they were not all those things. It took them a long time and considerable capital from American wallets to improve even to the standards of their American counterparts which were suffering in quality due to the loss of market and other factors like gasoline shortages, timed to coincide with the media campaigns to convince Americans to switch.

To be fair, the Japanese have vastly improved the quality of their manufacturing and today make very high quality, world-class manufactured goods, but at the time, it was not evident to me and I dare say many others. The media propaganda campaign did work though with millions of amiable Americans buying into a false message, because eventually the common popular public opinion changed and it became a big deal to go out and buy the Japanese stuff and shun the American made products. American industry suffered tremendously as a result.

Today that same move has advanced to a point where virtually all of the American manufacturing, technology, and heavy industries have suffered some degree of decimation and wholesale movement to anywhere but America, with the average American buying into the myth about Americans not able to produce anything but junk. It is a myth and we are suckers for believing it. In America now, virtually all consumer manufactured goods are made overseas and quality has only diminished for a great deal of it. As stated, much coming from Japan today is of high quality but much from other parts of the globe including China is very substandard. But do American's have a choice in the matter? No we do not. Try to find a reasonably priced pair of comfortable shoes from a department store. I believe it is still possible but it will be a long and arduous search.

Now virtually every consumer product is made in foreign countries, mostly asian, and most of it truly is Junk with a capital J. The consumer crap we are able to purchase at retail outlets is made by people that may not even understand what it is they are manufacturing, and may never have the opportunity to use the product or anything like it. How can they make a quality product for the American market? The simple and obvious answer is they can not.

That is the sad state of things today. We are way underemployed in the industries we pioneered and not allowed to make adequate products for our own everyday use, while slaves in sweat shops on the other side of the world are expending their lives to make cheap crap to send to us. This equation is unbalanced and does not make sense.

To understand why things have gone this way, we must examine the *"follow the money"* line of inquiry and ask who it is that benefits from this arrangement? Who benefits? Is it all the links in the supply chain including the end user in the American marketplace, or is it the American worker who's fore-bearers pioneered the marketplace and the industry? Sadly the answer is no; the beneficiaries are only those who purchased the right to access the marketplace from those who brokered it, and some in the middle; large banks, investment houses; politicians; importers/exporters; shipping companies; and multinational corporations. Is it not time to, as they say, *'Cut out the middle men?'*

I bring this up to point out that there is something at work and has been for at least the last 150 years in which media mass conditioning in America and Europe has resulted in us being persuaded to abandon our own identity and past history as innovators and creators; the undisputed world leaders in scientific, industrial, technological, cultural, and economic development. We pioneered what the world does and uses today. We are the most adroit of any culture or race at science and technology and virtually all modern endeavors, which is evident by what we have done in the last millennia, having invented and created the entirety of the modern world. Most everything that affects the life of virtually every living soul on the planet has its origins in a laboratory or garage in the world of the European diaspora. That is something that shouts very loudly about who and what we are, what we have done, and what we can do and where we will continue to lead the world.

Why us? Why is it that we have this ability while the rest of the world seemingly does not? Well, first, does it really matter in the overall scheme of things? The fact is, we can do this as we have demonstrated and the rest of the world is a beneficiary. We can and we will continue to create fantastic technology and invent the future just as we have done with the world up to now. Other cultures may take exception to the characterization that white Europeans and Americans have innovated the modern world and will continue to do so, but we have demonstrated that fact while others have not; and we have done it miles ahead of the rest of the world.

In the '50s, '60s, and '70s we were millions of miles ahead of most other cultures around the globe in terms of technology which gave us a very high standard of living. However in the 9th through the 15th centuries, we Europeans were the 2nd world while Asians and cultures of the mid-east were miles ahead of the west. So things will ebb and flow. Europe did not just invent everything from scratch but borrowed a lot from others in the centuries leading up to the ascendancy of the west, however we accelerated discovery and innovation like no one in history before.

What does all that have to do with the current situation today? The point is, we demonstrated the ability to discover and create technology which significantly advanced the entire world, but the fruit of that development is being taken from us and moved wholesale to the rest of the world while we Euro-Descended folks are suffering the stagnation and decline of our culture and economy as a result. While this may seem natural and innocent, or innocuous enough; something like the natural rise and fall of a civilization, I believe there are more sinister forces at work.

There are global interests that are purposefully causing the collapse of our industries and base of productivity and this assertion is bolstered by recent polls where many people agree that there is a global base of powerful interests that are calling the shots. They seem to be tying an anchor onto the west and are in the process of tossing us overboard. At this point, they seem bent on destroying, or at least, significantly diminishing the American and European ability for productivity and thrift and replacing it with a culture of irresponsible consumerism, apathy, hedonism, and just plain destructive habits and attitudes. That is not to say that we are not ultimately responsible for the mess we find ourselves in, but that does not excuse what is purposefully being done to us through subterfuge. They can not use the excuse, *'I did not kill the man, I merely poured poison into his coffee when he looked away. He drank it!'*

You may ask, why would someone want to do that? I am not sure anyone really knows the answer to that, even those that are being used to bring this sorry state about do not seem to know, but a simple educated guess is that knocking us down a notch or 5 will make it easier to command and manipulate us into the ultimate plans for the planet.

I was first introduced to the possibility that there were powerful forces orchestrating world events when I joined the John Birch Society in the early 1990s. When I first started writing about this subject, I thought I would have a tremendous uphill battle convincing folks that there indeed exists a force of such organized power, bent on destroying the west with hedonism, communism, and consumerism, described as the aims of groups like the Illuminati, or

Bilderberg group, Skull and Bones, freemasonry, Rosacruciens, Kabbalah, and so on, and even the more obscure esoteric forerunner groups like those associated with black magic such as the Hermetic Order of the Golden Dawn from which renowned occultist and self-proclaimed evil-man, Aleister Crowley, was ultimately spawned. I was led to believe that these groups took extraordinary steps in concealing the truth about their activities and their existence.

Now it seems that their secrecy is not as easily kept because there is considerably less skepticism as has been the case in the recent past. I have witnessed a change in attitude. Now I have less to do to persuade people that such a shadow force is among us and find it less necessary to do so. People are readily accepting that there is something terribly wrong. Indeed a majority of people now believe in the controlled or conspiratorial view of history and events, whereas in the early '90s, when I first learned about such things, there was no way you could talk openly about such things in mixed company because people thought you were full of it or off your rocker.

With the emergence of the Internet, Youtube, etc, people are exposed to what I learned almost 2 decades back. I was so frustrated then when I tried to convince others to understand that what I had learned, answered so many of the inconsistencies I saw involving how and why things are the way they are and are not what we are being made to believe. Also, books by authors like Dan Brown, 'The DaVinci Code', which explored and popularized material that was standard fare for the John Birch crowd for decades before his books were published, made it plausible that such secret and organized power with the clout to arrange the affairs of the planet did indeed exist. However in my opinion, the Birch society as well as myself would have considered these books and similar material to be more misdirection, false-flag, or for Hegelian[5] purposes, nonetheless it opened minds to the possibilities.

This kind of material was always among the standard tenets of the John birch society. I have to confess that I am no longer with the Birch society so I am not pitching them, I am simply stating that my introduction to this knowledge was by way of the JBS. I have not visited their websites nor read any of their publications for at least a decade and a half, however, once you see the world in those terms you can never see it blindly again. One of the first books I read on the subject was carried and sold by the JBS. It was called *'None Dare Call It Conspiracy',* by Gary Allen, in which he discussed how the shadow powers, which he referred to as 'landscape painters', were involved in painting a false picture of reality in the minds of the public. He included an illustration with a hidden picture in it, which really opened my eyes and stuck with me. It was an image composed of many hundreds of small circles of various sizes and line thicknesses that seemed to be randomly arranged. When you first looked at it, you could not really see much of any pattern, however the more you stared at the image, the more you began to see a hidden picture emerge which was of a boy and a donkey cart. Afterward, every time you looked back at the image you would immediately see the hidden picture. He said, once you see the world as it really is you will always see it that way. This is because your mind will connect the dots each time and you will start to view the world with that information and view in mind. You were told to distinguish between what he called the *'accidental theory of history',* in which everything that happens, happens randomly and without any real purpose; or the *'conspiratorial theory of history',* in which little to nothing of significance in world events happens without some unseen shadow power planning and executing it. If you did not see the image, you would likely go on viewing history as a series of random occurrences and vice versa if you saw the picture emerge. The 'landscape painted' world is barely hidden purposefully but once you see the

---

[5] Hegelian Dialectic

telltale signs and verify the real stories behind the events, you will see the real picture emerge from hiding. Once you see the *'New World Order'* you will always see it.

Why do I bring this up? My concern is not convincing you that there are nefarious powers that are eons old, and organized, who want to order your life against your will and against the interests of the American nation; as far as I am concerned that is not even a question. If you are reading this and you do not see or believe that then you are on your own because I am not going to try to convince you otherwise; that is not my purpose. The evidence for global power structures of this nature is overwhelming and readily available for anyone that will search it out. No, instead, at this point my only aim is to attempt to communicate with you regardless of whether you will accept that reality or not. So now the question is, regardless of the cause, what do we do about the approaching failure? In my mind that is the only relevant question. Now that we see the monster in the room with us, how do we get rid of it, or how do we live with it? How do we maintain some level of autonomy and sovereignty in order to maintain control over our own lives and that of our nation? That is my concern and I hope you share the same concern and want to learn ways to change it.

I run the risk of leaving a false impression that the power of which I speak may be construed as so complete and powerful that it is futile to attempt to work contrary to their purposes. Nothing could be farther from the truth. We, the American nation, like the balance of humanity joined in purpose, are considerably more powerful than they if we only realize it and act properly. Each generation has to deal with the same forces that are arrayed against our interests as members of the human family. Our struggle today is no different than those of the past, but we are certainly blessed (or maybe cursed) with a vision of greater definition into the extent of their power and what they intend to do.

Feminist Folly

What happened to the American economic and cultural landscape when the feminist movement was sold to American women, inducing them and telling them they had the 'right' to go to work, and the duty to prove themselves worthy to the rest of the human race, the status of which no one had previously questioned except the feminists themselves? They convinced women they had to prove their humanity as they were not as worthy as men unless they were willing to challenge the men in the workforce. They had to prove they were as good as a man and could do the same job just as well if not better, but only if it could be demonstrated. This brilliant line of reasoning, which was really designed to appeal past the limited intelligence of those who entertained such a fool's deal, instead appealed to foolish pride with promises of the glory of a liberated lifestyle and more money to live the material dreams which they were also sold. American women were encouraged to sell their children out despite obvious loss to their family which had been pointed out by detractors of feminism, and even after considerable warning by wiser members of society who saw through the charade and lies.

The effect of a massive influx of new workers into the American workforce; a virtual doubling of the workforce; which after taking the law of supply and demand into account, resulted in a significant reduction in wage rates for most labor intensive sectors and eventually all sectors of our economy. Women entered the workforce enmasse looking to prove their worth and humanity and expand their living standard, only to lose ground, because not only were they in competition against all the other women also entering the workforce, but they also competed against their own breadwinner husbands thus putting significant downward pressure on wages and the family income. Double the workforce, halve the prevailing wage; it is simple supply and demand. I have talked to hardened feminists on this issue, explaining to them the reality of how it worked only to be met by snide and ignorant denial of the hard reality of what is wrought. They roll around wallowing in abject ignorance and denial having made their bed in it.

It also created the current bumper crop latchkey[6] population of worthless and functionally retarded children our nation enjoys, who grew up without the nurture of a mother during vital years of mental and emotional development. These children instead emerged more influenced and nurtured by fine exemplary models of humanity; the heros and stars of the idiot-box, along with their morals, the values sold by corporate America, and the all-penetrating and oh-so wholesome, uplifting, and objective media. They were also raised with all the morals, ethics, and wisdom exhibited by the previous generation of teenage babysitters who had recently graduated summa cum latchkey. We are now on the 4th or 5th generation of this and the conventional wisdom says that by the 5th generation, it is too late to correct their minds; the first completely lost generation of Americans. Not generation X, or generation 'why', but generation ZERO.

It turns out that societies are vitally dependent on what women are good at, and that is being mothers; raising smart, well adjusted, healthy, emotionally stable children, who are next inline to inherit the nation and the world. This part can only be accomplished by women. Men are not even minimally equipped by temperament or emotional or physical makeup to do the job. Without their voluntary participation, the society is rendered crippled and on the short path to complete failure, just as assuredly as if men refused to do what men are equipped to do; there is no getting around it in either case.

I have a first hand experience so I know what I am talking about. When my son was born, he slept comforted by his

---

[6] Latchkey Kid - A child who returns from school to an empty home because his or her parents are away at work.

mother in our bed until he was 5 years old. There were many times when I was particularly annoyed by his presence, but my wife would not leave him alone. She nurtured him like only a mother can through those critical years when he was emotionally and intellectually developing into the person he became. He turned out to be one of the highest caliber persons I have ever come across. It was well worth what his mother and I gave up to insure he turned out. While it is true, there is not always a guarantee as to the outcome of the child, it is a sure bet that the likelihood of a good outcome is increased significantly if he/she is nurtured and raised by a loving mother and allowed a fully immersed relationship with her, than those not so raised and that has been proven. Consult any expert in early childhood development; virtually all of them will agree on that assessment.

Now with women in the workforce and both working, men earn and keep considerably less money, about 1/2 of what it was before the so called *'feminist revolution'*, while women earn and keep about 3/4th of what the men do, so together the family has lost about 20% of the income over the previous era and they have severely compromised the integrity of the family and their children's self-worth.

Women were sold the slogan 'women's lib' on the notion of liberating them from the responsibility of being a mother and to refuse taking a secondary role in the family and society; to challenge the men as the leaders. They were told to question and challenge their traditional role as demeaning to them, which was supposed to lead to their 'liberation.' Eve was hardly liberated but instead only secured her place and fate as a demeaned laborer, whereas before her role was simple, respected, and dignified. There was no need for her to work outside the home. Taking a second bite of the apple, she accomplished the repudiation of the pinnacle of human existence in the bargain. Falling for the lies told by rabid feminism only further wedged her into the role of economic slave, and insured her family was now completely dependent on her remaining a slave.

Cultural Hegemony

The application of Cultural Hegemony to the American landscape and its effects are lightly discussed to illustrate a point. It is a topic too broad for this book, but nonetheless essential to understanding what is happening to the American landscape. In a nutshell, people of European ancestry and traditional Euro-Centric American culture in-general, are being marginalized by interests and influences hostile to traditional American culture and people. *Cultural Hegemony* is simply a dominating control over the mainstream culture. In our case, it is control from influences that are Anti-American, foreign, and destructive to the soul of America. It seeks to replace our identity and cultural heritage with something toxic, leading us down the path toward self-destruction.

If you are white, Christian, and male, you have a huge target on your forehead by the commercial popular media culture. This is particularly true if you live in, or your cultural identity or affinity is in what is contemptuously referred to as *'fly over country'*, by the cultural elitists in the popular media. Fly-over country is the area in-between the Northeast (New England and particularly New York), Chicago, and Los Angeles. It is particularly biased against the traditional culture of the Southern US, but also the mid-west and a great part of the west.

If you are white, Christian, and female, you also have a target on your forehead, but a smaller one. If you are white but not Christian, you also have a target on your head. White people are being pushed out of positions in government and corporate America through affirmative-action and set-asides in record numbers, and replaced by considerably less competent and less qualified minorities including recent immigrants. Immigrants have traditionally started at the bottom and took the lowest positions in our culture then created some value proposition, something of value to the rest of us in order to earn their way up. Now they are entitled to reserved and favored jobs and status right off the boat, mostly in government, but also in corporate America; but payed at our expense. This is outrageous. White europeans founded and carved the country out, and are the owners and politically endowed; **they will not be marginalized or pushed out!!**

Whites are systematically marginalized when speaking their minds. If they express any sentiments of the traditional American values or the traditions of what created and built the country, they are called racists, criticized, chastised, and told to shut-up, mostly in the media but also through all phases of the education system. They are now expected to accept and conform to an orthodox mindset, which is not acceptable to them and very much foreign to their view of the world and cultural alignment. Whites form the majority of the population; it is their right to determine cultural orthodoxy and norms, but instead foreign and domestic engineered cultural hegemony is interfering. The largest voices attempting to redefine American culture and mores, are:

1) The crass and corrupt popular commercial media culture which continuously insults traditional values and ethics with any ties to traditional Euro-Centric history and culture. This it does for many reasons, but one is the fact that considerable government financial support and welfare money flows to foreign elements and minorities in our society, which corporate commercial interest are attempting to serenade for those government dollars thus the degrading commercialized insults aired in our midst; and...

2) Institutional influences; mostly public k-12 education and universities. Their not so subtle vitriolic indoctrination seeks to poison the minds of the young by controlling the public dialog, attempting to transform and remake the culture into a morass of self-absorbed contradiction and all-consuming

hedonism, while rendering the traditional culture obsolete along with the members of that class which define and maintain traditional culture inorder to marginalize them. They promote profane street-gutter culture, which is not conducive of healthy or sustainable societies but is destructive. They are foreign and hostile to the mainstream of America along with the fringe members of our society which these bankrupt cultural elements represent.

Minor but accelerating examples of such are the rise of the drug culture along with fringe occult influences. Heavier examples are the *'freebooters'* and entitlement cultures': drug saturated and violent criminal street gangs and the gang-banger 'music' culture; much of which is composed of marginalized blacks and Mexican street culture. Hip-hop and rap 'music' which are filled with vile and profane language and attitudes, demand cultural deference for what traditionally is considered profane and shunned by the mainstream, but nonetheless it is put up on a pedestal and glorified as examples of acceptable American culture for the young.

The gutter culture is put forth with the air of moral authority, expectation, and entitlement, and a pretense of outraged oppression and victim status. They propagate that their culture and racial elements have been denied by the dominant Euro-American culture and their imagined right has been suppressed so the bill is now due; they claim they are owed a fortune, having been denied whatever they believe is their heritage, as they blame the middle of traditional America, wailing their profanity toward us with venom filled rants. The facts are, the same people from a previous generation have contributed greatly to the American cultural landscape and the mainstream has not denied them that contribution but has embraced it. The issue is that the nature of the current cultural elements are not acceptable to the mainstream population, but are being massively promoted and marketed in an aggressive *in-your-face* manner nonetheless. Much of the black population from older generations detest the new cultural elements as degenerate and destructive, painting very negative stereotypes and destroying their own American cultural identity.

Why it is that every time you turn on the news, about half of what you see are foreign faces? Ken and Barby are still there and they get top billing often, but they are way outnumbered by the foreign (non-European and non-American) faces? Could this be an attempt to indoctrinate American's into believing they are obsolete? Then consider that it is not just in America but most of the European nations as well. How about the nordic countries being overrun by 3rd world people mostly from islam? Why is there a need to so dramatically change the ethnic makeup of the white European nations, who are responsible for creating the modern world? What is that agenda about?

Understand, virtually no one would pay even an inkling of attention to the obscenity of gutter culture, but it would quickly die if it were not heavily promoted through commercial media. However, it is not the entertainers and performers that are behind this move; they are simply tools being used by global commercial interests who use these profane cultural elements as a weapon to destroy then reshape the mainstream of American culture and identity. Their aim is to create a generation of insolent, mindless, hedonists consumers.

Other examples are several decades of media depictions which claim *'mainstream'* and *'normal'* status, but only indulge the fantasy and prejudice of equally profane fringe elements of society against the traditional American white male hero archetype. Men, and white men in particular are depicted as villains, wimps, perverted molesters and rapist, and self absorbed pariahs in movies and television, while women, gays, and racial minorities are now the hero figures. A complete reversal of the traditional depictions. The new super-hero class are depicted as having to make excuses for, and compensate for the inept, incompetent, 'dinosaurs' that are now barely tolerated by enlightened society because they are now just in the way.

The *'dinosaurs'* are depicted as wimps, barely able to defend themselves and their balls against all of 105 pounds of *'Sally Kickass'* who is morally superior and justified in her outrage when she kicks wimpy's 220 pound ass without breaking a sweat. She righteously plants the pointed tip of her number 6 fashionable heeled-pumps in wimpy's sack, because he justly deserves it; which excites the rabid audience to great cheer; then she single-handedly takes on and whips an army of bad guys, each one having fallen by her lethal blow, nary able to stand again but only slink away in humility and disgrace.

In the absurd fantasy world planted deep into the very shallow simpleton minds of way too many that are persuaded by this tripe, Wimpy deserves everything that comes his way. He is depicted as a real threat to society; a potential molester of children, beater of wife, and oppressor of minorities. He is a potential powder keg of angry with a lit fuse; the proverbial *'angry white male'*, used to getting his way with everyone and everything. He's had it coming for a long time and now its here. He's been needing a good lesson from women-kind, who is the epitome and upstanding example of pure virtue; not prone to any character flaw or faults, never tempted by vice or driven by greed. Only Wimpy fits that mold.

Flipping to the very next channel brings hoes and bo-atches, from all racial groups of the lowest caste of socio-economic humility, dressed like their true hoe and bu-atch selves, throwing chairs at, and pulling off the wigs and bling of their rivals, in a petty feud over a single worthless example of wimpy. Occasionally its the real wimpy, again from all racial and socio-class of males throwing punches to preserve their 'honor' when one or several of their baby-mammas are insulted..., cah..., sunt'in wah diss'ed. The depictions are fodder for a frenzied mob maniacally cheering on the spectacle with howls and hoots of bloodlust approval. The entire disgusting display is meant to program and reassure the pea-brained audience into their acceptable societal roles.

Sally Kickass is forced against her '*up-righteous-ed-ness*' to perform these incredible heroics because of her children who desperately need moral examples of feminist heroism and character because Wimpy can not provide any kind of moral compass, and can not be relied on to provide meaningful life's training for the young; and because her children are threatened by having to live in a world where white oppression and injustice is tolerated. Her role as protective super-mom is preserved as the highest exemplary model that any society can embrace, while Wimpy is depicted as a sorry and pathetic example of something to be ashamed of, dealt with, and shunned, but, who thankfully is becoming less necessary and passing on into submissive compliance and history.

The target of demonization is all too clear. The depictions only serve to weaken and degrade the strength, stability, and resolve of our society by diminishing the traditional role of men, while usurping that role by 'strong' women and other minorities who are depicted as smarter, more judicious, naturally better leaders, and better equipped to deal with the problems of the world. This depiction and the insidious philosophy behind it, fly in the face of millennia of Euro-centric Christian patriarchal tradition and roles, honed to generate and maintain a very highly advanced society which not only functioned effectively and thrived for thousands of years, but came to culturally and economically dominate the world.

These lies only lead to the wholesale dismantling of the structure of our society. They embed into the heart of the culture, depression, confusion, and violence, where sadly outside of the fantasy worlds of Hollywood and Madison Avenue; in the actual world, the more vulnerable members of the society, the women and children who are ostensibly those to be uplifted are instead rendered real victims. They suffer tremendous psychological and emotional harm as they are left with overwhelming impressions of hopelessness and uncertainty. Children are victims of growing up without fathers, and the women are victims of abandonment and divorce, having alienated their men, the accomplishment of insidious intent.

This is corruption of an entire nation by design and intended to displace the majority population of whites of european decent and their traditional definition of family and culture, who are accustomed to self-reliance in determining their own sovereign future and captaining their own ship; and replace them with dependent people of the 3rd world or the extreme edges of society, who are more predisposed by cultural or ethnic origin and background, or by sexual role reversal, but considerably less equipped to deal with the complexities of the modern world created by the European descended people.

All is designed to transform our population to be compliant and passive, and rarely rock the political boat. However, this is only a fragment of the agenda of the transformation of the population from one of sovereignty and self determination to one of control, passivity, and compliance. We have absolutely no reason to trust in the benevolence of those who would put us in a cage, so we must understand that putting us in a cage is their agenda, then step up the struggle to set that agenda back as far as possible.

I intended to set the tone and give a hint of what will be discussed by bringing attention to where we have been, where we're at now, and where we can go as a nation which is why I called this chapter *'Something is Wrong.'* That much should be evident to virtually any American with a breath and normal body temperature. I could go on with many, many more examples of the decline, degradation, and failure of the American civilization; where it is failing, what lies were told, and what devil told them, but that would take volumes. My intent is to deal with where we are now and how we can extricate ourselves from the situation.

American Broadside

The following is a manifesto; a mind and spirit dump; even a rant, and represents the essence; the shear distillation of the frustration and seething anger of that which has been culminating in 10's of millions of people in the US who have endured a continuous insult for most of the 20th century by elitist-statists. It was created out of the dissatisfaction over the destructive path the country has traversed to this point, and the predictable destination in the very near future. Many signs of that place are already on the horizon.

At this writing, October of 2006, there is nothing new about Americans being disgusted with the way things are going. A lot of decent middle class Americans see changes taking place faster than ever before and those changes seem to be not only at their expense, but at the total loss of virtually everything of value to them. Speaking for the masses, we are tired of seeing total loss referred to as 'change' at the expense of our sovereignty, culture, heritage, rights, wealth, money; all the things that free people have to this point believed were theirs by virtue of the fact that they created it and it is theirs in perpetuity.

We have lost:

....trust in authority;

....trust in our neighbor;

....trust in the government sworn to uphold our rights;

....trust that if we may obtain some small particle of wealth someone will not frivolously steal it through the courts, or by breaking into our house;

...And we are...

....tired of being told that our communities can not impose standards of decency, but must give deference to perverts and criminals;

....Tired of seeing gangs of homegrown and foreign criminals roaming free in the streets and our law enforcement powerless to do anything about it for fear of being charged with violating their civil rights;

....Tired of watching an encroaching police state emerge. Tired of hearing how law-enforcement is brutalizing innocent and helpless law-abiding people for frivolous reason. How they are instructed in methods of baiting people in attempt to solicit a natural human response of anger and resistance, as a pretext to justify their brutality. Tired of hearing how this is done to condition the masses.

....Tired of our government lying to us and attempting to scare us into submission and support with bogus threats of terrorism, pandemic disease, financial collapse, global weather threats, ad nauseam;

....Tired of being told that we must give deference to foreigners and their culture or we must accommodate them and have respect for their culture and backward 3rd world ways. This situation is backwards. If they are here, then they should pay deference to Americans and American culture, not the other way around.

....Tired of foreigners imposing a burden on us by consuming and loading up the hospitals, roads, schools, courts, civil authorities, law enforcement, insurance and on and on...

....How do you keep a mexican from breaking into your car? SEAL THE BORDER!

....How do you keep a mexican from breaking into your house? SEAL THE BORDER! There is no other way.

....Tired of endless serial wars costing trillions that enrich the elitists in charge of stoking the flames of war who then sell it to the public on the spurious basis of threat to our very survival.

....Tired of the 2 parties that control the congress, the executive, and the courts, pass then uphold a succession of one after the next destructive acts upon the nation, and against the express-will of the vast majority of the populace for their monied benefactor patrons.

....Tired of seeing one free trade agreement after another gut the wealth creating productive capability of the country.

....Tired of seeing the multinational companies that were cradled in the US forget what they owe to the country, while they move operations offshore but expect to retain access to the market that was bought and paid for by the American producers, laborers, and consumers. The people that created the marketplace also own the marketplace.

....Tired of seeing small companies that would otherwise like to stay in the US and give back for what they have received being forced to outsource their operations, or face the scrap heap.

....Tired of being referred to as a 'taxpayer' as if that is the sum total of our reason for existence, and as such we must assume the responsibility for bailing out the losses of multi-national mega-banks and corporations that have been absolutely irresponsible in their business to the tune of trillions; and the idiot congress that mandates those same banks must make irresponsible mortgage loans to people that would never qualify to own real estate in the name of a destructive asinine leftist doctrine called '*social justice.*' Social justice is a doctrine that says in a 'just and equal' society, separate public bathrooms for men and women is discriminatory and oppressive and must be done away with.

As I see it, the inmates are running the asylum; the fox is in the henhouse; the bull is in the china shop; the toast is burning in the toaster; and the poison is in the cup! OUR CIVILIZATION IS WAY TOO TROUBLED AND IT'S TIME IT WAS COMPLETELY CREATED ANEW!

Three Wishes

Remember the story of Aladdin and the lamp? In the story, Aladdin finds a lamp and when he rubs it a djin[7] appears and grants him 3 wishes. The first two go very badly because he used them selfishly, and so he uses the 3rd to ask for something noble thus averting complete disaster and defeating the evil plan of the djin. The story has given rise to a popular folk myth and a puzzle; if you were given the same opportunity and assuming a similar outcome for the first 2 wishes, what would you do with your last wish? The answer is usually something like ***"I would wish for more wishes"***, meaning that although it has gone bad previously, if I could have a few more chances, I'm sure I can get it right.

More to the point, it is about the desire for an unlimited chance to get what we want, to avoid the pitfalls of life and circumvent the consequence of bad choices made in the past. Another analogy along the same line is the idea of, ***"wouldn't it be great if we could go back in time and correct the mistakes of the past?"***

Some generally accepted principals need to be brought into view to bring perspective, frame the discussion, and serve as the basis for preparation to put things back on the right course. In the next few chapters I will outline what we must understand and do to move down that path.

---

[7] Arabic word for English Genie. Demon.

CHAPTER THREE
Authority

Mission

To change the dialog concerning the people and their place in our civilization in hopes they will stand and take it back. To create conditions necessary to focus a movement of people to extricate our nation from the stranglehold of increasingly corrupt government regimes, and the criminal shadow interests that have co-opted it. To educate the public and demonstrate an alternative to the erroneous contemporary belief about the relationship between government and people. To restore the correct chain of authority in the relationship. To establish a new social contract that respects the sovereign rights of the person and individual states. To further the evolution of the modern state by establishing new systems that are orders of magnitude more immune to corruption and co-opting by criminal interests.

Advocate for Dependency

An advocate is an agent who intercedes on the behalf of a supplicant.[8] The intercessor generally pleads the case for the supplicant. This describes the degeneration and degradation of our society. It operates mostly as a nation of supplicants

---

[8] An entity which asks or pleads with another for favor.

begging for handouts. Our republic does not function as envisioned where the *Trustees*[9] of our republic represent their constituent's interests in a relationship of negotiation with other foreign entities, sovereign individuals and states, individually and as a whole.

In this discussion, I used the model of a *Trust*, which is a legal construct, with a Grantor; one who entrusts their interests property and such (rights), and a Trustee; a servant charged with looking after the Grantor's interest, because the parallels are very close. The relationship is germane, where the trustee as a fiduciary is supposed to be a steward or custodian and look after the property and interests of the grantor or beneficiary. Instead, it has degenerated to become a *free-for-all* where the grantor's (sovereign people and states) interests have become locked away from them, as it were, and only accessible through supplication. In the abstract, even though America and Americans have become the wealthiest on the planet, functionally, they have become as penniless dependents and not as the proud owners, able to freely exercise their sovereign will.

In the relationship, the grantor or beneficiary has been seduced or tricked into giving full Irrevocable Power of Attorney[10] over to the trustee, who effectively dictates the use of the resources as well as the activities of the grantor. Think about how a shyster attorney will swindle all or a portion of an estate from a vulnerable, usually older person, with probably less acumen for the affairs of the estate than is required.

Americans have been persuaded to, and so now view themselves by government and powerful institutional classified groupings for manageability, arranged by dependent interest-categories such as race, ethnic or national origin, language,

---

[9] In this context it means representatives of sovereign people's and individual state's interests.

[10] The power to act as if they are another person in legal, business, and personal matters.

occupation, profession, age, sex, sexual orientation, gender, handicap, education, ability, proclivities, habits, desires, vices, diseases; their status in relationship to family members, strangers, government, clubs, organization; members of a group, etc.   All of these classifications have a status per government policy which are considered and enforced under horrendously unconstitutional 'findings' for what are fallaciously lumped under one umbrella, that of *'Human Rights'*, and its evil stepchild, *'Civil Rights.'* These distortions make a mockery of legitimate human and civil rights.   Both are something that humanity must uphold and religiously guard, but these are not them.   Legitimate human and civil rights are more in harmony with the preamble of the US constitution; regard for *life* and *liberty* and *Due Process*.   Legitimate human and civil rights never enforce tribute or the consuming of resources supplied by another individual or group.

The begging is formalized to hide its true character.   It is called lobbying instead, where professional advocates for all the special dispensations are brought to the seat of power as it would have been in the day of king and court.   It is made to seem very dignified, all the begging and beseeching at the court of favor, with special consideration and lofty justification given each particular request.   Grants are given with an expectation of a vow of fealty and allegiance.   The Advocacy Industry figures very prominently in our society, from the largest group in the nations capital to the smallest corner of America.   From its home in the national seat of power, it has grown extensions in every city, county, berg, and municipal building; with allies in all avenues of media, academia, industry, and government; it is a monster and pervades our society.

All who have been made party to this trampling of rights in the name of rights are supplicants begging those entrusted for a false and pale token of what is already theirs, however ignorant of the fact. Most would not like the characterization as beggars, but that is exactly what they amount to.

Minorities, racial, sexual or otherwise, beg for welfare money and special services, and special rights of protection in employment and accommodation in public service, which infringe on the free exercise of the sovereign rights of those who provide such services or employ people, while employers beg for compensation for the infringement of their right caused by the mandates guaranteed to minorities. Middle class workers of white traditional America will not shun special money from others for the education of their own children, or their own neighborhoods and pet projects, but are inline with the rest, hands outstretched. One would think these of all should know better.

Large, wealthy multinational producers and small business alike; all beg for protection against government regulation and from foreign competition, and for unfettered access to foreign markets; they want protection from unions begging for government enforcement of their demands on the corporations. Union workers beg for favor for extracting more than they are entitled from their producer employers, and from competition by other non-unionized workers, which they obtain by government mandates, and all of which infringe on the free rights of producers, employers, and workers alike. Elderly Americans beg for a litany of welfare and special privileges in accommodation and protection from other Americans exercising their free rights.

Foreign nationals and entities, and illegal aliens, who have no rights vis-à-vis our civilization, beg for, and are granted the same status as Americans, and for protection against deportation as well as the same litany of illegitimate 'rights' as what is enforced for the rest of the nation. Governors and the legislatures of states beg for money for infrastructure and to fund the unfunded mandated 'free-money' programs imposed on them by the big provider in the sky, while they are also begged for favors and illegitimately grant them. All of these groups beg for and expect money and resources from everyone else to fund their special protections and privileges. It is a zero sum game for most; all except for those that have the largest pots of money and influence, and the government which gains power by brokering the non-negotiable rights of the populace.

This supplicant mentality which is endemic in our society is very destructive because it does a number of things that distort the proper relationship of grantor and trustee:

• The population view the government not as a servant but as a master; a provider; a hander-out or rationer of favor, not a trustee of their own interests.

• The populace has developed an unhealthy attitude of expectation toward the resources of others, and expectation that the 'others' are obligated to provide it to them. If they do not get what they believe is their right, they become vocal and violent; the squeaky wheel which threatens to harass and embarrass any noncompliant representative or provider who is laboring under any unorthodox or false notions concerning their right to someone else's resources, and their obligation to provide it.

• Supplicants believe they receive favor not of their own right or resources, but as a result of extraction from someone else. They believe it proper because the 'others' have obtained it unjustly. This is the poisonous exploitation which the *envy-trade* brings to a society to destroy it.

• The populace loses all the power of civilization and become wards, or subjects of an all powerful state. This is similar to the relationship of an oligarchy of nobles with that of peons or serfs during the feudal age. We fought a revolutionary war to throw off the shackles of serfdom and indentured servitude only to trade that freedom and self determination for a few handouts and some shiny beads.

• The relationship puts the bureaucracy firmly in control as the broker of all the goodies everyone expects to get. Those in the seat of power may then play one group of beggars off another, and all against the middle, strengthening their illegitimate hold on power. This is not sustainable, nor the proper order.

• The middle has degenerated to a class of dependents where it is commonly reported that over 50% of our population is a recipient of some measure of welfare from both federal and state governments, while the balance of the population is tasked with supplying the emoluments for the government largess.

• A populace of dependents have no power, and are no more valuable than a herd of livestock to those who wield the power. This threatens the lives of everyone in the civilization.

Karl Marx[11] said it best, *"From each according to his ability, to each according to his needs!"*

In the next section I begin the long discussion of how we have degenerated to this sorry state, and for gaining the proper perspective of where we must go and what must be done to restore our civilization.

Remake the Nation

I have named this chapter *'Authority'*, because I intend to demonstrate that *we the people* do indeed possess all the authority in our civilization, and why we need to recognize and embrace that fact and its implications. The next chapter is titled *'Declaration'* for similar reasons, and I hope it will be made clear that recognizing and embracing just these two elements is 90% of the effort needed to solve the bulk of the problems plaguing the nation.

'That to secure these rights, Governments are instituted among Men, deriving their just powers from the consent of the governed.'

This passage is from the American Declaration of Independence. The words were written by the same men that gave us the US constitution and the Bill of Rights. They are

---

[11] Author, The Communist Manifesto, 1848

shown here to demonstrate that the founders of our republic believed that government derives its power from the **Authority** of the people.

However, I am not here to give a treatise on the virtues of the US constitution. Many will be initially disappointed in what I have to say about that, because I believe the US constitution is obsolete and does not live up to the beliefs, nor serve the expectations of Americans today. For lack of a better word, I will say that the US Constitution is defunct.

This is important because we must get past the bothersome but persistent false notion that our rights come from the government created by the constitution, or that they come from the constitution itself. Both ideas are false. We, Original Americans, were born with the highest order of political right, which establishes our authority.

Many argue that our rights come from God or nature. While I do not want to argue the merits of that now, I will say that, that notion creates a whole other set of problems that are not particularly helpful in understanding the reality of the present situation. I will deal with the origin of rights later on, but for now, suffice it to say the political rights which gives us the authority to create, destroy, and empower government, are rights which we inherited from the founders of the nation, not the founders of the Republic, whom many proudly refer to by the moniker, *'Founding Fathers'*, nor the Republic itself.

Continuing with the passage from the Declaration of Independence:

...whenever any Form of Government becomes destructive of these ends, it is the Right of the People to alter or to abolish it, and to institute new Government, laying its foundation on such principles and organizing its powers in such form, as to them shall seem most likely to effect their Safety and Happiness...'

This indicates their recognition that we have the authority to recreate our civilization whenever it suits our purposes. It shows the principle which they operated on when they established the US Constitution and the Republic. Again, it must be understood that the principle expressed here is not what gives us authority, nor is authority derived from any document or accord like the constitution; we have authority regardless.

The Republic is not the nation. The nation exists above the republic and is superior to it. The nation was founded several hundred years before the republic. The nation created the constitution, and the constitution created the Republic. The nation consists of the people and the land, not the form of government or those who hold office. The nation, our heritage, and identity are considerably more important than the federal republic or the constitution; that is what must be preserved. The republic and recent history involving law and events are temporal; they will end, and in my opinion it is close to failure at this time but the nation and all that entails will endure and must be preserved. This idea is paramount and must be understood. A few vital observations are enumerated in the outline that follows.

1) The current US Federal Government is a strictly self-serving entity.

Advocacy Government, Special Interests, Political Parties and their patrons dictate all of the policies that govern the country now, not the people's voice. This is justification enough for all or most of the current states to un-join the current union and form a new one.

The current US federal government has become too powerful and is completely self-serving. It exists for its own purposes and not the mandate for which it was created which is to protect and guarantee the sovereign interests of the politically endowed people and their states. It has no other purpose or reason to exist. This makes the current one illegitimate!

Our government today mostly responds to advocacy voices. This means those organizations and groups with the most money or connections and backers get heard and their agendas are enacted into law regardless of the expense to the people and the nation as a whole, and since the USG now holds unprecedented power, it actively assumes and enforces authority over and brokerage of that which it does not hold title. The entire system in Washington DC has deteriorated to operate virtually exclusively in conjunction with lobbyists, policy institutions, and other powerful advocacy groups.

Political parties are special interests. As of now the USG does not pay any heed to the voice of the populous but virtually responds only to the interests of the highest bidders; actions which are not within its authority. This perversion, for the most part is orchestrated through the democrat and republican parties, large shadow organizations, domestic special interests and foreign entities. Both the democrat and republican parties and political parties in general are in reality special interests and grew out of advocacy organizations and now completely dominate the political process and policy. Parties do not represent the interests of constituents or voters and certainly not the population at large, but instead they serve as strictly advocacy organizations for narrowly defined interests. This is sadly the current state of affairs in our country.

The keys to the kingdom are passed more or less to one of the 2 dominant parties every 2 to 4 years. These parties have time and again demonstrated their willingness to compromise the sanctity, wealth, and security of the nation in order to wield power over the affairs of state. These actions are characteristic of an illegitimate and reprobate government. The motive for most of the participants is age-old; greed, money, and the lust for power.

Government is a **For-Profit** *entity.* The USG has become a de-facto for-profit organization similar to a corporation and allows elected and/or appointed members of one of these parties to enrich themselves by brokering those sovereign rights reserved to the people and the states. This is tyrannical and will not stand. It actually operates in a manner similarly to the way an organized criminal gang does business using bribes, payoffs, and intimidation to extort what it wants. The similarities are striking. Our government is reaching the depths of what most 3rd-world, despotic, tin-horn dictators would consider indefensible.

Enumeration and limits on power. The United States Federal Government mandate does not include the guarantee of the rights of any person or entity outside the borders and territories of the US. By the Constitution:

• With the exception of diplomacy, it has no authority to intervene, act, or govern outside of the relationship between the state and the people or any other entity with which it has no enumerated authority; a power which it has assumed. An example is working with the United Nations for what is called *'Nation Building'*, as done in Iraq and Afghanistan.

• With the exception of the very narrowly defined oversight of interstate commerce, it does not have the authority to intervene in the relationship between any entities in which neither are the state. It has no authority to govern or regulate the relationship between one or more people. The same applies to the relationship between one or more individuals and corporations, institutions, other entities or any combination of these in which neither party is the state. To put it another way; with a very narrowly defined exception of things directly related to actual interstate commerce, which does not include anything **not** directly involving interstate commerce, it only has jurisdiction in a relationship where one of 2 parties is the state itself. It is expressly charged with protecting against abuses by the state and prohibited from acting in any other business or relationships not involving the state. This power it has assumed. When it does act in this relationship, it is mandated to restrain the state from injuring all non-state partie(s).

• It may not interfere with the sovereign affairs between individuals or private entities or institutions. This means that all federal laws such as the so called civil rights laws that ban discrimination by private companies or individuals are patently unconstitutional and have been ruled as such by federal courts including the US supreme court on more than one occasion[12]. Subsequently, 'findings' and rulings undoing this correct interpretation were accomplished by the frivolous, erroneous, and false application of the Interstate Commerce[13] clause of the US Constitution, declaring intrusive power through the dry-creekbed of federal authority given through the commerce clause, in which an entire battleship of federal authority has now been allowed to pass.

• The constitution expressly charges the USG with the protection of the people and private entities from abuses by the government and foreign entities, yet both are routinely abused by the government and foreign entities alike.

• The US Constitution was crafted to strictly operate in the relationship between the individual or private entity and the state and nowhere else. It expressly prohibits the government which proceeds from it from having jurisdiction or the power to act elsewhere. This is disregarded wholesale, so the federal monstrosity at the behest of its patrons, interferes where it has no express authorization. The founders of the republic never envisioned nor authorized federal power intrusion into the personal private affairs of individuals or entities, therefore this is a perversion of the intent. It is illegitimate.

• One person or private entity can not violate the constitutional rights of another and by the same token, is not charged with observing or upholding that right either because neither are the state. The state can not censor your speech or

---

[12] The Civil Rights Cases, 109 U.S. 3 (1883): United States v. Stanley; United States v. Ryan; United States v. Nichols; United States v. Singleton; Robinson et ux. v. Memphis & Charleston R.R. Co.
[13] Article I, Section 8, Clause 3

discriminate against you but I can. The rest follows as well. This describes and should illuminate the nature and intent of the architects who saw it as a set of rules that strictly limit and govern the power of the state in the relationship between the state and individual persons and private entities and gave no authority to intervene or act outside of this relationship. It was never intended to 'rule' the people or the citizens as a king or oligarch would.

• It further affirmatively enumerates express-limits on the powers of the USG.

The USG has no authority to act on behalf of foreign special interests. It has no purpose vis-à-vis foreign interests or people. It has no authority to recognize and act on the United Nations or any of its laws or mandates. It does not have the authority to guarantee any person of any nation what the United Nations fallaciously calls *'Human Rights.'* The sovereign people of the United States have never recognized the profane leftist utopian doctrine called the *'United Nations Charter on Human Rights'* which would restrict and burden Americans and threaten their sovereignty by forcing every American to assume the responsibility for the worlds impoverished. It has no authority to engage in what is called *'Nation Building',* nor engage in any foreign or domestic war to enforce any extra-national directive, or guarantee the rights of any foreign entity, or engage in any police action that has not been sanctioned by the sovereign people through the constitutional process.

2) Government can not solve societal problems.

We as a people have forgotten where we came from. Applying the chicken and egg riddle to civilization gives a very definitive answer; people came before government; it was us who invented it. In more or less harmony with the natural order we long ago discovered the solutions to the problems associated with living together in groups for economic advantage, which required the invention of government.

Government, like other obstacles is the problem solved, which established the people as the problem solvers.

Problem solving is not the mandate nor in the domain of government, nor should it be. The effective role of government is strictly to function as a utility in providing reliable service within the mandate it is given. In its given role government should never be a net burden on the people but only enhance their station and their lives. Governments derive their power from the people who are to benefit from its governance, however, government can not solve societal problems and the best solutions designed and executed by government are seldom able to do so. Even though the advocates for more government action and authority tell us that government can solve problems, they are mistaken and history proves this.

Society in general gets the government that it has decided for itself and it will get whatever level of government that it tolerates. Common people and communities, not politicians or bureaucrats have always solved societal problems. Politicians and bureaucrats are generally of low character and not prone to flashes of inspiration or genius so problem solving is certainly not within their skill-set. Even if they could generate solutions, it is not within their authority to enact solutions. It will always be within the domain of common people.

Societies get what they deserve. Moral and just societies will have responsive government and prosper while immoral societies will get tyrannical government and digress. Government can not create a moral society from an immoral one. Governments can not impose egalitarianism on society or create equality of persons, nor should it attempt to. Governments can not create a just society. These things fall strictly within the realm of morality, religion, and philosophy and are best derived at the community and family level. Indeed, a moral nation comes from social mores and societal expectations imposed by religious, moral, and responsible communities and families. A moral community will expect, admonish, and finally demand compliance from their neighbors instead of primarily relying on the police power of the state to enforce modes of behavior on those acting outside the acceptable range of decorum.

3) **Societal self-governance.**

Solutions and power flow from politically endowed people. If people want something done by the government they must give a directive to the government, but must not abdicate their own authority nor ask the government to solve their problems. The solution to societal problems can only come from the people. The solutions to most societal problems come about by small groups and communities who put into practice and refine over generations, those things which through trial and error, nature, history, and custom has already proven work. This is to be done mostly without the help or hindrance of government. Governments empowered to enact solutions outside of their mandate will only yield disappointment, fracture societal cohesiveness, impose burden, and lead to the reversal of the correct chain of authority. The people must provide directive and authority for government to act in their interest, but that society must not relinquish that responsibility to government.

Most problem issues have already been decided, but are rarely what is codified in law today. Examples of societal problems long ago solved are: Labor Versus Management; Racial Relations; The Individual's Inviolate Right to Self Defense; Homosexual and Alternative Lifestyle Agendas; Wage Standards & Rates; Income Disparity; Funding of Governance; Welfare; War & Defense; Immigration; Political Rights; Civil Rights; Haves and Haven'ts; Sanctity of Life; etc., all having been decided long ago by the society at large should be codified in law and upheld by government.

Such are the most divisive and politically draining issues of our day due to governmental bias and meddling, however the people have already spoken long ago on these and unambiguously decided them, but government, prodded by its activist patrons are in denial of the will of the populace at this stage and actually sows discord. Most of the laws dealing with these issues are at odds with the natural order.

The current laws and court rulings regarding most of these issues are at odds with stable, sustainable societies, therefore they are mostly temporal and will fail and be corrected again. If not corrected voluntarily by the people, the natural order will come into play to put things back in line with what works. What we have today is mostly as a result of dictates contrary to the will of the populace by reckless liberal experimentation; it will not remain.

4) Effective government has only minimal power to execute limited function.

What should government be doing? The preamble to the current US constitution defines the role of government. It is strictly to protect and enable the pre-existing rights and interests of the people it serves and can not be trusted with authority or power beyond this.

In addition, its worth noting that it functions as a utility to provide *efficient service* to a society for **only** those things which are best done by the group or public. National defense, consumer protection, regulation of industry, diplomatic representation, national foreign trade representation and negotiations, law enforcement and adjudication, customs and immigration, construction and maintenance of vital infrastructure, and so on are examples of such services which may be considerably more efficient when done by a national or supra-state body.

5) The US Federal Government can not be fixed or reformed. A new system must be created.

The Federal Government is broken and cannot be fixed. Our government is broken and can not be fixed by reforming the broken system; it is beyond correction. In what may be used to refer to losses from a natural disaster or in the parlance of automobile accident repair, *"It is a total loss."* It must be re-created; Why? Because the government was created by the US Constitution which is obsolete and broken.

6) The US constitution is obsolete.

Many would disagree that the US Constitution is a 'bad' system or anything other than perfect and believe, *"if only we would restore our laws to those that the founding fathers intended, all would be ok!"* This is just wishful thinking and any meaningful reform enacted would soon give way to a furthering of the insult. However, the nation is fine. The nation was established by founders from Europe in the 16th century while the US constitution given to us in 1789 also gave us the republic which is failing. The constitution is not a divinely inspired or sacred document; it is strictly a creation of flawed humans who established a very good system for the time, but it has served its purpose and is now defunct. The case for the demise of the constitution is evidenced by how much it has broken down and is now only selectively enforced or considered by our government and elitists. Further evidence is in the fact that it has broken down. For a constitution and the government it provides to be of effect, it must remain in effect undiluted. It must protect its own integrity and remain immune to erosion by elitists and special interests. The constitution that we know was simply a victim of time, corrupt interests and interpretations, changing customs, and eroding mores and values.

The founders of the republic designed the federal system to govern based on the character of the people of their day, the late 18th century. They were more of an honorable and moral people, less prone to the consent of pervasive societal license and therefore the doctrines and functions of the constitution, although revolutionary and profound, could be written in a simple manner and left seemingly vague or even omit much of what today is distorted and interpreted in extreme ways or contrary to the intent. A moral people, particularly with a Christian background are already governed by a higher power and so the heavy hand of human institution was not considered as necessary. One of the founding fathers of the republic, John Adams, stated that the constitution and the government that it created would only work as long as the people that it governed were of high moral character, but would fail altogether if it were applied to govern an immoral people. As a nation we have arrived at moral bankruptcy and are suffering that failure now.

7) Sovereignty and Pecking Order.

People are the Sovereign. The US constitution was created by agreement between the early sovereign colonial-states which were created by the conquering, sovereign, founders of the nation thus defining the pecking order. The constitution created the federal government. Therefore since the constitution created the federal government, and the states created the constitution, and the people created the states, they through the same process can also dissolve all then create it all anew. Restating for clarity: The sovereign founders of the nation who conquered the land, created the sovereign states; the sovereign states then created the constitution, and the constitution created the federal republic of the United States of America. The **Sovereign Politically Endowed People (SPEP)** are inheritors of the founding of the nation, not the citizens. They have the highest order of right and must always have the option of dissolving any constitution and any government system whenever it becomes abusive, illegitimate, or out of control. As discussed above, the conquerers in the American revolution and founders of the Republic told us as much.

However, the dissolution of the defunct federal system which our constitution created seems to be an immense undertaking due to powerful entrenched interests and the perceived lack of anything practical to replace it. It can however be done if enacted carefully. The main obstacle is not in convincing the masses that it need be done, that is self-evident. The obstacle is in convincing them that there is a viable alternative that would vastly improve their lives and fortunes, for them and the generations to follow. Failure to act at this juncture may result in a worse, probably irreversible condition in the short term.

States may form a New Accord. As I have discussed; the highest sovereignty and order of right belongs to those who inherited political right. They are heirs to the *'Right of Conquest'*, or *'Founders Rights.'* That right is followed by the right of sovereign states and the constitution is subject to the sovereign will of the states, and the federal republic (government) is subject to the constitution. This line of logic is used to show that the sovereign states do not need the consent of the government, the congress, executive, courts, not the constitution nor anyone else to un-join the current union.

One or more states may leave the current union by resolution to form a new body by the creation of a new accord. A sovereign-body within a state may declare proposal for the state to un-join (secede) the current union by amending its state constitution, or by whatever means the sovereign-body and the people of the state so determine. It may join a new accord by the rules of the new. The new accord established may accept or deny entry by other states. States may need to reform or recreate themselves to meet acceptability for entry into the new accord and body.

A New Accord means a New Nation. A new association of sovereign states can be created from within the current alignment, which will constitute a new nation. The new accord would be based in-part on what was actually good and effective from the old one along with some new measures suitable for the era. This would be a quantum step towards an effective new civilization. It is not the end but a new beginning. However there is no reason or compulsion to create the same type of system as the old, which has proven to be flawed. New thinking and new design will need to be implemented.

I started off this chapter by stating that I intended to demonstrate that we the people possess all the authority necessary to remake our nation. Implied in that, it follows that any new body or function of governance commissioned by the nation on their behalf and allowed to operate is to be subservient to the people.

Authority is the 1st of several keys that I will discuss throughout the book as elements necessary for regaining what we have lost. I hope the point about authority has been adequately demonstrated, but if you are not yet convinced, I will continue to make the case in hopes of informing, educating, changing minds, and shaping attitudes and belief.

Original Interpretation

Although I have declared my belief that the US constitution is irrelevant to the long term disposition of our nation, I would like to throw out an observation concerning the way the constitution was marginalized over time inorder to effect the current state of dysfunction. The point made may give some a better argument for its interpretation. I make no claim as to my ability to interpret law. I am not a lawyer, and I have not researched the following inference with any rigor. It is a simple observation and argument.

Many argue over what is called 'original intent', or what did those that wrote the constitution intend for it to mean and enact? In theory, if original intent were known explicitly, then there would be little to no question as to how fine points of policy disagreement between advocates should be ruled on by the courts. Clear intent would have driven correct rulings based on what was clearly intended, and would not tolerate perverse and twisted rulings by those in robes to be pushed through weak or gray areas of the language. However, there is really no way to obtain intent explicitly, because many parts were intentionally left ambiguous, or the drafters extrinsically[14] argued contradictory opinions and views, leaving us without a clear exegesis[15] as to what the intent of absolute limits on power, duties, authority, jurisdiction, and so on were. While many argue the intent has been clearly articulated, nonetheless there are many twisted arguments in gray areas that persist, allowing perversion and weakening the effect of actual intent. A great deal of the disagreement focuses in on areas of bad policy, recently adopted and based on a liberal interpretation of the Interstate Commerce Clause.

I believe the larger question which trumps the idea of original intent is: What was the understanding or interpretation of such questions by those who ratified its enactment? The document and all it brought forth came into existence and authority based on the interpretation of those who accepted their own understanding of what it was supposed to enact. To consider otherwise would be do accept the validity of sham contract.[16]

To a large part, the understanding of intent was put forth by those that endorsed and 'sold' it to the rest. Regardless of what if anything may have been cleverly hidden or covertly intended in the document's clear, or ambiguous sections, one thing is clear, it would not have been ratified if it was believed to have been fraudulently represented, having contradictory or hidden meaning, or nefarious intent buried within, nor would

---

[14] Outside of the object of interest.
[15] Critical explanation or interpretation of a text.
[16] With hidden meaning, cleverly disguised in language. Containing fraud.

such practice be sanctioned today. That is what sham contract is. Therefore, it should suffice that no such corrupt elements were in it, or if they were, they are void as having been misrepresented, so the document can **not** be interpreted (ruled) in the distorted fashion it is today.

This is important when considering many parts such as the interstate commerce clause that has been used as a wedge to rip a gigantic hole in the intent as interpreted by the ratifiers, removing virtually all of the protection from federal usurpation of power, allowing it to interfere, even to the point of micro-managing the sovereign affairs of state and person. If the ratifiers believed that the interstate commerce clause would render all of the protection and virtually the rest of the document ineffectual, leaving them and theirs in a position of servitude, with considerably less right, would they have ratified it regardless?

I believe no!

They would have sent it back to be corrected before ratification. The fact that it was ratified in good faith, while it clearly articulated iron-clad restrictions and the enumerations and limits on the power of the federal government, means that they were satisfied with it. If the current interpretation, which is that the interstate commerce clause allows the unlimited power of intrusion as is the case today, were suspected by the ratifiers, it would never have been left as it was, but they would have sent it back to have the language made clear.

Restating just to be absolutely clear; if it was intended for the federal government to wield the extent of the power it does today, the document would have clearly articulated that, but it did not; but the opposite was clearly articulated. Therefore it must adhere to the interpretation of those who ratified it in good faith, and not to the distortions under which it has eroded. Anything less is an acceptance of sham contract. Regardless, I don't expect that clock to turn back by ruling.

By corruption it arrived today, and by corruption, it will remain, while we must move forward.

CHAPTER FOUR

Declaration

Attitude Adjustment

History has revealed how things are really decided to a large extent. It may come as a shock to some to learn that the reality of how things work is different than the romantic (Hollywood) version which they have come to believe. Americans are proud of the erroneous idea that we are governed by ideals of law and the principles of western civilization, meaning we believe we are more civilized when we are governed by laws which are embodied in lofty grandiose wordy documents with names like ***The Magna Charta***, ***The Declaration of Independence***, ***The Bill of Rights***, ***The Constitution of the United States of America,*** and so on. It is true that most of these documents have embodied the ideals and aspirations of western civilization, and hence have been useful and served those who created and established them, but time, the inclination toward evil, and the cleverness of men has limited their effect.

History has shown that the winners in any contest usually write the history that is left to be interpreted by future generations. This shapes our view of the form of civilization. We proudly believe that in our modern age we have transcended the petty ways of the past when conquering tribes and empires subjugated their neighbors and far off lands. We like to believe that "*We do things in a more civilized, diplomatic way now*"; "*we decide things democratically*"; and "*we have risen above our primitive tribal past and now we are much too sophisticated for barbarism.*" The truth is, and history bears this out, that often when a determined people no matter how primitive or inferior encounters a more sophisticated and established people, the winners are often those that are determined and not afraid to resort to more primitive guerrilla methods to get what they want while the 'sophisticated' and 'civilized' rules of engagement really have less to do with the outcome.

An example was our own American revolution where the far inferior Americans went up against the mighty British forces and beat them in two humiliating wars. The difference was that the Americans were in a really desperate situation. For them it was all or nothing. If they win, they win everything including a nation of their own and the right to determine their own destiny, whereas if they loose the leaders are hanged and the rest suffer the humiliation and oppression of being under the thumb of the British Crown. On the other hand, if the British win not much really changes for them, and if they loose it is humiliating but they can go on with the rest of the empire. It really comes down to attitude. The more determined people usually have a lot more at stake. The fallen British Empire has many more examples to instruct us in this lesson as well.

The American civilization today and for the past 100 or so years finds itself in a situation of invasion and conquest from within as well as from foreign power. Speaking plainly, America has been seduced. That is, a growing population of people and interests that would like to redefine our civilization to favor their particular political, cultural, and economic paradigm are painting the landscape. This is nothing more than the age-old lust for power. We, meaning the American white middle class established culture wield much of the power that comes with wealth and founding, while the others, meaning racial and ethnic minorities and immigrants, funded by multinational mega-corporations and local/international leftist organizations, having made headway in the last 100 years in garnering some political power, desperately want to control it as though they are entitled to the banana-republic style coup they seek.

They believe this is their day and their turn and the 'Old Dinosaur', Euro-centered established people and culture are obsolete and therefore, 'illegitimate.'   At least that is the perception. The truth is a lot more complex in that while it is true the white European descended Americans have defined, and do currently control the waning established culture and paradigm of power; and ethnic minorities, while they would like to think that they are charging ahead and making great strides in 'social justice', 'civil rights', and 'equal rights' and that they are on the ascendancy by their shear determination and the 'righteousness' and 'fairness' of their cause, and while if given the chance to call the shots, they would in-fact impose-on and oppress all the rest with their notions of culture and rights; the reality is they are really pawns in a much larger game that is being played against the whole of the American society, meaning both white 'traditional' Americans and minorities as well.

The society is being split by a global cabal of money and influence mostly foreign, meaning not American, but also not established or characterized by any particular nation or ethnicity. The ethnic identity behind these powerful interests are mostly white and of European extraction, and as entities may have had their origin on Wall Street, Silicon Valley, or the halls of academia. As International leftist organizations, they may have initially been funded by the US department of state to address some National or Global Security interest such as the United Nations and the myriad of alphabet NGO (Non Government Organizations). Funding and directive may have come as the result of an endowment by an ostensibly well meaning billionaire from a past era, or it may be from a

Washington DC or Massachusetts based so called Policy Institute, Foundation, or Think-Tank.

Many of these have particular influence with the American ethnic minorities and foreign ethnic interests which they use like a battering ram to force destructive unconstitutional and elitist globalist ideals such as 'social justice' which is a code phrase for socialism and the forward progression of government control, down the throats of Americans. Regardless of the origin of these interests attempting to reshape the American landscape, in my view, they are proof of the adage that we have sheltered and nurtured the seeds of our own destruction, cultivated them, and given birth to a monster which now seeks to devour us. Indeed we have given shelter to and incubated much of the foreign elements who now believe themselves to be the heirs to the American civilization, who are being used to reshape the landscape to suit very powerful narrow-interests.

In the case of the Multinational corporations and even the foreign political and economic interests embodied in the US inspired and funded United-Nations; these believe they have the right to gratuitous influence over the affairs of our Nation, including the right to buy the will of the congress and the executive branches to fulfill their particular world view; a heretofore right which was the exclusive domain of those Americans legitimately endowed by right to determine policy through the political process. This reserved right, which in the recent past was mostly held by the American public, has now been marginalized through corruption of the process. Through lobbying, politicking, and bundling of funds, they routinely buy and sell votes to get their way in every conceivable issue of domestic and foreign policy, and when as a result things go terribly wrong and there is created a *'systemic risk'* threatening our *'very existence'*, the same recommend that it is up to the legitimately politically endowed middle class, now referred to as 'tax payers' to bail everybody and everything out.

The process described above has given rise to a particularly twisted view of the relationship between the populace and the government that is presently almost universally accepted and certainly propagated by the think-media. In fact this view has almost entirely replaced the proper constitutional view of the role of government serving and responding to the will of the people and accepting its responsibility for protecting our political rights from those criminals in high places that so corrupt the process. This new view, which is shared not just by government and the think-media but also surprisingly, the mainstream populace itself, has been adopted no doubt due to the mental and educational conditioning over the last 100 years.

It is a view that the nation as a whole and everything in it is owned, possessed, and controlled by the elitists class and their rights to such are protected by the government, and the populace masses should be grateful when in their great benevolence, they allow us some privilege. It is the view that the government and these large patron interests and organizations are endowed to run things and determine the rules that we who are lucky enough to be here, shall live by.

Thirty Flags Over America

Have you ever heard of the theme park called **Six Flags Over Texas** which is a nationwide chain theme-park named for the 6 nations that at one time or another ruled Texas, or how about Disneyland? This describes an analogy and the current thinking. We can expand on this view with an example like an amusement park, but ours we'll call 'Happy Land Park', where one pays the entrance fee and is admitted and gets to go on all of the rides. This is increasingly the way we view our nation and government. Any person, whether native or foreign-visitor has the same rights with respect to 'Happy Land Park', which are becoming increasingly narrow, but nonetheless, we are all in the same boat with respect to our limited rights with no distinction as to our origins. No matter who we are, American or foreigner, founder or immigrant; if we have paid the entrance fee we are equal and we can go on the rides, eat at the concessions, walk the grounds and pet the animals; but none of us really have any voice with regard to how the park is run.

We can not say what hours or days the park is open, what rides are provided or who may get into the park, who manages the park, or what the admission fee is, etc. If we are unhappy with our lot in this situation and seek to have more influence or complain, we are reminded that since we are merely guests and not owners, we are limited to just riding the rides so we should just shut-up and be thankful for what we have, after-all it is a happy place; the land of happy, so stop complaining and be happy. It's even getting to a point where the park is beginning to oversell admissions so the lines are getting unbearably long, and many of the rides often break down and they are now charging an additional fee to ride some rides because of the cost to maintain them. Now they are even going back to some well-to-do patrons and asking them to pay the entry fee again after they have entered because the park is facing a *'Systemic Risk of Failure.'*

They are even making all 'pay-abled' patrons pay an extra fee to cover the cost of others, foreign as well as local, that 'have not' the ability (pay challenged) to pay the entry fee for themselves. But as bad as this deal is getting, there is nothing that anyone can do, so we had better just make the best of it; after all we should count ourselves lucky that we even have a 'Happy Land Park' to go to. This view is furthered by the lie that we are all the same in terms of status because 'Happy Land Park' was handed down to us from heaven as a gift to mankind; a kind of world heritage treasure open too all that wish to come, and we all discovered the park where and as it was and had nothing to do with its founding or creation, and so none of us can claim any greater right than another because we are all really just immigrants to the park, or the descendants of park immigrants.

Now, as to our nation, a parallel view applies to us and the government which has simply come by definition over the last approximately 150 years or so, and to a large extent it has been illegitimately codified into law by many decades of legal precedent and constitutional 'findings.' Current generations of Americans are totally clueless as to their own heritage as founders and owners of the nation and so not willing to even challenge the politically correct status quo. They are aware of and speak about the nations 'Founding Fathers' and the founders of the republic, but perceive them to now be some bygone irrelevant fact of history with which we have no heritable link. The reality is that the majority white European descended American middle class are legitimately heirs, and politically endowed, and have their right by way of inheritance from their forbearers who were not merely immigrants but their status far exceeds that which comes from the erroneous simplistic and destructive rationale that *"we are all immigrants."*

In the above comparison, a further analogy is drawn in that the Six Flags Over Texas park is more like thirty (30) flags over America, and can represent the extent of the influence and corruption brought by the globalist and foreign interests that dilute our own. These foreign usurpers currently have more to say about our governance than we do.

The Power of Declaration

Earlier on we discussed how our modern decent societies like to believe that we have entered an era of enlightened thinking in which 'Democracy' or some other such failed system has liberated us from older more tyrannical forms of social order such as those under kings, while we have entered a new age of justice and truth. However, the reality is, when a small diabolical group of determined entrenched interests can change the entire system by which we govern ourselves, and take possession and control of virtually all of our individual and national heritage, wealth, and rights, simply by redefining the rules with which we govern ourselves, by declaring the original rules invalid and declaring a whole new set of rules, without the consent of those that have the legitimate right to determine those rules, then have we really gained anything? How is this any different than the less civilized age of brutal conquest and oppression by armed tyrants? Have we really entered a superior era where justice, peace, and the 'dignity of man' is paramount? The reality is, there has been no real change but things continue the same way unabated.

Our American Republic was born by a declaration, *The Declaration of Independence,* which preceded the constitution in which was embodied a set of supreme laws which expressed our values and beliefs in how we chose to run our civilization. However, our constitutional system of governance was flawed, so it really only lasted about 60 to 70 years from its ratification before traitor agents of elitist interests like Abraham Lincoln, Woodrow Wilson, FDR, Linden Johnson, the Clintons, the Bushes, the Obamas, ad nauseam saw fit to broker our rights and fortunes off to those tyrants that have assumed the right and stuff to rule over us.

Have you heard of the United Nation's *'Universal Declaration on Political and Human Rights?'* This document and virtually any others from that corrupt organization are in the same vein and are completely at odds with our own declarations and the embodiment and essence of those we have made, because it would give our rights vis-à-vis the American civilization to others simply by declaring it so, thus diluting and cheapening our own right. That is to say, foreigners and multi-national organizations and institutions interests have equaled or supersede our sovereign rights regarding the government (protector of our rights), our property and wealth; we, who were born here and whose ancestors founded the nation and the republic and whose rights are to be defended by the constitution.

The UN charter and those that espouse its ideology further declaring that we do not have what we have declared and believed we have because we have obtained it illegitimately through oppression and theft, therefore the rest of the world and all oppressed people will now assume the right to own and control what Americans have formerly owned and controlled. It is the agents of these voices that are now operating in our midst. They live amongst us and influence us daily. How perfect a betrayal when domestic enemies are asked to take the oath to uphold the constitution and defend against *'enemies foreign and domestic.'* If you believe the lies, lofty justifications, and heightened rhetoric designed to separate the naive from their heritage, you deserve and shall suffer the severance of your right and enjoy the slavery that is sure to come upon you.

So then, if those are the rules of the game, then perhaps *"we the people"* need to reaffirm some declarations of our own. After all, if the principles laid out by God fearing men of decent standard are not regarded and are without any more a semblance of honor than would be granted by a rabid mob controlled only by their tribal instincts and destructive impulses, is the real order, then we should by all means take advantage of this because we certainly could measure out a demoralizing rebuke against the chaos of the hoard and their scheming masters. We are certainly not helpless but capable of the judicious application of power. We have proven that in the revolutionary war when diplomacy failed. Did we just roll over in compliance? No, but swiftly moved, first to enumerate the abuse and then to declare our identity as Americans and our independence, our mission and right, then to the utility and pure persuasiveness of war when upon considering our options, the least of which decent people turn to is war. That is not to say that a declaration of war is what is needed now, far from it. This just states and brings into scope the range of options available to us. We will not be denied and we will not roll over and succumb to the most primitive and evil among us but with God's help we will throw off this evil.

Our future progress lays in playing the game better than those that have us at a disadvantage now. We believe that the higher aspirations of man come from the application of laws, the 'rule of law', good and noble indeed, but history has proven intrigue and brute force more persuasive. We now express our aspirations in accordance with the rules of gentility and respectable debate which seems proper, but again the power of money and corruption has come to overwhelm us.

How then should we fight? Firstly by knowing what and who we are. We must ask, then answer the questions, *"What is an American?"*, and *"Who is an American?"*, then having regained our identity we must ask *"Who owns America?"* Can our nation and the national identity we have rediscovered be separate from the land? What does this mean other than our nation, our heritage, and our identity are inseparably tied to the land. We are the land and the land is us. The land is everything; without the land we possess, there is no America or American. And if we own the land, does it not follow that we then determine all within our domain? Everything is built upon our identity and our possession and control of the land. Our enemies understand this as well. They understand that *"possession is nine tenths of the law"*, and that is precisely the reason that after failing to remove us politically and militarily, they are redefining our identity and the title and ownership of the land we possess.

They know they can declare legal control over the land and that decent, God-fearing, law abiding people will acquiesce, believing they are acting correctly. They can not take control by the persuasion of socialist ideology, they can not take control by taxing it from us; they have attempted to obligate us by debt to then sign over our rights, but the most potent of their weapons to separate us from our heritage, to pervert the foundations of western civilization upon which we have built our nation, is to convince us that we have no right to the land and never have.

Among these voices is the United Nations and the other globalist interests and organizations, which have made wide sweeping declarations about the rights of foreign persons, powers, laws, and interests with respect to our land in which they have declared and given title to that which is not theirs to give. While our own government, having been compromised long ago is there to enforce the theft under the color of law. The declarations enforced are hostile to the very people who commissioned the government; the ultimate betrayal. So to answer the question, how do we fight against that? We simply re-affirm our previous declarations and draw a line in the sand.

The Ruse of Law

Illustrating further, some amongst us are proud of saying that we are a nation that obeys 'The Rule of Law', but without further qualification and correct understanding, I believe this to be a trap. Many believe, and are fond of declaring that if it comes to a contest between the will of the majority deciding an issue vs. the rule of law, that the majority will tend to be tyrannical and tromp on the rights of the minority, but the opposite is true more often than one might believe. With a universal view, law should serve, obey, and be subject to the higher elements of truth, justice, and righteousness. Its only purpose is always to enforce and protect the elements of the higher order such as the rights of individuals, but it is also used to destroy those rights or award them to others in employing a divide and conquer strategy.

Recently a man I know founded a company and worked hard to launch and nurture it through the uncertain and unpredictable market conditions to become productive. Indeed, he was the creative and driving force behind the company, and with planning and action he took risks and invested virtually all that he had. Then upon the first green shoots of success, his partners decided that they would like it all for themselves, so they conspired to boot him from his creation and enrich themselves. The legal description is loosely summed up as 'Freeze-out and Squeeze-out', and it is rather common behavior amongst small corporations. This is the classic story of one reaping where he has not sown. This man, having put everything into his company and having been kicked out of his own creation did not have the wherewithal to take the evil usurpers to court immediately, so he could do nothing about the injustice for a period, but when a season had passed and he now had the substance to employ the law to win back his rightful property, he found that the laws were not really on his side because past case-law and precedent had perverted the justice that should have been his through the law.

The judge in his case decided based on current law, but the law had already decided that this man had no right to his property because he would have needed to bring his claim within the statute of limitations time frame which he could not afford to do because he had nothing left after having invested all in the company. Now understand and everyone agrees, and the law recognized the man had a right to his property on the day he was forced out and his property stolen, but two years later, even though nothing had changed in principle and the higher order elements recognized his right still, the law did not but legitimized the theft of the evil usurpers.

The law was supposed to enforce and protect the higher order of property rights and the right to profit from ones own creative initiative, but now the law is used to enforce the theft of those rights. This illustrates that although the higher order principles are ideal and trump law in principle, the laws which are declared by men, as corrupt as they may be will usually be respected although with protest.

This is the 2nd key to the people taking their civilization back. Understand that the root of law is simply declaration and precedent. Now a loud, clear, and firm voice is the root of power and power trumps corruptible law. It all must start with declaration.

A few examples are illustrative; consider that:

a) The courts have held and the laws on the books have **declared** that illegal aliens have the right to protest their immediate deportation and have a right to a hearing and accommodation which can take years in which many are free to carry on business. This tends to clog the efficient disposition of the problem and lays a burden on the country. Where did these rights come from, and more importantly, where did the laws that establish this outrage come from for they are not in our constitution and certainly at odds with the sovereign will of the people? The answer is, judges and courts at some point made 'findings' that suited narrow interests and made rulings based on them. Other judges and courts then upheld the bogus 'findings' and rulings, then it was codified by precedent. This is more or less the process that leads to a wholesale eroding of our rights over time. Make no mistake, it is not by innocent misconstruction or well intentioned oversight, but corruption is at its root and it is at our expense. Why must the people endure and be subjected to this burden when they in their sovereign right choose not to? Were any of you consulted about this? I certainly was not, but there was someone and maybe several, probably in robes with the power to pervert that which the people have clearly not sanctioned.

b) The federal government having a constitutionally enumerated power giving it charge for the protection of the nations borders against the infiltration of dangerous or otherwise undesirable elements, and having abrogated or otherwise deliberately ignored that charge, thus endangering the security of the nation is in the process of preventing states from filling in the gap by passing their own enforcement laws. This done at the behest and benefit of political and corporate special interests, to the detriment of the country as a whole. Again, this is nowhere in the constitution but is done using 'findings', which are in-fact, **declarations** by the courts which justifies such outrageous and dangerous behavior by elected government. Somehow these 'findings' are always at odds with the sovereign will of the politically endowed majority.

c) The legislative and executive branches have decided and the law **declares** that every person is now responsible to expend resources against their will in order to purchase national health insurance. It constitutes a burden and obligation in direct defiance of the explicit will of the populace, and now renders them no longer persons with a sovereign will and right but subjects, as if they are property to be exercised by the whims of an oligarch. What clause in our constitution gave the federal government the power to direct the people's use of their own money? Again I ask, were any of you consulted, and if so what was your response? Even the interstate commerce clause of the constitution, so often used by judges and politicians to justify federal expansion of the dictatorial power of intrusion into even the most mundane aspects of our lives can not justify this insult; so by twisted rationale, it was 'colored' to be a tax, a defacto declaration by the court making it 'legal' under the constitution; another 'finding' by the court. This demonstrates that there is simply no limit to the extent they can use any rationale to **declare** then force whatsoever fits their agenda upon us. We stand in a large sandy field; is it not time to draw a line in the sand and make a few declarations of our own?

d) The law allegedly **declares** and indeed precedent has demonstrated that the government can arbitrarily confiscate all or most of your property based on your productivity, or imprison you without due process if you do not comply. This is the income tax. Again, find this one in the constitution, or for that matter find it in the written law; it is not there. Again, this power, although not in the original social contract, nor any properly executed law is however enforced through the administrative state.[17] It has nonetheless found its way over a few decades through precedent and 'findings' and is now unimpeachably reinforced in the 'rule of law.'

Many additional examples of outrage can be added but note that these are examples of the abuse of the government and those who have co-opted its utility for their own purposes, justified by the rule of law against the will of the significant majority and codified by corrupt declarations and 'findings' that create false precedent, which must be respected by the law abiding.

What About America?

After we have rediscovered who and what we are, then we must determine to discover, define, and implement how our civilization will be structured. The following are critical questions that Americans must answer then declare to the world, affirm, and unwaveringly defend in their own minds and hearts from any and all interests before any progress can be made in restoring our rights, our land, our identity, and our heritage.

Who owns America?

Is it the current corrupt co-opted government that daily manipulates and diminishes our rights through laws which separates us from our property, and is currently engaged in brokering off our heritage and our land block by block?

Is it the multinational corporations that threaten economic ruin if they do not get their way, and demand that the *'tax payers'* vow fealty and tribute and bail them out when they through their own shear greed and hubris bring financial disaster and collapse? Or is it the multi-national corporations

---

[17] The Administrative State is a shadow or false executive state masquerading as the legitimate one. See Administrative State in Appendix.

that after having been incubated and nurtured in America and fed the milk and meat of the great American middle class workforce and market? They have left their American family and married a global whore, and now routinely buy the influx of hoards of cheap 3rd world foreign workers to dispossess the American middle class, who's labor can not even pay for their own keep, the cost of which is passed on to the 'tax payer' masses?

Is it the international leftist coalition with their armies of have-nots from here and around the 3rd world who employ threats of racial violence to empower the envy political trade and is represented by the United Nations and powerful shadow advocacy and shakedown groups?

Is it the corrupt Republican and Democrat parties who have demonstrated on numerous occasions their reckless disregard for the stability and soundness of America, and further, have demonstrated their willingness to destroy the country in order to wield the scepter?

Or is it the sovereign people, legitimately endowed with political right by birthright, with affirmation of previous declaration? *We declare and affirm that we the Sovereign Politically Endowed Heirs to the American civilization are the only ones that can legitimately assert ownership of America.*

Who has the right to the land?

Is it the federal government that claims to have jurisdiction and the right to regulate all land and its use? And further uses the power of government to outright confiscate or through regulation, diminish the rights to property through non-ratified so called 'treaties' with corrupt globalist agencies and world bodies? Or is it those who claim through corrupt interpretation, imagined 'constitutional findings' of power that mysteriously emanate from the interstate commerce clause?

Is it the leftist international and globalist governance bodies, and NGOs (Non Governmental Agencies), UN bureaucrats, or so called 'human rights' groups that declare any 'world citizen' that makes it to US soil has some imagined right to remain which supersedes the right of native born Americans?

Or is it the native born Original-Americans whose ancestors were pilgrims, and founders, and frontiersmen, and settlers, and pioneers, and explorers, and warriors, and conquerors, and the architects of our culture, who invented the modern world; who through their shear perseverance and necessity defended the land and formed the nation out of a wilderness, and who are endowed with political rights through these and hence ownership by that heritage? *We declare and affirm, we the Sovereign Politically Endowed Heirs to the American civilization are the only ones that can legitimately assert the right to our land, and the right to determine restrictions and the use of our land.*

Who is an American?

Is an economic refugee, or an illegal alien that crossed over our border without permission, or one that abused our hospitality by overstaying our generous visa in order to seek economic opportunity, an American?

Is an economic immigrant who has come to make *'a better life for themselves'*, but who's culture has no concept of our system of ethics and its flip-side, the uniquely American version of Christian values, defined and refined by Americans for over 200 years? They have no idea of who we are or from where we have come. No concept of the values we learned by raising oneself up by his bootstraps or carving out something from nothing, without a government hand-down, defending it, to see it prosper. Is this an American? No, but potential is there.

Does this newly arrived immigrant add to the richness of the already defined American culture, or do they detract and pervert our sense of identity claiming their right as defined by globalists, with 'Global Citizens' status which shields them from having to learn our culture or ways when they enter here? Refusing to adopt American customs, language, and culture, they instead demand we give deference to accommodate them and their customs, thus Balkanizing our fair land into enclaves of warring tribes with no sense of community or commonality? It engenders in them an attitude that we Americans are the odd ones, out of alignment with current world views on culture and identity, which in-turn solicits contempt for us and our culture.

Or is it the Original-Americans, American v1.0, who obtained that right by bearing the weight and burden of sacrifice, and have passed that right on to their heirs? *We declare and affirm, we the Sovereign Politically Endowed Heirs to the American civilization are the only ones that can legitimately assert we are Americans, and as such are natural citizens. We have the right to determine who if any other may enter here and enjoy status as citizens.*

Who can determine the laws of our land?
Do the international leftist organizations inspired by the UN whose corrupt socialist doctrines presume the power to determine the laws and rules that all nations must adhere to simply by making declaration and passing resolutions, then dictate that these have the power of law without any recognition, authority, or accountability?

Is it the corrupt and increasingly illegitimate US government who at this time exists only to serve its own ends, and whose dictates routinely only selectively observe the constitution and the rights of the people in order to garner favor with its benefactors? Is it this same government who passes laws that obligate one group with the maintenance and expense of another without any benefit, and burdens all of the people with regulations and the ever increasing burden of taxation and debt? Or engages in foreign adventurism and wars, fostering national enemies while increasingly destructive of our rights in the name of safety and national security?

Is it the people who inherited that power from their forefathers, who carved out a nation and thereby established a perpetual right to their domain, and who intended that it be passed on to their heirs? We declare and affirm yes of course the heirs are the only ones that legitimately have that power.

Do foreign peoples or powers have the right through treaty to supersede what we have decided for ourselves? Does our government have that power?

The simple answer is no. A treaty is established if those legitimately endowed with the authorization, negotiate agreements in harmony with the universal principles of the founding of the nation, and only if such treaties are in accordance with natural law and justice. It must also be only in the interest and benefit of, and in no way contrary to the interests or benefit of us who are legitimately endowed with the power to approve such treaty.

If you hesitate, even a little in your mind about the answers or are tempted to rationalize the current flawed ideology imposed on us, let us make it very clear by way of a little declarative credo:

We, the Sovereign Politically Endowed Heirs to the American civilization declare in no uncertain terms, the land contained within the borders of the 50 states currently joined in union, belong in entirety to the same, and to the states and nation respectively. We have the absolute sovereign right to determine all things that are now, and will be in our land. It is not up to any other person, people, or power to make any determination concerning us, our land, or our affairs. This is the truth in perpetuity and any person, people, or power that attempts to subvert this declaration; we now declare to be an enemy and do hereby swear to defeat them.

We declare and affirm that we are the sole heirs to the foundation of the nation. We share this with no other.

We further declare and affirm that we are the stewards of the civilization built upon that foundation with the absolute sovereign power to renew and remake it as is necessary; to restore, further, and improve our civilization.

We declare and affirm that we are the sole heirs to the right of political participation, inherited from the founders of our nation.

We declare and affirm our power to possess our land and that we have the sole right to determine all laws and matters within our land, and that no others have the power to supplant or supersede it.

We affirm the virtue, validity, and supremacy of this declaration as applying, having applied, and applying henceforth.

CHAPTER FIVE
Gaining Perspective

Looking To The Future

It is important to move past the obsession with the problems plaguing the nation and look to the future. We as a people need to stop obsessing about the mountain of problems, and start talking about solutions. If any patriotic and conscientious person dare realize that not all is well in the magic kingdom, then ask what can be done, they will likely hear crickets. However, if they further investigate where one would naturally look for the expected forthcoming answers, they are met with a barrage of confusion and noise, most of it intentional. Mainstream media is quickly ruled out and it is evident that they deny there really is a problem.

Why is it that most look for answers from the sources that are the least likely to offer any? What about those in the public opinion and talk industry; the liberal or conservative political talkers? Upon close investigation, they are usually recruited and settle into a myriad of erroneous views and schools of thought that all amount to a continuos recital of the litany of problems that plague us, with absolutely no solutions, or even a clue, as evidenced by the lack of any viable measures proposed. They play a game for our benefit, to entertain and indoctrinate us, not to educate us.

So where else might one inquire to find a wellspring of wisdom and answers; the internet, or the alternative radio, or other media? Maybe the completely dysfunctional government itself holds some answers, but then its not likely to be of any help even if it did. Maybe the halls of academia or the cave of a wise oracle? To all of these I say no; if there are answers to our problems forthcoming, they are most likely to come from the ranks of the common people; those individuals, and organizations that when focused together have the greatest power, and the greatest stake in the outcome.

Let us examine where we are at this juncture, and where solution for our future lay.

What are the views and attitudes necessary to lay the foundation for the future; to ensure we are the architects and not just passive observers, along for whatever ride others may have in-store for us?

Note: *In this discussion, I will limit the matter to that which applies to the US, and not the rest of the western world, even though, it is also mostly applicable.*

We have entered a new millennium as well as a new century, so old ways, and old thinking must give way to new thinking, and new ways must be designed to deal with life on planet earth.

Civilization continuously ebbs and flows between the evil forces of corruption, decay, and death, and the good forces of life, renewal, and restoration. The trend over time is unquestionably toward the rise of sovereign individuals and groups from the ranks of the common, and away from the powerful cabal.[18] Our government and the rest of western republican, democratic, parliamentary systems, etc. are failing; at this time all are dying. This means the current Republican structure of governance created by the Constitution of the United States will cease to exist. I will repeat that just in case

---

[18] From cabala (Kabbalah)

you were asleep, or glazed over what I just said; **The current Republican structure of governance created by the Constitution of the United States will cease to exist.** That is; the office of the President, both houses of congress, and the court systems; the US military system; all federal statutes and laws will become void then end; and the currency issued by the US Federal Reserve system; all will cease to exist, and it is likely to be in the near timeframe. However, the states which created the constitution, the sovereign people, and the nation will remain; thank God!

These failing systems cannot be resurrected, nor should that be attempted. They must die, inorder to allow for a better system to emerge, which the people will institute. The likely outcome is a complete collapse of the world economy, with significant financial displacement and disruption to everyone. This must be recognized universally and established as a qualified certainty. It is going to happen, and is likely very close in time.

It is time to start recognizing that we must design and create a new system and stop the hand-wringing about the old failing system. Stop looking to preserve the old which is dying, but embrace what the future will bring, which is liberation and the elevation of humanity to new echelons if we make it so. The future for us is not one of enslavement as many believe and advocate. It is not one in which the small narrow-interests of rich and powerful will have more and more control, and wield more and more oppressive power over our lives. Instead, it is one of liberation and a new beginning. History bears this out as the cycles of birth, death, and renewal have shown.

To insure this future, it is imperative that we begin to visualize and describe that future. It is within the power of men to believe then achieve whatever he may conceive, but it must begin with a vision. This means stop agonizing over the failure of what we have had in the past, or what you have imagined is the ominous future of slavery and the oppression

77

of the common, but begin to speak and accept that we, the common, are the architects of the future, if we will only realize that we have that power.

Many will take exception to this assertion and instead counter that those that are oppressing us are gaining more control and more of the ability to put us in a box. Again, history supports just the opposite. We have moved from past civilized states in Europe and even before where the common were considered as having virtually no worth or right, but instead were viewed as chattel at the whims of kings and the noble. We have arrived at a point in history in which most of us believe in the democratic voice of the masses. Whether it really works as expected or is limited in practice, at least most believe that is the way it should be. That makes all the difference in the world, as now the powerful can not really put that genie back in the bottle or turn us back much from here; we will never accept that. We have arrived at this point in time and with the understanding we have gained; knowing from whence we have come, we will never accept going back again. That limits their power to force anything on us beyond what the majority, or at a minimal, what the masses of the simple and the most uninformed will accept.

We must imagine then conceive our future civilization, then design it, begin to believe in its plausible and realistic implementation, then imagine the possibilities, and talk about it, and teach others the concepts, then solicit their support in creating an army of others that see their future in alignment with what we do; who are willing to do their part, make their sacrifices, and dedicate their lives to insure its fruition. This involves vivid and detailed descriptions of the system with stories and projections about what it is we want, and how it would come about. This needs to be the dominant topic of discussion, and leave the worrying in the past. It is up to us, and we will never arrive at the desired future without going through that process. These are steps along the path that must be trodden to arrive at a desirable future paradigm.

Some like to make the analogy that we as a civilization are in a war against the forces of corruption and control. If you believe we are in a war, then you have to answer what extent you are willing to go to secure victory? Are you willing to stop, and give up clinging to the dream of what America once was (the so called American Dream), in order to bring about another chapter for future generations, because that is what is required? The 'American Dream' was really part of a media marketing campaign to make people believe in something that did not really exist. That is not to say that America did not present extraordinary opportunities to the average person, but it has now turned into some imagined right, without any basis in right, with misguided people decrying its denial. It is my belief that we may see the real American Dream in the future if we are willing to let go of foggy ideas and embrace the work and challenges set before us.

Many who believe they are alerting the masses to the impending situation of doom and calamity, are in reality, hindering the natural progress of civilization by painting an ominous picture of the future, leading people to believe there is very little they or anyone can do to head-off the impending disaster. Paraphrasing a common nugget of wisdom, believed to have been attributed to an ancient Chinese war-lord[19], who said, *"You can defeat your enemy without a fight, if you can get him to believe that it is futile to fight, and impossible for him to win."* That is the outcome of continuously churning the language of defeat by endlessly reciting the impossibility of the problems and the dire circumstances, but saying nothing about what we can do to shape our own future, or where we go and what we do after the dust clears from the impending implosion of a system gone bad. If it has gone bad and is near implosion, then rejoice, it is time to start looking to the future. The sooner we start down that road, the faster we can get a glimpse or a complete vision of the future we decide for ourselves, and with God's help we

---

[19] Sun Tzu. The Art of War

will ease into that future having endured whatever degree of pain and displacement he determines for us. Do not pray to salvage a corrupt system, but pray for a new system where righteous people will lead and give good counsel to the rest.

Reducing the Perception of Threat

I have formed viewpoints concerning the public dialog that has cropped up in radio and on the internet concerning the power of global forces that seek to rule the planet and dominate the lives of everyone. If you are not sure what I am referring to, give the Republic Broadcast network a listen. First let me re-iterate what I have already stated; that the nature of the progression of civilization will always include a contest between constructive and destructive forces, so there is nothing new at this point. This is much like the reports of increases in certain types of weather or other natural phenomenon; frequency and intensity of earthquakes, etc. The phenomena have probably not really changed outside of normal probability, but what has changed is our ability to detect, observe, and catalog such occurrences, so it seems as though there is an increase in them. Some of the rationale for the 'fear-speak' portending doom and gloom stems from the same effect but let us take a more rational look at it.

If one takes a sober and balanced view of things, especially with a historical perspective, the fact that there are powerful and scary groups that have made ominous statements and taken actions that threaten civilization is no reason to despair, that accomplishes nothing. The fact that they may have tremendous influence over large segments of the global economy is alarming, but still, no one should panic just yet. These groups have always been there, mostly unseen and unknown by the masses. The fact that they are more known today than in the recent past is nothing to be alarmed at either. In fact, there was pretty good knowledge of the same threats back in the early part of the last century, before they monopolized the media, and cleansed their presence. In the 18th and 19th century, when their ambitions, and plots were found out, the groups were removed from the society they threatened.

The ability for nefarious forces to control the populace, although it is now thought to be more easily accomplished by them, that is in-fact not the case. To the degree that technology bestows an advantage to powerful groups, it also gives an even greater advantage to the masses to combat and neutralize their ability. Their recent past monopoly in news and media are quickly fading due to the internet media of the masses expressing viewpoint and opinion. Their faces and secrets are being exposed. Globalization, forced against the judgement and willingness of the nation, along with unchecked debt accumulation, has setup conditions for tremendous loss in terms of economic power which some would argue is all part of the plan, but I view it more as the unintended or uncontrolled consequences of mismanagement, free-for-all attitudes, too much greed, and too many bodies that need to be payed to play. The consequences of all of this has yet to play out.

It is really incumbent on us to pull back the curtain and expose the little man loudly barking mighty threats. Its in our interest to unmask him; demystify him, so we can understand the actual magnitude of the threat. This cuts him down to size and yields a realistic and relativist perspective on the future. To accomplish this, there are many lessons that can be given, and one must be a student of history to cite them all, but let us examine a few. The first, and best example is what happened to the architects of the French Revolution who had similar aims as today's cabal of globalist, hegemonists; which is a world government with an elitist ruling-class handing down dictates and imposing their warped ideas of how everything should be run onto the rest of humanity. It ended badly for them with heads filling baskets. The ones that move in those circles today, are, or should be, acutely aware of that fact and know that they must move carefully.

The second example is what happened after World War II. The Nuremberg war trials[20] were held to deal with the aftermath of the nazi menace. It was a trial in-which war-crimes charges were brought against several accused, and according to the charges, acted believing they were justified with barbaric and inhuman treatment of innocent people. It is notable that many of those charged with crimes against humanity, used the defense that they were not culpable because they were only following the orders given them by superiors. This excuse did not wash and 12 were sentenced to be hanged, while others, to lengthly prison terms because it was determined they were duplicitous in guilt.

I debated illustrating this example due to a few reasons that have to do with the use of the trials for propaganda purposes. It is argued that the trial took advantage of the Hegelian dialectic principle by creating the condition necessary for, and highlighting justification and ratification of powerful and intrusive global laws and institutions which were highly influenced by the trials and instituted afterward. It is also argued by some that the spectacle was mostly a 'show-trial' and those accused would have been convicted regardless of guilt. In any case, it serves as a useful and powerful example for us today, which is to hit home with a powerful message of the swift, sure, and serious consequences of one's actions, particularly for those in positions of authority, or who may be tempted to egregiously violate the humanity of others.

Those that make similar pronouncements about the fate and disposal of humanity today should also be acutely aware of that reality. In Nuremberg, most of those charged were found guilty and hung, as have been tyrants throughout time. These trials were held and made public to send a chilling message to

---

[20] Nuremberg Germany, 1945/46

future generations of opportunistic tyrants and criminals. It was made clear, they are not in-fact, omniscient, omnipotent, invulnerable or anything other than weak and frail humans, just as the rest of us are. They eat, sleep, eliminate, and bleed, and they put their pants on one leg at a time. They employ others to do work for them, while those employed are also human, and usually work for a wage, regardless of their position in government or industry. Take away that paycheck and they will not show up to carry out the work.

This discussion is really to put a human face of frailty and vulnerability on an image or perception that has been hyped and built up into something greater than what it is in reality, which those that propagate it fought hard to create and have successfully accomplished. We need to work toward neutralizing that perception; to face the demon with a man's face and stare him down, which will help remove our own *'deer in the headlights'*, catatonic state of fear, and our unwillingness to act in our own interests toward building the future.

Patriot Legal Stew

A great deal of the so called patriot movement preaches the gospel of a false messiah. Their message is doomed to failure if you listen to their rhetoric and their reasoning. They are good at researching and finding the letter of the law where the nation has been betrayed. They can cite chapter and verse, the treachery and legal plunder of our constitution and our laws. The problem is, this information is not of much good when you realize that it is mostly true. Our system has been completely plundered as if it were done by a hostile foreign power operating within our midst, because for the most part it was.

Indeed our Article-I and Article-III[21] courts, called 'constitutional courts' and legal system has been completely

---

[21] US Constitution

hollowed out and replaced wholesale by a foreign system without our consent. The legislative branch defers responsibility and policy to private interest organizations, or simply allows Administrative State agencies[22] (bureaucracies) to run roughshod over the people, the states, and industry. For examples of how this works, consider that the IRS, EPA, FDA, and virtually all the alphabet soup government agencies are free to make arbitrary rules (codes) and enforce them as if they are law, which they are not, and do not carry the weight of law. However, that hardly matters. Challenging these arbitrary rules is fraught with pitfalls when attempted. Usually when challenge is brought through the phony administrative courts operating not under the constitution, but under the jurisdiction of maritime law, the challenges are simply not allowed, thus reinforcing the power of these agencies to operate by fiat.

This state of affairs came about by way of an unlawful and unconstitutional act designed to serve the interests of a foreign private body which operates as a hand in the glove of constitutional government. It operates stealthily in and throughout the structure of the original constitution, just beneath the surface in such a manner as to not allow the American public to overtly detect or discover the reality of their own status vis-à-vis the illegitimate-pretender state. The presence of this corrupt, illegitimate state for the past 150+ years has had a very profound transformative effect on the nation and the people, having entwined itself into the very life and fabric of our law, history, and traditions.

To understand how this could be the case, think of what happened with the recent American invasion of Iraq and Afghanistan. The United States made war on them, and militarily invaded them, then set up a military occupation, taking political control inorder to remake those countries into something which suits their purposes, which in no-way is in

---

[22] Administrative Procedure Act, 1946

alignment with the interests of the American people, our nation, or the people of the countries targeted. Approximately the same event happened to our nation with the civil-war, and occupation of the sovereign southern states afterward in the 19th century during the reconstruction era. It was during this period that the political occupation occurring there was extended to the entirety of the nation. We have been occupied by an unseen foreign power ever since.

This event and *'change of status'* was *'accomplished'* through an act of treason involving several new constitutional amendments, one of which in particular, the 14th amendment,[23] and many that followed were patently illegal in terms of passage and standing, for a variety of reasons involving procedure, but in my estimation it is due to the chief reason which is seldom cited; it is because the constitution and its amendment process does not have the power to fundamentally alter the sovereign status of the people or the states which is claimed by the amendment. For the 14th amendment to be in effect, it could only be considered so if it were enacted by way of a Coup d'état and maintained by force.

I used the terms *'change of status'*, and *'accomplished'* above with quotation marks, and I am repeating it to highlight the fact that the constitution and its amendment process do not have the power to alter the sovereign status of either the people or the states. That chain of authority is reversed. In actuality, the amendment changed nothing because it had no authority to do so, therefore, the original status of the **Sovereign Politically Endowed People**, the **SPEP**, remains intact, however the sovereign right must be exercised to prevent further erosion.

---

[23] 14th Amendment to the US Constitution, 1868. Ostensibly transforms sovereign people to mere citizens of the Corporate United States, however, without possessing the power to enact such a transformation. See *'14th Amendment'* in the appendix.

Now that 150+ years have passed since the act of treason was accomplished and it has significantly ingrained itself into the current culture and law, does anyone really believe we can put Humpty Dumpty back together, ever again? Can we ever go back to the previous state? In my view the damage to the integrity of the American system is irreversible and is in totality, therefore a proper system must be structured anew from the ground up.

To quote wise old crumbs of wisdom; continuously decrying the betrayal of our nation by criminals is *'crying over spilt milk'*, or *'closing the barn door after the horses have left.'* It does little to mitigate or rectify the situation, or to educate a mass movement of those that should be employed to put things right. It should be recognized, especially by those 'patriots' that are continuously selling the problems; those who have corrupted our system can and will continue to do so at will, until a structure is put into place in-which they have no power.

We need to understand that the solution to our problem does not lay in using any existing system of laws with the power to correct the situation. It cannot be done. The *'rule of law'* does no good because they can make or ignore laws at will. Our legal system is subject to the whims of the prevailing political regime. Law is trumped by political power and corruption. Law is a tool; a big hammer in the hands of those that wield political power. Only by regaining political control can we put things back on track, and that only by force, rendered through the strong voice of the SPEP.

Stop preaching the legal betrayal sermon. Stop selling the problem; stop reacting to it and stop engaging in it; it makes no difference to anyone in the long run. The rhetoric of betrayal and endless, untenable dysfunction only sows confusion and a spirit of hopelessness. It feeds those that churn the capital of fear. You can not rectify our current trajectory by merely informing anyone of the treachery; those who matter significantly already know that it is occurring, and those that will not hear and will not join the fight are irrelevant. Those elected to operate our government were compromised long ago; if they remain, they have sanctioned the betrayal and they can be counted on to continue the betrayal. With the same vigor and energy used to research and expound on the problem, these 'patriots' should now employ to research solution and focus the rhetoric on that, and *'stop beating a dead horse.'*

Above the Law

Most have heard the expression *'no one is above the law.'* While we would like that to be true to protect all of us, it cannot be true in any practical way. This is the root of the misunderstanding made by most of the patriot groups like the Tea Party, Libertarians, etc, and the myriad of individual groups believing themselves a bulwark, holding the beast at sway. The reason why the idea that *'no one is above the law'* is not true is because the law came about by the sovereign will of a body, the *'Sovereign-Body'*, of people who put it into effect, therefore, the same sovereign-body will always hold a status above the established system of law. This is important because so many attempting to fight a loosing battle against our eroding civil order, argue their rights from a perceived subordinate position, meaning they look for legal arguments to justify their reasoning and their right. They allege to speak for all Americans, but cling to the all but failed constitution because they instinctively and correctly know that the constitution is a higher authority than the government, even the impostor shadow government operating in our midst. However, the argument fails because they put themselves and all they speak for at a status of subjection to the government. In other words, they believe the government gives them their rights, and some believe their rights emanate from the constitution. They are in error on both accounts.

While it is true that individually we are all subject to the laws established by the higher order sovereign-body and under the jurisdiction of the constitution, a significant portion of us are also part of the body that is above all. This is the part of our right that should have heretofore held a defined and codified recognition in law as it does in tradition, but it has not, thus the confusion. We must recognize that our sovereign rights emanate in a minor way from our sovereign status as members of the human family, and this has a legal basis that can be argued, but which is probably beyond the scope of this book; but these rights emanate mostly by inheritance through the **Law of Conquest**. At the very least, although not necessary, if we wanted a legal justification, an argument could stem from the western tradition of property rights and the right of kings, called the **Right of Conquest**.

The right of kings also has a religious basis in the Bible in 1 Samuel 10:1:

"Then Samuel took a flask of oil and poured it on his head and kissed him and said, "Has not the Lord anointed you to be prince over his people Israel? And you shall reign over the people of the Lord…"

In the middle ages, the kings of England, Scotland and elsewhere sought a particular type of oil[24] believed to be the same type used by Samuel, so like Saul who was anointed by Samuel the prophet, they could be anointed by the regional priest, bishop, or recognized representative of the Church, inorder to firm-up and justify in the minds of people, their right to the throne. This idea of 'right' is very intrenched into western tradition and is a part of the basis for the founding of our civilization.

Some will argue that we are not kings. What is a king if not a conquerer or his heir? The right of kings in actuality comes from conquest, however, it is somewhat secured and

---

[24] Anointing Oil containing jasmine, oil of bensoint, oils of orange, roses, cinnamon, musk, civet and ambergris.

recognized by ordination as suggested. The tradition also recognizes that conquerers pass-on the right of conquest to their heirs.

Earlier I suggested that legal capital is not needed, nor is any other, to establish our sovereign right, by the simple fact that 'right' ultimately comes from the application of force which I take up in the next section. It is imperative to recognize the proper order of right (food chain) that governs the structure of all civilization.

Rights

I like to think of 'rights' as something that is more a construct of ideas and ideals. I apply to the idea of **rights**, the definition as what is presented in one dictionary for the definition of an 'object', derived from the word objectum, *'a thing presented to the mind,'* which is a more utilitarian way of getting to a good understanding of what I believe a 'right' is, how it can be defined, and from whence it is derived. It is easier to view it this way simply because it is easier to remove some of the confusion about what it is and is not. Rights are like laws, mathematics, philosophies, and other such constructs or inventions which humans use to define and understand their world. A concept is derived, labeled with a name for the sake of discussion, then pontificated, and philosophized endlessly, attempting to categorize, and define it, to determine its significance in our world. Throughout all of this there is the hope that somewhere along the way, it is simply understood and agreed upon by most about what it 'is', what it 'means', how it works, and where it fits in. The problem with the usual taken meaning of a 'right' is that, it being what most people relate as an object implies it is 'real' or foundational somehow. The concept of a right is real, although in my view, it is not some nebulous moral foundational principle established by God and handed down or imbued by him into humankind; it is more arbitrary than that. Instead it is something that results more as a balance of the forces of nature that mankind is subject to, and which he encounters daily.

A simple and practical definition of rights and this means all things that can be called **rights** is, *'authority which is secured by the application of force.'* This also practically nullifies the rhetoric in the preamble of the constitution which declares that men have certain *inalienable rights*. The fact is they only have rights if they can secure them for themselves and then they are never inalienable. Alienable means that it can be transferred to another, or taken away, so 'In-alienable' means the opposite or that it cannot be taken away and of course this then leads to the introduction or invocation of God, or mother nature in the emanation of those rights. Isn't the definition of rights as an outcome in the balance of the forces of nature, the same as saying they emanate from the invocation of nature as the provider of rights? That is an argument that could be made, but I am simply stating that the idea that there are inalienable rights is simply not the case. However I will amend this principle with the assertion that sovereign political rights are not transferrable via any method with the exception of heritable conveyance.

Is there such a thing as an inalienable right to life, liberty, or the pursuit of happiness? Not that I can tell. It was decided long ago that societies may remove life, and liberty, and while the pursuit of happiness sounds wonderful, its exact meaning is elusive; somewhere in the ether I suspect. I can not think of a single right of those fondly and repeatedly listed by constitutionalists and patriots as qualifying under the US constitutions preamble as being inalienable, however I can think of one that may qualify but which is rarely if ever mentioned, and that is simply the right to think and believe as you wish. Until the day when someone figures out how to get directly into your head, and direct your very thoughts and convictions, that one remains.

The 'inalienable rights' spoken of in the US constitution may be considered to be recognized or espoused 'ideals' and believed to be as rights but they do not fit the criteria, and neither are they 'natural rights' because although nature will enforce its own order upon the world, these so called rights are not exactly part of the natural order so nature does not enforce them. By the definition given, they can neither be considered rights.

I will again temper my remarks about the inalienable right to life, liberty and so forth by saying that if the case can be made for their inalienability, it is simply by example of what would likely transpire, regardless of legal status, if an individual or group were to go about denying individuals their lives. Since this threatens most everyone, or at the very least, some in the vicinity, it is inevitable that force would be employed to put a stop to the activity. However this makes the force and effect of inalienability very weak indeed, however, law certainly strengthens it. The same applies to 'liberty.' If this can be used to construct and support the notion of inalienability, then so be it. I view it as questionable and unreliable at best.

I expect most will take a great exception to this discussion and disagree heartedly with me on this, but I changed my opinion from the very popular but erroneous view which I once shared when I began to really cut through the crap that is said by others and make examination through my own initiative. Indeed, when you scrape away the layers of fluff and rhetoric, and yes the founders of the republic used fluff to sell the ratification of the document to the convention, you are left with a similar conclusion.

I do not wish to be taken as someone bashing the US constitution which was a superbly drafted document for its time, which embodied most universal and good principles with which to found a republic, and it served well for the 70 or so years it was in effect, but it is really of little effect now. So I believe we need to look beyond something which is now defunct, to something that will serve us into the future, and extract and incorporate into the new those good and universal principles that were included in the original, sans fluffy rights. The concept of rights is something that must be properly defined and understood in order to do that effectively.

A good example for understanding the wellspring and existing status of rights vis-à-vis the constitution can be drawn from the Bill of Rights. The 2nd amendment states:

"A well regulated militia being necessary to the security of a free state, the right of the people to keep and bear arms shall not be infringed."

Note that it recognizes the existing *"right of the people"*, and mandates that the preexisting right *"shall not be infringed"* by the federal system. That is, the people's right to bear arms precedes the constitution and the bill of rights, which this amendment only recognizes and spells out. The phrase, *"shall not be infringed"*, puts a limitation on what defined governmental power may do and may not do with regard to these preexisting rights; it shall not infringe them. The 2nd amendment does not bestow the right to bear arms, and the government may not use the application of force in an attempt to alter or diminish the preexisting right.

Keep in mind, this is not a discussion about the right to bear arms; instead it is simply to illustrate that our rights do not stem from the constitution, nor the established government, but we have them preexisting; preceding and post any established civil system. They are of a higher order than the constitution and the structure of government which it put in place to recognize and secure them. Numerous other examples can be drawn from both the constitution and bill of rights to further illustrate this fact.

I mentioned before that a significant majority of our population, as a sovereign-body, are above the established system of law, but individually we all are subject to the law; which is where citizenship comes in to play. There is a place for the definition of the rights, or better ***privileges*** of citizens, which can be articulated, accepted, and codified in such accords that spell out the duties and liberties of citizens, and so forth. However, these only embody that which a simple contract would, and carry as much significance; and any rights bestowed may only emanate from that level.

So, we have rights (sovereign) which supersede the constitution and government, and we retain them under the jurisdiction of the constitution and government as sovereign individuals. We also have rights as a sovereign-body which are always above the constitution and government or any established system of law, while we have only privileges as citizens.

The SPEP have the right of ownership which includes the supreme political right of participation and it transcends citizenship and is inherited from the foundation of the nation. This stems partly from recognition of millennia of the western tradition of respect for property ownership and western jurisprudence, but mostly it comes by declaration; we declare it, thus speaking it into reality. It is really, as are all rights, a declaration that *'we shall retreat no further'*; a stance, a line in the sand which we are not willing to compromise, but we will stand and sacrifice all in defense of it. As I have already asserted, our political rights, like all rights, stem from declaration and the application of force. Our struggle is against those that similarly use declaration and the application of force, attempting to take it from us.

Six Keys

For the sake of organization and distilling the thoughts expressed in this book, I have boiled down the message to 6 keys, some of which I have already discussed. In my opinion, the 6 keys listed, taken as a whole, give us a very powerful tool for altering the current declining trajectory of our civilization, steering it back to one of health and vitality.

1) <u>Authority.</u> I have already thoroughly discussed this one, giving rationale for our complete authority to make the necessary wholesale changes. It assumes that we can confidently identify the necessary changes.

2) <u>Declaration.</u> The same with this one. The rationale for a firm and loud declaration has been discussed already. Again this assumes that we can confidently identify what declarations are needed to define our civilization, and put the world on notice.

3) <u>Obsolete Political Profession.</u> Advances in civilization has given us a 2 part key consisting of:

> a) Knowledge

> b) Survival

This will be discussed later. It outlines a very powerful rationale that the political profession is obsolete, which means the entire political establishment is no longer necessary. It performs no useful purpose, but instead only holds the door open, facilitating narrow-interest criminals and predators the opportunity to prey on the people and the nation.

4) <u>Structure.</u> Proper structure will ensure and maintain the integrity of a new and better form of civilization. This rationale states that a better model for civilization is one that takes into account that structure is vitally important. The structure must employ the energy and natural forces of human behavior to put in place the proper set of incentives and deterrents for governance.

5) <u>Alignment of States.</u> It was recognized by the early pre-union states which instinctively did not trust an imperial central government, the necessity for maintaining the status of a sovereign and independent political entity. The structure may well have been established with the abolishment of independent states in favor of one big happy family, but instead they left them in-place and with good reason; they feared the situation we find ourselves in today and wished to

give themselves the ability to abandon then remedy a corrupted and degenerating system. The writers of the Declaration of Independence informed them of such and recognized their right to do so. The same men in recognition of this fact sought to facilitate that situation should it ever become necessary by creating a constitution which loosely tied the states voluntarily so as to not complicate the process of abandonment if necessary. That fact of history must be recognized today. The abandonment of the federal monstrosity gone bad by individual sovereign states is the most effective path to renewal and restoration of the civilization.

Many tested and exercised their sovereign right with the secession[25] of independent southern states in the 1860s, however it was short lived, but that hardly altered the status or the structure as it was forged by agreement among sovereign entities precisely for that purpose; so it remains to facilitate the disposition and recreation of our civilization recognized in the Declaration of Independence. This is important because the task of recreating our civilization can be made considerably easier by directing the power for changes toward certain individual states with populations that are more willing than others less inclined. With the states, the commanding power wielded for change is much closer to the people and allows them considerably greater voice, while allowing a buffer against the power and influence of the illegitimate federal system.

6) Opportunity. If all was great with the nation, we would have nothing to worry about. However, the situation is rapidly degrading and it is assumed that at some point the situation will become unacceptable for a critical mass of people. At that point it is an easy assumption that there will be enough minds open to the possibility of making the appropriate change. ***That is our opportunity.*** There is an expression which states that success happens when opportunity

---

[25] The act of withdrawing formally from membership.

and preparedness meet. We must work hard to ensure there are enough minds with adequate understanding who have prepared, by laying a foundation. We must insure we have sufficiently laid the ground-work in the right states and have a movement in place to take advantage of the catalyzing energy of collapse, which will create the conditions necessary to propel the appropriate change. To be sure, those that would put us in a cage are thinking the exact same, and when the time comes, they will be prepared to take advantage inorder to accomplish their own agenda.

Macro-view Summing Points

At this point it is necessary to sum-up the message of the book from a macro viewpoint by bulleting the major points, then flush out the details in the balance. Summation short-cuts much of the concepts and rationalizations and is intended to give a brief overview of the themes and message of the book rather than require the reader to plow through the considerable material, while giving points that will later make better sense when viewed in light of the balance.

• The Declaration of Independence informs us that the sovereign heirs to the foundation of the nation are politically endowed with the <u>Authority</u> to remake the nation.

• The nation can be remade by exercising that authority. This comes by loud and clear <u>Declaration</u>.

• The Sovereign Politically Endowed People (SPEP), not citizens, own the nation, having inherited it from the founders.

• The nation and every aspect of it exists to serve the will and interests of the sovereign people and the citizens and not the very narrow interests who currently dominate the culture, economy, and the political process; that status must change.

• The current constitution is obsolete and of little-effect and the federal republic which was created by it is also illegitimate as a result, and the fact that current government exists for its own ends and profit, and not the purpose for which it was created, proves the assertion.

• Government may not exist for its own ends or for those that operate it, but it may only exist to serve exclusively at the interest and whim of the politically endowed people and citizens.

• The current federal government was created by the constitution which was created by the states which were created by the sovereign politically endowed founders of the republic.

• The current government is in its death-throws with total failure imminent. It cannot be reformed, restored, or salvaged, nor should it be attempted. Any attempt will be futile.

• Financial collapse of the government is imminent, and close in time, probably within the current decade.

• Through the same process, the SPEP, organized and acting with authority as a Sovereign-Body, may create a new supra-state structure made-up of voluntary members from the existing <u>alignment of states</u>. Such new supra-state exists only to serve at the pleasure of the sovereign people and citizens.

• Reconstituting a new structure cannot be accomplished by confronting or overthrowing the current one directly, nor by reforming it. An easier route is to work through the <u>opportunity</u> presented by channeling the catalyzing backlash of fear and energy from a likely near-term economic collapse, into the political-will for creating a new system, absent criminal interests or partisan political agents and operatives, or large money interests. These can have no role in its recreation or definition.

• A new association or alliance of sovereign states constituting an alignment or association is formed with members coming from the current alignment of states. The new supra-state structure will have a new structure of governance functions, monetary system, definition of citizenship compact, body of law, etc. States wishing to join must adhere to the criteria for admission, and may need significant reform to comply.

• Civilizations, and governance has been evolving and improving for millennia. The next iteration to emerge should recognize and be built on the supremacy and sovereignty of the politically endowed common man, not narrow interests.

• The new <u>structure</u> must incorporate a Sovereign Democratic Majority (SDM) legislative operating form. Sovereign means *'Law Giver'*; the SPEP will make all laws.

• An outline for method of accomplishing the creation and operation of a new structure of supra-state, and state governance is presented. It must be structured through the SPEP (acting through a Sovereign-Body), who will originate, articulate, draft, and ratify all policy and law. There is no power vested in political middle-men, otherwise called politicians, neither legislative nor executive, or through any structure of trust, because the current Republic has demonstrated there can be no trust with the power to legislate, or execute. This effectively eliminates the Republican or elected representative form of government and many others which have become <u>obsolete</u>.

• There are no elected offices. All people that compose any power vested in running functions of governance are employees, and derive from private enterprise. They are hired and employed by contract only, and may be fired with their contract ended simply by act of the sovereign-body.

• An executive may be employed, but may only have a very limited power, and is a mere contract employee of the state. The sole responsibility of an executive is to serve exclusively at the will of the SPEP, and citizens and nowhere else. The executive, for all intents and purposes is a dutiful care-taker or executive manager.

• Funding for the executive and all functions of governance come exclusively by way of direct appropriations by the sovereign-body. Executive, legislative support, judicial, military, and any other function defined as state, are expressly restricted from any and all self-funding activities. They are all expressly restricted from borrowing or debt, and may only operate by direct funding from the SPEP through state channels. The sole source of funding is limited to that which the SPEP have articulated, budgeted on their behalf, and appropriated through apportionment from the states. Any and all debt incurred by any structure of governance must be authorized by the SPEP.

• Funding may come from many sources, but all are aggregated by states. Sources may not include direct taxation on income, neither personal nor corporate, but may be collected from non-resident or foreign sources, both personal and corporate. Examples of acceptable sources of revenue include Point-of-Sale excise tax, user fees, licenses, and trade tariffs. Estimations for all forms of taxation to fund governance at all levels (local, state, supra-state) should not exceed 6% of GNP. It is near 55% in total, and 25% at the federal level alone currently and growing, estimated to top 30% in the near term.

• All aligned interests, parties, and associations must be registered and licensed for political participation, and are dis-incentivized by relegation of all affiliated sharing a 20% maximum of total weighted vote. Parties are narrow-interests by definition, and as such they will always be involved, and cannot effectively be eliminated, therefore in recognition of this dynamic, aligned interests are allowed.

• Any and all organizations involved in the political process or which have coalesced with others are considered to be aligned interests,[26] and shall be bound within and share the 20%

limitation. Normal political weight is rescaled for representation within the full-scale of the shared limitation, while undersubscription cannot extend normal weighting up to the limit. The result is total weighted vote from all aligned interests may not exceed 20% of total.

• All adoption of policy is accounted in a system in which the vote is weighted by full qualification: by competence, and by right.

• Later chapters outline the current US government fiscal debt analysis in which the current public debt is shown to be a fatal problem for the federal system. Several methods are given for dealing with the debt, with one being preferred over others, however, it can only be accomplished under certain circumstances that are laid out in the bulk of material presented.

• Finally, there is a theoretical counterpart to the debt solution presented, which involves the re-definition of a monetary and banking system needed to support a debt solution and set a framework for growth and renewal for many decades to come.

---

[26] Aligned Interests are the same as narrow-interests.

CHAPTER SIX
Elements of Stable Civilization

Rules For Civilization

Civilizations must have rules which govern them. The rules are what provide stability and safety for the participants. They may be looked at as clauses in the social or civil contract. The right elements must be present to ensure harmony with the dictates of human nature. If the rules are not in harmony with that which drives human behavior, the civilization will be unstable and ultimately fail. I have attempted to compile what I believe to be at least a partial list of the elements necessary to enhance the growing, thriving civilization. It is by no means intended to be a comprehensive treatise but only to give a cursory idea.

Sovereignty

The sovereign status of individuals from all strata of societies, and the body of common is a growing phenomenon, as opposed to past eras when individuals and groups of common had absolutely no worth or right but were considered slaves and property by the elite members of the civilization. Sovereignty embodies most of the ideals of liberty in the society. Through liberty, energy for growth is fostered and the forces which propel considerable economic development is unleashed.

One of the greatest advantages of Sovereignty of the individual is it allows the individual to undertake risk through the capital systems; to create new and useful products and services that enrich every member of the civilization.

Sovereignty means the individuals are no longer considered as property or subjected to the arbitrary rule of corrupt bodies, so the endowed body of individuals that make up the civilization are the rightful owners of the civilization with the absolute right and authority to determine all of it's affairs.

Church

The issue that comes to the minds of most people when they read 'Church' in a list considered necessary for a stable civilization is the idea that church and state are supposed to be separate. A secular state and religion buried and restricted to the private home and the church-house, and not tolerated elsewhere; however that is simply propaganda programming. To clarify let me give 2 reasons why I have included it here:

1) I am using the word 'Church' in a somewhat generic fashion, although it does represent only the Christian Church. It is generic in the sense that it refers to non-sectarian Christian, but it could represent any religion in general. The same discussion could also apply as for Islamic or buddhist temple for those civilizations in the part of the world where those religions are predominant. I do not believe that a plurality of different religions within the same civilization fits the criteria for stability due to the inevitability of sectarian and religious wars that have always, and will continue to permeate multi-cultural societies, therefore in this discussion it is in the context of the American civilization and the Christian Church only.

2) I am not referring to state in this discussion. I am talking about the civilization itself which is a group of people; members of a society and culture absent any particular form of government or state. In this particular case the discussion is in

the context of the American civilization, which means predominance of the Christian Church. Let me also say I do not believe that it is desirable to establish an official State-Church, Christian or otherwise; the 2 serve different and distinct purposes. I do not believe anyone should be forced to subscribe to any religion in any form by coercion of the state; that is tyrannical and no different from anything which forces individuals against their conscience.

Churches function as the moral and spiritual center for the civilization; to provide vital instruction on successful living; how to live in such a way so as to bless the lives of others and thereby, the quality of life for the whole; instead of following the natural more basic instincts which would lead every person to attempt to live off of the labor and wealth of their neighbor. The Church is vital to develop persons who exhibit the highest qualities of behavior, which enhances the society and does not detract from it. It provides charity to those weaker or infirmed members of the society who are in-need of care. It provides spiritual guidance to those members who are driven to explore the spiritual realm and worship.

Churches provide religious and moral instruction, which significantly mitigates the need for the heavy and hard hand of civil regulation. People are instead admonished and more prone to honorable conduct and self-regulation. History has shown that civilizations which cultivate religious observance have considerably less need for police and jails, while civilizations which have eliminated or restricted the role of churches, and the free flow of religious exercise or instruction, invariably suffer decline and failure.

Societies that have a background population who were brought up with a moral and religious tradition; one that has taught its people how to treat others with respect and love, will be considerably more stable than those that have not. They will experience very high levels of success and happiness, and will nurture and raise their children to become very capable

103

high caliber members of the human family. They will be much less prone to pervasive criminality, violence, and vice. They will not tolerate crude or unacceptable behavior, violence, evil, or the kind of sick social ills that seems to be overwhelming our current failing culture at present, but will swiftly stand to eradicate abhorrence from the society. They will selflessly watch out for their neighbors and not ignore their need but help them when it is warranted.

Traditional members of our society, regardless whether they adhere to or practice Christian ethics, are nonetheless familiar with them which positively influences their behavior and instincts, having been brought up in our society where Christian ethics were freely observed and pervasive up until most recently. We became considerably more prosperous and capable, with a population more self-sufficient and more willing and able to generously help others of their neighbors and those in other lands. It can not be stressed enough the enormity of the value of the Christian ethic which has shaped western civilization in the last 2 millennia.

Sadly the Christian church and Christian belief and ethics have come under vicious attack by the secular powers of our Republic which have a passionate hatred toward it. They are not content to live and let the religious beliefs and practices of the population continue as they were, but they seem bent on driving it all but out of the life and tradition of our nation. We are beginning to see the ravages of that fact now as the American civilization slides ever more deeply into trouble. They have started a war against Christianity but it is my conviction that they will find it difficult to sustain that war as it becomes more and more evident to the people, the magnitude of what they have lost.

Homogeneous Culture

This is a difficult subject to discuss due to the poisoned atmosphere created in the last 50 or so years, rife with the campaign of subtle lies and programming of the public, starting in the 1950/60s and before. The subject of race has become a hot potato and is the most highly volatile subject, so much so that few people will talk openly about their real feelings and attitudes concerning the matter, and that includes people of all races.

I however, am not a shrinking violet. It is a subject which is verboten to speak about, outside of acceptable and strictly enforced orthodoxy, which is another way to say it is *'politically incorrect'*, because it is used as a very powerful tool in the hands of elitists to program and shape the attitudes and thoughts of the culture. Our nation should look much differently today than it does due to the hammer of racial innuendo and guilt used against the middle-class white population which is a perpetual storm of controversy. The programming effort seeks to make whites feel uncomfortable in their skin. It would seem to be a sort of turn-about agenda, but the motivation goes way beyond something as petty as that. People will naturally wear their race as if it were a piece of clothing due to the fact that they are stuck inside of it, like it or not. It is a big part of their identity and it defines who they are to a great extent, as does their native culture.

The source of virtually all of this *politically correct* culture programming is from 2 sources: 1) The mainstream commercial and government media, and 2) The academia programmed curriculum of public education. From the continuous media pounding of Nazi-holocaust propaganda shame in public television and radio, to the slavery memorial trade in-which the southern US must now repudiate its own cultural and racial pride and history to forever wear a banner of shame. Whites are programmed to act the role, and speak the language of contrition and shame anytime any private or public dialog broaches the boundaries of race. According to media programming, they are expected to cease from all objective discussion and pull out their shame-hat to wear with a long hang-dog face of contrition and expressions of deep shame for being members of the most evil clan on earth.

Lets cut right through all the crap. White people have nothing to be ashamed of, nor apologize for. All people are racist! That is right, I said ***ALL PEOPLE ARE RACIST***, just as all people tell lies and all people have to empty their bowels. All people think evil thoughts about their neighbors, and all people lust after many things. All people have some degree or another of preference and affinity for their own skin and culture. That is what racism is; So What? Discrimination based on a prejudice is nothing more than exercising ones preference and freedom to choose whatever they like. Is it passing judgment? Yes! How is it any worse than any of the other indulgences people engage in? There could be no more hypocritical an act as to speak against or condemn someone else for being prejudice, discriminatory, or intolerant. The person that does so will always find it justified when they do it themselves, while they also represent the epitome of what they accuse when passing judgement upon others. *"Judge not, lest ye be judged."* I find extremely dubious, the claims of those who regard themselves without prejudice or racial preference. Mostly they are bragging to demonstrate their knowledge and compliance with cultural programming, which is a deep seated emotional need for stars and brownie points in recognition. A massive and unmistakeable demonstration of a small mind, not particularly able to comprehend the realities of life. The entire race-bating industry preys upon the petty nature of week individuals to poison society.

By American standards of the day, slavery is unacceptable, in contrast to our past history; however, slavery did not start in America or with whites, or even in the southern US, but was introduced into our land by a northern state. It was introduced into America in Providence Rhode Island by merchant shippers looking for cargo to build their shipping companies. They learned it from the already burgeoning trade the Spanish established in the early 16th century. They engaged in a triangle of trade between west Africa, the Caribbean islands, and America; hauling sugar for rum, rum for cash, and black slaves to harvest the sugar and provide labor to build the new world, all in the name of the almighty Spanish Cob, Reales, pieces of eight; the British pound-sterling; and the American Dollar.

The entire historical account of slavery in America today, is rife with propaganda and lies inorder to inflame the wound and exploit the division, so the truth has been distorted and lost. The point is, slavery is past history; not constructively relevant to anything current and should be left as history. Blacks are not the only ones that suffered the indignity of slavery, nor Jews a holocaust. I am American mutt, but predominately of Scotts-Irish, Scottish, Irish, Cherokee Indian, and Armenian extraction. All of these nations have suffered extreme persecution, discrimination, displacement from their own land, slavery and holocaust, but I do not dwell on it nor do I define my life by what happened to my ancestors.

Slavery as an institution has been practiced from the beginning of civilization by EVERY race and every tribe, including black Africans. Let's also be clear, most blacks in America are also programmed by the same media and education system, so also think and speak as they have been programmed, and I suspect a great number of them are also tired of the media drum-beating about the politics of race. The race baiting industry today is not of the black race nor the white race, nor any race for that matter. It comes to our society solely from an elitist class of politically engaged people, and for the purpose of achieving a political agenda. It has little to do with history or race. Who is better able to recognize what racism is, blacks or whites? The answer is blacks. They know what it is better than whites because they are more subjected to it. The fact that they are better able to see it where whites will deny its existence also leads them to adamantly assert that all whites are racists. The fact is whites deny it precisely because they do not understand or recognize it. Blacks are correct in adamance about white racism in the face of white denial, however, many blacks believe that they themselves are not racist or they believe they are justified railing against white racism while ignoring their own. The views of both are equally ignorant. All people are racist, and prefer their own kind and that will never change. Lions will not lay-down with lambs in the current paradigm, so attitudes that divide people by race will only continue as it is imbedded into human nature.

Whites deny their racism because they view themselves as morally above the very human characteristic of racism. They have been led to believe it is a moral sin or somehow exposes the negative side of their nature.

The word 'nigger' was tainted to become a negative epithet through negative association in media and education, so the same is being done with the adjective 'racist.' It is a *fear word*; hurled at any noncompliant white person to invoke shame and panic, to shut down the brain and any objectivity or rationality concerning the issue; to control attitudes, shape belief, and stifle any views outside of the accepted elitist orthodoxy. 'Nigger' is derived from the latin word for black, 'negra', which morphed by slang or regional dialect into 'nigger.' In original usage, in both the old south and the old north, it was not a loaded word nor an epithet but became so when it served a nefarious political purpose. Now not only is the word verboten for whites to even think, but any aspects of black cultural or physical makeup is restricted for public discussion by the white population, however the opposite, where blacks and all other racial minorities may openly deride whites is not only acceptable, but encouraged. This type of cultural programming can only come by careful planning and execution through the expenditure of large sums of money.

Coming to America, every other ethnic group gained a place and learned how to fit in through trial and failure, followed by picking themselves up to try again. Blacks were denied this process, not by slavery but by the advent of the welfare system, so never fully discovered the concept of value proposition.[27] They began to discover this concept between the 1860's and the 1960's. They were making gains in sports and music and other areas of the arts, when they were exploited by government policy through the advent of big welfare. This made them suitable as a bludgeon in the hands of elitists to metaphorically beat and harass Original-Americans.

Our current government inflames racism by creating a system where minorities are beneficiaries of the largess of Original-Americans. While whites deny they resent racial minorities, in their eyes minorities are seen as an object of burden and resentment upon the white population, who are tasked with supporting the burden. It taints and blurs their view of them as humans first. Most Original-Americans are generous and somewhat naive about such things, so they also are much more tolerant than they should be and are willing to accept the abuse and double standard, erroneously viewing the minorities as victims of white culture. Blacks and other minorities are victims of racism but not in the way whites believe. They are not victims because they lacked equal civil rights or equal wealth and privilege; they are victims because they have been denied the discovery of their own humanity and ability which only comes by struggle and failure. They have only been denied the opportunity to demonstrate their ability and willingness to contribute and earn their own keep.

Multicultural societies are more easily exploited for their differences which makes them more prone to internal stress and fighting, thus strangling their own future. Diversity of race and culture will naturally create division; programmed, gamed, or otherwise. It is natural for one group to dislike and

---

[27] Something of value offered to others through commerce.

regard another as a rival. We hear the political slogan that *'Diversity is our strength.'* There could not be a stupider idea, nor a bigger lie. Our culture is only weakened by the continuous railing about race and infighting over privileges and so called 'rights.' It weakens the society and introduces tremendous unnecessary stress. The stress generates a continuous drain on energy and resources and makes us much less productive.

This is evident by the fact that before the race-bating era, when the country was not continuously browbeat and obsessed by it; a society at war with itself; America reached a living-standard pinnacle not achieved by any other nation. Parallel to that axiom is the inverse; we only started to decline coincident with the national obsession over race along with a massive influx of non-european immigrants. There are other factors at play, and the one fact does not prove the other, however, there is a very high correlation between the two. These are glaring examples of things which divide us, making us dependent and easy for conquest. The more racial and cultural diversity, the less cohesion in society. China is a great example of how this works. Very little racial diversity exists there compared with the western world, and their productivity exceeds ours.

In many examples from history, devastating wars have broken out to settle cultural differences. This is called *'Balkanization'*, which refers to the area of southern Europe called the Balkans, which has a history of different ethnic and racial groups fighting for centuries over ethnicity, culture, and land. The Balkan lands comprising much of what was called Yugoslavia is one example to instruct us. History has many more of the same lessons to teach us on this subject such as events in *Northern Ireland* and many other ethnic tinderboxes.

Small ethnic groups in a civilization will more or less keep their heads down and not rock the political boat, but as they grow in number, they will begin to challenge the established order pushing for cultural influence and expansion, then the wars begin. We are witnessing that now as a low-level culture-war mainly between American whites and the rapidly invading Mexican and Hispanic populations from South America heats up, whereas, from the early 1800s through the 1960s, America was a very homogenous white population with a black minority, and there was very little culture-war over racial issues. Low level culture wars can grow to become bloody civil wars to re-establish cultural order. The cry, *"Why cant we all just get along?"*, is a recent political slogan calling for the repeal of the natural laws governing human behavior, invoked as a repudiation of the possibility of American Balkanization, but ignorantly disregarding history and human nature.

People will always compare themselves to others and by whatever the defined norm is in terms of economic standards, creating considerable self-loathing for those at the bottom. If they find themselves and their race at less than the perceived economic standard, which is supposed to measure the average, it creates negative feelings of inadequacy with a desire to blame external factors and others for them being short-changed in life. Humans are not equal and will never be, despite the hysterical rhetoric to the contrary. We are not all the same but there are vast differences between races in terms of ability to perform economically and in other measures. Whites invented the modern world having conquered the exploration and understanding of science, giving them the tools necessary to tame the forces of nature to great economic advantage, while other races did not. It is that simple.

Whites as a race are able to excel and achieve much higher levels economically, which means they will occupy the top space in the food-chain, while others will occupy a much lower space. These levels are solely determined by race, but that does not hold by the individual. As a race, whites perform economically better than all others, however, there are many individual members of the black race who are able to economically outperform many whites and members of other races, and vice versa with everything in-between. The differences in standard of living is determined by the race factor more-so than any other. It is only rendered by nature and history, not by laws or the artifices of ill or well intended social engineering.

Recognizing these truths should render the envy-trade and the lies told obsolete, as people should accept that they will only live up to their level of ability as significantly determined by race, not by the external factors falsely blamed for their inadequacies. Let us hope the future will smile upon all men where the differences between them, which separate them now, will fall away to become considerably less important.

Governance

Governance is what is used to govern a society. It is not the same as government, which is an organization or civic structure used to employ governance, however, governance can come in many forms from a series of informal piecemeal structures not requiring a formal hierarchical structure, to full autocratic, top-down, command and control structures, and everything in-between.

No society can live in peace and security without a lid on human nature. The aggregate balance of the forces which govern the natural man in his unbridled natural state is destructive to himself and everything all around him. Governance is necessary to lockdown the whims and mischief of men. In the current socio-political-economic paradigm, there is a requirement for force to impose rules for governing society; it can not be escaped.

Having said that, the governance objective for a workable civilization is to establish and enforce a set of rules acceptable to all or at least a majority of the members of the society. This objective is free to take numerous forms and not just the current so called Democratic-Republic form or any of the past models, but instead, we are free to innovate new forms, and indeed, the function of governance will continue to develop toward systems which are considerably more tolerant of the sovereign autonomy of society, and liberty (or license), depending on ones particular moral view.

We have at current something that was established as a Republic which when you strip away all of the rationalized philosophical rhetoric, it really amounts to what is called a *'Trust.'* Whether the founders intended to create a pure republic, or a hybrid form which shared power between the people and the government but only resembling a trust, which then regressed completely into a trust; either case makes no difference; for all intents and purposes what we have at this point functions as a trust. Even if established as a pure republic, the nature of which would insure its inevitability of degenerating completely into the form we have today. The republic is the stepchild of the trust.

It is not necessary to adhere strictly to rigid definitions to make this point. Based on the legal descriptions of trust vs republic, it may or may not be evident. The only thing that matters is how they compare in function, and in that, the correlation is very high. The operative thing to note about the word trust is that it implies that we the 'governed' must trust those that are charged with operating and maintaining the Trust. The system is operated by trustees for narrow interests, while we the people are merely passive spectators and servants who's function is to supply emoluments.

Trust implies and really ***requires*** that we lay our lives, our fortunes, our families, our properties, our future, our liberty, our culture, our rights, everything that we are, do, or possess; the essence of our very being, in the hands of those that operate and maintain the Trust. Does that sound familiar? When we are so completely dependent on the trustees: the politicians, operatives, and bureaucrats; the whole establishment; when they control every single aspect of our lives, because we have ignorantly, obediently turned that control over, we are reduced to little more than caged animals or slaves.

Here is a question about our relationship to our current Republic-Trust: Knowing what you know about it, if you were asked to, would you put your trust in the same today? If not, then ask yourself if a republic is really the best form for the structure of governance we can institute for our civilization, or can we do better?

I am going to layout an outline for a much better system of governance in the chapters that follow. It is a system of governance much more suitable for the particular era we are entering based on our current level of knowledge, attitudes, expectations, and behavior.

Rights

As was stated earlier in the discussion about rights, a simple and practical definition of rights is; *'authority which is secured by the application of force.'*

I have listed **Rights** lower down the list because, although paramount in necessity, the implication and view of rights will probably always involve the idea of them coming from on-high which then invokes the specter of 'government' or governance which I have also put lower on the list of elements for a stable society, below what I believe are elements which measure the qualities of human beings. For a complete understanding of my view of rights, please refer to the section called 'Rights' in the chapter, 'Gaining Perspective.'

Monetary System

The monetary system performs a vital product and service for the civilization. In its basic form, a good monetary system is composed of many competing private, semi-private, or public corporate bodies which skillfully gather and concentrate capital resources, used for conversion to currency to supply the capital requirements of the economic system. The currency is distributed through commercial and retail money outlets called banks. Thus the capital is leveraged into the economy through loans.

The system organizes and facilitates the exchange of wealth necessary to build a vibrant economy. It is there to create a supply of capital for growing and operating the economic system. Monetary systems should consist of as many competitive discreet private banks as are required for operation at full economic capacity, but should never constitute a singularly monopolized system which only leads to economic conquest and the enslavement of the society. As a condition of license, all participants should be on a continuous basis, completely open to critical scrutiny and regulation as required to ensure the integrity of the many currencies issued by all disparate monetary companies. Free circulation of multiple currencies in a single economy is not desirable, so currency indexing should be employed for retail level transaction.

The status of the monetary system may be completely public, completely private, or a hybrid combination of the two. The preferred status is a completely private one but with very tight public regulatory oversight, while the key to maintaining the integrity is to ensure an openly scrutinized and wholly competitive monetary industry.

The monetary system of a civilization should never be completely owned or controlled by any particular group or person, however, currently in most of the civilized world that is sadly the case with what are called Central Banks. These are completely hostile to a civilized state and leads to the enslavement and destruction of the civilization. Total control is accomplished by monopolizing the banks and capital that compose the monetary system. A good and sound civilization must take vigilant steps to insure there is no ability for any members or groups of the social strata to do so. If such a condition exists, the civilization must remedy the situation or it will be held hostage and suffer tremendous loss of liberty, security, and prosperity.

Economy

In the current reigning socio-economic paradigm, a civilization can not operate without an economy. One definition of an economy as taken from the dictionary[28] follows:

Economy: noun

1 the wealth and resources of a country or region, esp. in terms of the production and consumption of goods and services.

2 careful management of available resources

I would add that an economy is composed of markets where goods and services are exchanged using a currency medium. It provides the basis for the necessary economic activities vital for the civilization to survive and thrive such as creating shelter, food, and leisure for the population.

Just as with monetary systems, the economy of a civilization must never be completely owned or controlled by any particular person or group, however, today great portions are dominated by narrow-interests. That is completely undesirable and leads to the destruction of the civilization. It is accomplished by the monopolization of the components that compose the economy. A good and sound civilization must take vigilant steps to insure there is no ability for any members or groups of the social strata to do so. If such a condition exists, the civilization must remedy the situation or the civilization will suffer tremendous loss of liberty, security, and prosperity.

---

[28] Oxford - American English

Trade, Commerce & Markets

There are costs associated with creating and building a marketplace for any class of products or services, therefore ownership is attributed. Those that build the market own the market. In an economy enclosed within national borders, markets are owned by those most affected which only includes domestic consumers and producers, not foreign suppliers, governments, or middle-men. Foreign interests including domestic importers are subject to the rules of the market as determined by the Sovereign Politically Endowed People (SPEP) and should have no power or voice in policy otherwise. Are there international markets? Of course there are, however, the vast majority of individuals are limited by locality. Global markets are favored by large interests; corporations and political entities. The SPEP are inclined to limit participation only to the extent they may negotiate and influence their own status vis-à-vis global markets, therefore, they are also not inclined to tolerate their inequities.

Foreign Trade is intimately related to the issue of domestic markets because most civilizations are not able by themselves to produce everything necessary, or even what is demanded, so trade with others is necessary to bridge the gap. Therefore trade policy should be determined in such a way as to favor the prosperity of the people and the nation and eliminate the tendency to favor mostly narrow-interests. Some have labeled this *'Fair Trade'*; the idea being that domestic trade policy should produce the optimum benefit to the domestic producers and consumers, which means balancing of the interests (cost and access to goods vs access to jobs) of consumers against the interests (ownership and profit) of domestic producers, marketers, creators, and maintainers of the marketplace. In addition to cost and access to goods, consumers also need jobs which are created mostly by the domestic marketplace in which their products and services are sold for profit, which is a trade-off. Notice there is no room for consideration of foreign or domestic narrow-interests in the policy.

Recent free-trade policies were sold to the American civilization on the basis of cheap domestic products imported into our marketplace with jobs for everyone, offset by our producing products to be sold into the marketplace of our *'Free Trade'* partners. However, like most other schemes of global hegemonists, it only resulted in gutting the American industrial base with very little job creation from the differential commerce or sale of products sold into the others; with the 'savings' from the cheaply produced products only accruing to the bottom line of the importers and multi-national corporations, not passed along in lower prices to the consumers as was promised. In short, in the case of America, there is no net advantage in free-trade, only loss for the domestic producers and consumers.

A marketplace is only 'free' if there are no associated costs in its creation and maintenance. Those refusing to acknowledge that fact advocate theft. We the American civilization have been sold the erroneous notion of the virtue of a *'Free Market'*, and the equally erroneous notion of *'Free Trade.'* The use of the word 'free' implies that there was no cost to those who originally created the marketplace, implying that any and everyone may 'freely' participate because unfettered competition is always good. This is a false notion because in a world where global free-trade between developed and undeveloped nations seems to be paramount, there will be a very small number of 'winners' that will grow exceedingly rich brokering access to the marketplace completely at the expense of the masses in the developed and undeveloped nations who carved the marketplace out.

The advocates of this flawed notion have conflated the idea of free and unfettered enterprise referred to as Laissez-faire[29]

---

[29] French, 'Let it be'

free-enterprise, espoused by early American economists such as Adam Smith[30], with the modern practice of plundering a marketplace by the free-access of foreign producers. Free-enterprise is generally accepted as healthy because it advocates allowing producers the freedom to produce unfettered while only subjected to market forces, which greatly builds the wealth of the nation without saddling the producers with unnecessary regulatory limits or taxing their gains away. Given enough latitude, free-enterprise will vastly improve the economy in which it is practiced.

With free-trade, the developed nations see their industrial capacity drained by cheaper foreign producers dominating the marketplace which drives domestic producers out of business or forces them to relocate their production to undeveloped nations. The people of the undeveloped nations are displaced by large and well capitalized multi-national corporations which dominate what may have been a fledgling industry in their own nation, and drive small producers out. In both cases, it is the classic example of reaping where one has not sown.

Audaciously, the 'winners' have been promoting the notion that free-trade is a win-win[31] game and all that are forced to participate may benefit eventually despite that in the interim there is complete economic collapse and the total loss for those that labored over generations to build the industrial economic base and marketplace. We have witnessed the industrial dismantling of America by this means in the last 50 years.

In the frenzied, propagandized, manipulated, media of today, for one to even suggest, much less advocate for even the slightest protection of or demand for maintenance of the marketplace the nation has built over the last 250 years, it is met with a venomous tirade of invectives, ridiculed with the manufactured epithet of 'Protectionist.' It is labeled as a

---

[30] Author, The Wealth of Nations
[31] Everyone wins.

reckless knee jerk response to fare and free competition by those that regard themselves as the gatekeepers and preservers of the capitalist system. They are fanatical about the doctrine even as it devastates their wealth and destroys the wealth of their nation. The reality is the largest beneficiaries are driven by the profit they will gain for plunder, and their ideology and rhetoric is nothing more than social lubricant designed to sway their army of halfwit defenders.

There is no such thing as a free trade ... and never has been. What is labeled *'Free Trade'*, or *'Free Market Capitalism'* and practiced today around the world is in reality old fashioned plunder and theft.

Markets and the producers and consumers that created them in developed and undeveloped countries alike are destroyed by unfettered trade. It is a zero-sum[32] game; if one party profits by brokering that which belongs to another without remuneration or their consent, that other party has been robbed.

To give an example of the necessity for a protected marketplace consider what the purpose of a patent is. In the United States currently a patent gives the owner of the patent exclusivity against market competitors for a limited term of 20 years. It gives the innovator the opportunity to realize some potential profit for their endeavor by creating an incubative market environment, which creates a considerable incentive to undertake the financial risk necessary to build the enterprise. The patent system was instituted at the founding of the republic because the founders realized that it was necessary to foster innovation for the development of a marketplace which in-turn enriches the economy and prospers the nation as a whole. The purpose of a patent is to create an incentive for an inventor/entrepreneur to initially create something new then

---

[32] The losses of one party equal the gain of the other.

to undertake the considerable financial risk in attempting to persuade others of the usefulness of his innovation.

It is estimated that 90% of the risk capital spent on the development of new products/services is spent on development of the marketplace, while only 10% on the development of the product/service itself. Indeed if at the first hint of a new and profitable marketplace, everyone from everywhere were allowed to sell the exact innovation as the inventor, the fledgling marketplace would never have sprouted. A patent gives the quintessential protected marketplace.

Free-trade eventually creates economic conditions akin to the soviet communist style of command economy where there was absolutely no innovation because there was no profit incentive. As a result of the practice of limited term patent monopoly, the United States and Europe have together virtually invented the modern world and become economic superpowers. It is a simple matter to extend this principle to established marketplaces after patents have expired, where the marketplace has matured considerably.

There are many that have a stake in the creation of the marketplace. The innovators, producers, and the customers all have invested considerably in the creation of the marketplace. For this reason it is axiomatic that they are the owners of the marketplace, and for that reason the 'freeness' of the marketplace only extends as far as the owner's consent. This places the policy which governs trade in the hands of the SPEP.

Graph 1

Referring to the graph (1) above, it can be shown that since the 1960s there has been a steady and widening erosion of American industry as indicated in the *Foreign Trade Deficit* measured as a percentage of GDP. This measures the percentage of what we import as a total of what we produce. It very clearly shows that as time goes by we are producing less and less and becoming ever more dependent on importing from others to provide what we consume. It also represents loss in real economic terms which can be measured in jobs. As an example, according to the graph, the peek deficit year was 2006. In that year, the GDP was approximately $13 trillion. For an average job paying $50,000, the 6% deficit represents 15.6 million jobs lost to foreign producers. Where have we recently seen unemployment figures? They have been at levels not seen since the depths of the depression of the 1930s, and the trend does not indicates slowdown or reversal. Notice up to the 1950s, we as a nation exported approximately the same as we import today as a percentage of GDP.

One more note on this topic is to consider the so called 'Chinese economic miracle.' Lets examine it. The Chinese are very capable but they came out of an old world agrarian society in the last century, into 40 years of communist style controlled economic stagnation; now they are expected to become a global economic superpower. They went from virtually nothing to super-power economic status in 40 years. While they are highly capable, they have never in their history demonstrated anywhere near that level of rapid development. How did it happen?

If you listen to the pablum propaganda press, you are told that they bootstrapped[33] themselves by embracing western style capitalism, and while it is true that our system provides a much better model for them than what they had before, the simple fact is in the 1990s they were given unfettered free-trade status with the United States. That means they had unfettered access to sell the goods and services of their 1 billion strong slave population directly into our markets, while we got very little in return other than a promise that we would have access to their markets 'someday.' The 'someday' is because despite that at the time the free-trade agreements between China and the US were 'negotiated', they had no market for our goods because they had no money or a wealthy middle class population with enough disposable income to buy our products, but we were assured they will 'someday.' Now after the effect of these and other free-trade agreements have plundered our economy, the Chinese have considerable amounts of money to buy American, but somehow they find it inconvenient or find numerous reasons to exclude our products from their marketplace. The private national US industrial-consumer marketplace, built over 250 years by American ingenuity, risk, and sweat, has simply been uprooted from America and transported wholesale to Asia.

Imagine what may have taken place in our economy if we had been given unfettered access to sell into another market equal to the size of ours in the last 23 or so years without any obligation for reciprocal acceptance of their competing goods

---

[33] From the saying, 'Lift yourself up by your bootstraps.'

and services selling into our market in return. If you know anything about sales and marketing; having access to that is like hitting the proverbial mother-load. We built that rich mother-load vein of gold that was our marketplace over the last 250 years through thrift and hard work, and as a result it made our nation rich. The Chinese were just handed-over that mother-load with the aid and blessing of our government without any reciprocal obligation whatsoever.

As it stands today, they will still not allow us to sell into their marketplace to the same degree as they have access to ours. The so called *'Chinese economic miracle'* is the building of their marketplace in a very short time solely by plundering ours. Ours is declining at a very rapid pace and theirs is exploding at the same pace which ours declines.

In addition to giving them along with virtually the rest of the world, the right to plunder our marketplace, we supplied hundreds of billions of dollars of investment capital with which to build their so called *'economic miracle.'* Again, ask yourself what would be the outcome of the US receiving the equivalent of double our national investment capital for 20 years in a row from foreign sources; what degree of economic miracle might we have sustained? The Chinese economy was virtually handed to them courtesy of the American civilization, but without our consent. It was handed to them wholesale, brokered off for short term political advantage by the establishment in Washington DC. The so called *'Chinese economic miracle'* is purely a manufactured fantasy; absolute unadulterated hokum.

Justice System

A system of justice is necessary to maintain order and serve the civilization when individuals are wronged. I am no expert on justice, but our current system was designed during a bygone era which makes it less than adequate today for several reasons. It was instituted with protection against abuse of overzealous prosecution called 'double jeopardy', however, that introduces the possibility for abuse. A person accused of a crime is entitled to the presumption of innocence and a trial with a verdict rendered by a jury of his/her peers before conviction[34] and punishment. However if acquitted[35] in trial, they cannot be retried regardless of any evidence of guilt which may come to light afterward. The accused, in essence, gets away with the crime. But if convicted, the accused is entitled to another trial if evidence of innocence is discovered after the fact. Why not the same standard for acquittal?

The double-jeopardy protection was instituted to prevent an overzealous prosecutor from fishing for a conviction, meaning, trying their accused target over and over in hopes of getting a jury to convict. That is certainly abuse, however, why not institute that double-jeopardy applies unless new evidence of guilt emerges which if measured against a threshold would have altered the original verdict? The system is unbalanced in this regard, and there are many cases in which a guilty person was acquitted due to lack of timely evidence, never to face justice again.

Another problem is how our legal system is structured in that it is biased toward advocacy of either guilt or innocence, where the objective in both cases should be biased toward advocacy of truth and justice. This is an adversarial system which also makes it a contest or a game of competition, where the lives of the accused, along with justice for victims, hang in the balance. Currently, the job of the prosecutor is to prove the accused is guilty regardless of any knowledge of innocence. Contrarily, the job of a defense attorney is to prove the accused innocent regardless of any knowledge of guilt. In both cases, there is motivation for abuse. I am not an expert so not aware of whatever safeguards are in place to prevent abuse,

---

[34] Found guilty.
[35] Found to be innocent.

other than sanctions for unethical behavior, so it occurs and probably more often than it should.

Often prosecutors are motivated by political ambitions, so will deny justice in favor of a conviction to put a political feather in his/her cap. That may entail withholding exculpatory[36] evidence which would acquit the accused. Contrarily, a defense attorney is paid to keep his client out of jail and to avoid any verdict of guilt. Often the prosecutors have an advantage with considerably greater resources to prove their case. Again, where is justice in that? Note that in both cases, attorneys and prosecutors are not free to act as their conscience may dictate but they are bound by the rules governing the justice system.

An ambitious prosecutor with less than an upstanding moral compass will wrongly convict and send the innocent to jail, while defense attorneys will concoct incredible cock and bull stories attempting to get their criminal clients off the hook. In case the point has been overlooked, the accused if guilty is not entitled to protection from justice, and if innocent, it is a perversion of justice to punish them; justice is demanded in both cases. The controlling mechanism to ensure justice must come from the structure and rules which govern the system of justice.

A better system would make both sides work as advocates in the interest of truth and justice first, then for their clients. This would entail a duty to disclose and declare any knowledge of innocence on the part of a prosecutor, and withdraw any advocacy for conviction. It would likewise require disclosure of any knowledge of guilt on the part of the defense and a call for conviction with a pleading for lenience. Both should be required to serve the interest of justice first, which is what the civilization and the accused demand and are entitled to.

---

[36] Evidence which proves innocence.

Criminal Deterrent

Sometimes I believe that engineers should design the policies of civilization which encompasses many of the functions of government, because they are taught the basics of the behavior of physical systems, whereas most politicians are lawyers and accountants, so are not taught the basics of physical sciences and not equipped to deal with the particular part of nature which we humans compose. Being an engineer, I was taught about the physics and mathematics of what is called closed-loop feedback control. It can be quite complicated with advanced mathematics involved in making a system work properly.

These systems are encountered everyday by most people and are often used to regulate or govern something. Examples are thermostat and heating/cooling systems; natural systems which regulate the temperature of the earth; voltage regulators in automobile electrical systems; speed and position control of an elevator or escalator; biological systems which control the production of certain body chemicals in response to external stimulus; and so forth. These systems occur in nature very often so it is natural to apply the principles in controlling human behavior as a deterrent to criminality, and while it is recognized that most criminal deterrent systems are somewhat based on the same principles, current systems are poorly executed due to policy decisions by unqualified designers and administrators.

The science and technology of control systems has been developed over the last several centuries. Let's apply the concept to control the level of crime in our society. We'll start with a few very simple common characteristics:

1) Set-point. This sets a desired target to achieve and maintain. In the case of criminality, the set-point is ZERO.

2) Virtually infinite force applied to drive system behavior. This means the maximum punishment possible as a deterrent.

3) The application of negative feedback correction. In this case we are talking about applying a deterrent punishment force up to the maximum possible, until a diminishment response of the criminality is measured, then the deterrent may be reduced proportionate to the effect. In other words, maximum punishment should be applied to any particular class of criminality until it begins to diminish, with the aim of making it disappear altogether.

This is a simplistic explanation, but if we were to execute policies along these lines, we would see crime all but disappear from the civilization. The proof of this is that there is very little crime in certain muslim countries like Saudi Arabia where they apply swift, sure and severe punishment for even minor offenses. I am not aware if the principles of negative feedback control are applied there or not. It works because maximum force sends a clear message of deterrent, which only those with limited intelligence or who's desperation and defiance exceeds the perceived penalty for non compliance. In western civilizations, it would be more appropriate to apply maximum force until the desired effect is measured, then back off the severity of punishment proportionately to the decline in criminality. This can be thought of as increasing the pressure on the accelerator of a car to speed up until you reach cruising speed, then you can maintain speed with very little gas applied.

Some argue that punishment is not an effective deterrent to crime. These arguments are of course ridiculous. A little thought exercise can be used to see why. Since we are talking about driving a car, the example of the speed limit can be used. Do you obey the speed limit? Most people if asked will say, *"no, I go slightly over the posted speed limit."* This is analogous to being taken as proof that deterrents do not work because most people ignore the posted speed, and drive faster.

Ask yourself what speed you would drive if the speed limit was lowered? Most would still drive slightly over the posted limit.

Ask yourself what speed you would drive if the speed limit was raised instead, and how fast do you think most other people will travel? The answer is, people will still drive slightly faster than whatever the posted limit is.

Now ask yourself how fast you might go if there were no speed limit at all? Most would say they would use their judgement to determine a safe speed, but we know the average speed at which motorist would travel would gradually climb until unsafe levels are achieved. Of course this is the same as a deterrent and sets an absolute limit on how fast we should travel while driving. This proves that a deterrent will not completely stop or control all illicit behavior because humans are not machines, but any deterrent if applied in sufficient strength will have a measurable effect, even if it is not 100%.

Media

Nothing is more important to a free and sovereign society than objective, reliable, and truthful news, opinion, and the dissemination of public information. The operative figure of merit in the measure is the level of integrity of the information put out by the most trusted and beloved sources, which garner the admiration and trust of virtually all of the society; unfortunately at this juncture we have none of that.

The media in the US and probably most of the rest of the world is referred to as the 4th and the 5th estates. They have as much importance and sway as the others; Religion, elitist narrow interests, and the common people. I see both the 4th and 5th estates (the press and opinion-makers) as really part of the second estate (elitist narrow interests) in that it is really controlled by them and used for their purposes.

I discussed earlier how nefarious globalist narrow-interests and their agenda are being exposed and their monopoly power of the press is coming to an end due to many factors, but mostly because the internet offers an attractive alternative. This however does not mean that we are emerging into a paradigm of completely balanced and free media. Indeed, we the people are experiencing an advantage by the diminution of the monopoly on media, because it can no longer occupy exclusive influence in our thoughts and lives, however, while the monopoly is being replaced to some extent by independent voices, alternative views, and some truth, it is mostly now replaced by the background noise of the mindless masses.

In my opinion even though the quality of much of the information one gets from the internet is suspect at best, at least now it is not a hole bored directly into the head with-which uncontested lies and propaganda are poured in. Truth, opinion, and news are now much more disperse than in the recent past, coming from many different sources mixed in along with new lies and old propaganda, and a considerable amount of purposed misinformation. Just the same, while now it is not balanced nor objective reliable truth, neither is it any longer purely unadulterated sewage.

It may come as a shock to some to learn that the idea of *'freedom of speech'* as a noble and desirable element of a free society, does not really exist and never has. The press and the ideas that flow through most social structures have always been controlled, manufactured, bought and paid for, prohibited, suppressed, etc. It is that way because of the value to those with the power to disseminate their version of truth and values, and suppress anything that opposes those views.

For the reasons given in this discussion, it is an acceptable rationalization that; if freedom of speech is really only an ideal and can not really exist in the form we have been led to believe, then it must be controlled, or better, regulated. Therefore we the **SPEP** must see to it that whatever information is disseminated freely to the masses is acceptable before it is dumped into our midst. It is precisely because it is so powerful in influencing the views and thereby the decisions people make, that it needs to be licensed and filtered. More to the point, as long as it remains disperse in tenor and effect, it can remain relatively unfiltered and uncensored. However, there must not only be an adequately broad range of sources, but there must also be oversight on large and influential sources of media to deter mischief along with a limitation on how much media is controlled by any single entity and their interlocking entities.

Publicly disseminated media channels should be thought of as public utilities and licensed. It is allowed primarily to serve a public purpose, therefore publicly disseminated sources should only be allowed for private purposes on a subordinate basis, and that only if it does not harm the interests of the nation. Because it is in the interest of the public, it must serve the interests of, and be subjected to the scrutiny of the SPEP and the Sovereign Democratic Majority. The aim is to ensure narrow-interest media monopolies are no longer allowed nor tolerated. The airwaves, netwaves, and brainwaves of the nation belong to the people of the nation, not narrow-interests. We can no longer allow them to dump malevolence into our midst, or sow discord with impunity, anymore than we would allow them to dump poison into the nation's water supply.

CHAPTER SEVEN

Elements of Stable Governance

Legislative

The function of a legislature is as a deliberative body to analyze, evaluate, articulate, and debate, the needs confronting the civilization then draft workable rules to address, compensate for, or work around whatever obstacles exist. The rules which result are called policies. All policies are supposed to represent the sovereign will of the people who are affected by the rules; why? Because the civilization is about us, the sovereign politically endowed people; the owners of the civilization, and not about anyone or anything else. The legislature exists for this reason only, and if this function was not needed, a legislature absolutely, comprehensively, and unconditionally, WOULD NOT EXIST otherwise.

The function of legislature has traditionally been done by an elected body ostensibly representing the will of those who elected them, however, human nature being what it is, a representative legislature is generally responsive to the extent that corruption and bribery is held at bay then they will do what the highest bidder demands. This is where the form of civilization based on the Sovereign Democratic Majority comes into play. Sovereign means 'Law Giver', therefore, the Sovereign Democratic Majority through the sovereign-body is the legislature and makes all laws.

Note that in a Sovereign Democratic Majority, the legislature is above, and drives the constitution which codifies the accords, and embodies the law, with the narrow exception of threshold criteria in-which it will need a super-majority or other defined super-criteria to overcome. This is opposed to the current system where the legislative body is not above the constitution except with a super-threshold for amendment. In this case the constitution can only be altered by amendment. That is because the current US constitution was created to define a government. In the SDM form, the constitution does not define a government, it merely reflects the civilization.

Our current system is controlled exclusively by power brokers that extract favors to bilk wealth out of the system at the expense of the nation as a whole. There are very few legislators free to do what they believe they were sent to do. Any independent inkling of thought or action by elected legislators, whether federal or state, is quickly met by sanctions and marginalizing them for defiance of one of the 2 dominant parties. This hardly serves the needs of the nation or the sovereign will of the politically endowed. Corruption of the process is completely stopped under the SDM since they are the people and not prone to cheat themselves.

The notion of the SDM legislature may seem to be at odds with the philosophy of others that believe the legislative branch of government is put into place to deliberate policies that serve and preserve the state itself. This is oxymoronic as the state itself can not be self-serving and can not exist for any reason other than to serve absolutely at the interests and behest of the sovereign people, whereas in the past when it served kings and the elite. Today we have none of that so a legislature that does not serve exclusively at the sovereign will of people is illegitimate.

Today that function needs to be constructed and arranged bypassing the free-agency[37] representation by men who are corruptible, so that policies are presented, debated, deliberated, and adopted by the people themselves. It will ensure legitimacy to serve its mandate and force legislative efficiency, creating and maintaining only laws critical for integrity of the nation and nothing else.

Constitution

Usually a collection of documents forged through the consensus of the sovereign politically endowed which defines the structure and enumerates the extent of governmental function and power, defines restrictions on operation and parameters, and the social contract that governs the relationship between the people and the structure of governance which they have commissioned.

The above describes traditional ideas of a constitution, but there are other models. Further, the defined structure and its operations are called a social contract. Ideally these should emanate forth from the sovereign power and interest of the SPEP not the state or narrow-interests, simply because it is all and only about the SPEP and will greatly affect their lives. Men have sought social contracts as ways to live in a civil order for as long as history records. The SPEP have the power to bring it forth and must retain the power to dissolve it at will.

With a Sovereign Democratic Majority, the constitution is what results when sovereign people design their civilization, but it is not used to define it. It merely codifies, or records in documented form, what accords have been reached from time to time concerning the operating structure and parameters between the SDM members who establish the civilization. In practice, the SDM as a body, the *Sovereign-Body* are above the constitution and all laws, but individually they are not.

---

[37] Free to represent their own interests, and bothered with the interests of another.

In current practice, traditional western styles like our own has sought to embody all of the ideals described, balancing the sovereign rights and liberties of the people against keeping a lid on mischief and maintaining order, but it has failed. This has happened due to poor definition and structure which results in somewhat of a compromise where the sovereign people are supposed to limit their own rights and power and give some of it over to the government in a share arrangement. This is done by empowering a body of men-governors; in our case 3 units supposedly equal in power. This forces what results to take a particular form which is not particularly respectful nor expressive of the sovereignty of people. That form, in terms of effectiveness and utility must enumerate the rules of the system of governance itself. The rules are there to keep everyone in check. In our constitution, rules were created to keep the lid on the mischief of the 3 units; courts, legislators, and executives entrusted with power. In-turn, they were given the power to legislate and enforce rules to restrict the absolute freedom and movement of people, although with limitation.

In a legal analogy, even for the traditional style, a constitution should never be intended as a charter for ruling the nation, any more than a contract for one person to provide service for another, charters him to rule over the first. It should be limited in intent and power to nothing more than a contract used to employ a service; no more than the contract one would use to hire a builder to build a structure or a waste disposal crew to pick up the trash. It must contain safeguards against abuse, degradation, or distortion by narrow-interests, their use for personal gain or for use against others. The letter of the contract must be met and it should not be vague or left to specious interpretation and enactment.

It may also spell out the qualification, requirements, duties and liberties of citizens, which is also by contract. Most participants in the civilization maintain citizenship status. Citizenship accords usually emanate from the constitution, but may reside or emanate from sources separate to, equal to, or above the constitution.

Because of the nature of western tradition and the democratic/republic style of civilization, the constitution is forced to be a ruling document to define the civilization, like a set of specifications are used to define a product or like the operational by-laws of a corporation. It must maintain a status as the highest authority, and although the sovereign body has authority above the level of the defining document, in-practice, that is rarely considered or used to effect any great change, but the people are subjected to the authority of the letter and court interpretation of the document, and the laws which the constitution allows the legislative and executive bodies to impose upon them.

When it is changed by the sovereign-body, it is usually very tightly limited in scope and called the amendment process. This is supposed to be the power and will of the sovereign-body exercised to enact something important. However, the change considered is virtually always brought forth and defined by narrow-interests and sold to the masses who enact it through a super-threshold mechanism. In the abstract, the constitution defines the civilization and is an authority higher than any single individual or entity, and although it does not exceed the authority of the Sovereign Democratic Majority or the SPEP who have the power to amend the document which defines their civilization. The effect of our constitutional amendment process is greatly limited and historically it has empowered the narrow-interests more than it has the people.

A better model is the one for an SDM, which does not have a single document or a set of documents, viewed as the highest authority in the land, define the civilization. A civilization should never build a prison then put themselves inside of it; so neither should they put themselves under the authority of a document nor be defined by it. Instead, exactly the opposite should be the case. The civilization should be defined by what the owners decide about it and what they enact to shape it; not limited by what the political class or courts interpret it to allow or to force.

In this way, the constitution is not the ultimate authority, but only a set of documents which **constitute** what the civilization is, does, and wants, but does not define or limit it. It simply reflects the civilization at any particular time. This makes it fluid; reflective of the changes that take place as time and events demand, not rigid and fixed, and not putting restrictions on the necessity for change. This is the case with a SDM form of civilization where the SPEP embody the legislature which controls all executive management and judicial process. When the usual layer of legislative and executive bureaucracy is stripped away, there is no need to have a document define rules to limit their mischief regarding the people, therefore the constitution only chronicles the civilization and stands to embody documents which reflect their will.

Even in this context, still, there is the requirement to put some absolute limitations on what the most authorized body of people may do. Again, in the abstract, the people are the highest power and sovereign in whatever they do, but the reality is, the people themselves need to be protected against themselves. This demonstrates the need for super-threshold mechanisms. A civilization does not need to define rules for restricting elected rulers if there are none, but it still must have rules that define operational parameters. It still must codify whatever absolute limits there are, and the process to change them.

It must hold the SDM in-check against whimsical or rash moves or tendency to react out of emotion. This could be a requirement for a 'cooling off' period for reflection, a super-majority threshold, or in combination with convening a special authoritative wise counsel to review and make recommendation to the sovereign-body. There will need to be mechanisms for the sovereign-body to amend the absolute limits by a threshold other than a simple majority FQWV (Fully Qualified Weighted Vote).

Foundational vital fundamental operating parameters and principles which define the working functions by which the civilization operates are examples of where super-threshold mechanisms apply. Parameter which define the Sovereign Majority; the Sovereign-Body; the SPEP; allowed forms and restrictions on revenue generation; qualification for voting; limitations on aligned interests; laws governing the fundamentals of money and banking; FQWV (Fully Qualified Weighted Vote); maintenance of military force; trade policy; requirements for the admittance of states; media activities, etc. These are generally parameters which after being adopted and then found to need alteration would potentially change the fundamental nature and structure of the civilization. Altering them must be held to a threshold level higher than a simple majority of **Fully Qualified Weighted Vote** because they cannot be altered frivolously without doing harm. A shortlist of examples are:

• *Allowed forms and restrictions on revenue generation.* Taxation should be held to a minimum and fixed as per methods and restrictions and not a running policy as is the case now. It should never be employed frivolously, so a super-threshold is a mechanism which spells out the adopted agreement and operating parameters, and the necessary criteria to change the rules regarding the protection of sanctioned minorities like wealthy individuals, and religious institutions and observance. This is important especially in a democratic process inorder to limit the temptation for extracting disproportionately from producers and the wealthy.

• *Use of military power and the provocation to war.* In normal peace-time, Military Power should remain dispersed amongst the individual states. If the need should arise to allow that power to be more concentrated under an executive manager in terms greater than the agreed upon contingent threshold, then a super-threshold mechanism should be employed to alter it.

Democracy

The simplicity and power for furthering the organization of people toward a civilized structure and espoused in the ideals of democracy can be summed up by 2 words, 'Majority Rule', and it is no more complicated than that despite volumes of sophistry attempting to justify unworkable and defunct systems. We all grew up being educated into the truth of this definition and it is universally accepted and it greatly influences how we naturally tend to behave in social situations when it comes to recognizing and respecting the ideas, rights, and will of others when making decisions affecting an entire group. Yet at the same time we have been conditioned to make excuses and exceptions for this when it comes to civil order, arguably the most intrusive aspect of our civilization. Majority Rule almost applies in certain circumstances like the outcome of elections, notwithstanding our convoluted, ridiculous, and heavily biased electoral-college system for electing a president which disregards the will or numerical vote of the majority; or the fact that there are 2 senators for each state regardless of the disproportionate populace distribution and the fact that the senate is one half of one of the 3 supposedly equal branches of government; something which the election of members of the house of representatives attempts to compensate for by apportionment. The excepting and skewing of this fact regarding the Senate seems insignificant, however it is enough to perpetually favor the smaller and northeastern states; It is a joke. Regardless of whether you agree with the analysis or not, one thing with which we can all agree is that it is not a proper or fair system in the abstract. It is antiquated and we have the tools to do better.

Then there is the outrageous fact of so many exceptions to Majority Rule by political rules established by court 'findings' over the years, giving all kinds of special rights to minorities at the expense of the majority. How does this square with the notion of *'Democracy'* when the system is rife with scads of exceptions where small groups have minority protected rights and special privilege? We are told this is to protect these minorities. Let's cut through the crap! Why should they be protected? From what pool of eternal wisdom and blessing to the nation does this special right spring, that the majority need suffer the outrage? Since when does Majority Rule, taken in its proper sense, mean enacting the will of a political or for that matter, any minority? A minority loses by definition which is how it works in real life. There can be no exceptions except those granted by the majority themselves.

We are told that if we do not protect the rights of minorities we risk the 'tyranny of the majority', 'mob rule', but it is OK to have the 'tyranny of the minority mob.' Somehow that is less tyrannical, except that it is not; tyranny is tyranny. At least by the definition of democracy, the tyranny of the majority is justified by the fact that they have the right to tyranny if they so decide. There is no universal law to prohibit such and no force to stop it. Civilizations rise and fall on the decisions they make as is their right to do so; who can argue otherwise?

Is it tyranny when an owner of a house gives uncontested directive to the crew he has hired to keep his yard up, but does not consult them on interior remodeling or allow them to move in? Is it tyranny when a corporation decides the outcome of business issues based on the majority of shares held by an absolute **minority** of shareholder individuals and not by the majority of shareholder individuals themselves? We would never make such foolish arguments, but we make exceptions when it comes to special and narrow-interests that are slick and persuasive in their deception.

Given these facts, it is not in the interest of the majority to be tyrannical with those things that are vital for their survival or those things that are truly good and of value to the civilization, therefore, they will instead cherish and preserve them regardless of minority status and would not destroy them. Anything else is excess and can not, nor should it be sustained or preserved. There may be a few exceptions to this rule, but by and large Majority Rule is a natural and workable system, thus universal recognition. All phases of civilization including governance should adhere to the principle in its purest form.

Majority Rule however, does not fit with the stated and demonstrated agenda of the current elitists in charge who are a very small minority indeed. With Majority Rule, their position would not last long at all, so they fear the loss of their own protected and privileged status which explains the great weight of indoctrination and misdirection concerning the issue and the ferocious fight we have regarding this monumental tenet of civilization.

Majority Rule would not result in the immediate equalization or redistribution of wealth as it is supposed, or that the majority-mob would elect to take the wealth away from the rich; this is sophistry. With a majority of the politically endowed qualified vote, rights to property and wealth would be respected, preserved, and viewed as vital for the sanctity and security of the civilization.

The notion of mob rule '*stripping the shelves bare*' is based on the idea that we would all fight to '*get what we can while the getting is good*', a kind of mob mentality akin to what happens in a riot. This is only true if it comes to getting what is perceived as someone else's loot. When it is your own you will not behave that way. This illustrates another aspect of why our current system is so broken, because it makes those at the political apex, brokers in a position of handing out favors to those deemed as their friends, while using the power of the state to take away from their enemies. People under this system are then predisposed to get what they can under a system where what is already theirs is really only theirs through authorization and favor from on high. They are also then inclined to support those who construct the sham order. Remove that system of elitist favoritism, supplication, and advocacy, meaning, remove the system that allows individual and organized positions the brokering of power and the dynamic of the behavior of the civilization completely changes.

Democracy and by definition, Majority Rule alone is not suitable as a form of government; it can never be anything more than a component of civilization. Democracy is only a component of stable civilization as mortar is only a component needed to build a wall. It can no more serve standalone as a form of government than mortar alone can be used to construct a wall absent bricks, lumber, or other components. It can not work effectively absent many other vital elements working together.

We are told that currently America is a democracy but what American democracy is not, is democratic. Instead, it is a mislabeled, perverse, jumbled, patchwork-mix of inconsistent rules that favor the status quo, used as a set of tools in the hands of those privileged interests that would drive the nation as a whole further down the path of instability and ruin. The American republic was initially founded employing the democratic process but today it is neither a true republic nor a democracy, but increasingly resembles an oligarchy where a very small group of elitists adhering to a globalist agenda capriciously make arbitrary rulings for the populace to observe while they exempt themselves from the reckless consequences and fallout. This is the stuff that bloody revolutions are made of.

Citizens and Citizenship

The concept of citizenship was borne out of the practice of subjecting a population to the authority of a ruling state such as a king. Citizens were subjects, which is really property. Today however, the idea of the status as property is not recognized, but that repudiation does not elevate the status of citizenship to another level.

Citizenship is by way of a contract and the privileges and rules of citizenship may be enumerated in the constitution, or other accords. Citizenship usually entitles the person to certain **privileges** regarding political participation, and responsibility. It may also provide certain protection status regarding travel in foreign countries. Organizations in general such as clubs, corporations, businesses, or institutions may not acquire the status or privileges of citizens; It is only held by individuals.

Citizenship is not the highest order of right for an individual. The highest order of right is the **Right of Conquest** which may only come by conquest or by inheritance, thus foreign born, immigrants, the children of immigrants, and the naturalized may become citizens but may never be founders or attain the sovereign rights of founders.

Funding Governance (Taxes)

Governance requires money to operate. While revenue may come from numerous sources, in the aggregate it must come from the broad population who expect to benefit by the governance. Currently it comes from a broad range, however, it comes not in an equitable fashion. Our current system of taxes is based on the 2nd plank[38] of the *Communist Manifesto* calling for a heavy progressive graduated income tax. Currently, despite the argument some make that the 16th amendment was not legitimately ratified, if we assume it was,

---

[38] A heavy progressive or graduated income tax.

even so, there is no basis in law for a broad based general income tax. The amendment gave no authority to tax individuals outside of a narrow class.[39]

The income tax today is foist upon the broad population illegally because there has never been any enabling legislation passed allowing it to be levied on individuals outside of the narrow class, nor small business or corporations. It is done by the rules of the bureaucratic administrative state,[40] which makes it illegitimate.

The current US tax system is created by and operated for the narrow-interests who control it. Graduated Income taxes are not equitable to the broad class of people; neither the wealthy producer, nor the poor worker. As a system, it only benefits a syndicate of narrow-interest capital monopolists who set it in motion, expanded it broadly, and now maintain it through iron-fist enforcement using the power of the state. The motivation is not to fund the needs of the nation as much as it is to limit the power of people. The system cheats the wealthy productive class of business owners and people of means, because the real objective is to limit their wealth and the capital they may otherwise use to expand the wealth of the nation, taxing away any excess above a certain threshold.

A graduated tax system does not serve the poor working class either because it limits capital and growth by which they may earn a living and increase their standard of living. I have never understood the envy of people who have bought into the redistributionist, graduated income tax lie. It appeals to the envy motive which is extremely short-sighted. Taking away the resources of someone who has more than you, does not benefit you in any way; it merely limits the wealth of the civilization as a whole, thus limiting the prosperity of everyone. Too many are comfortable with the idea of

---

[39] Those doing business with the federal government; residents of the District of Columbia; or dealing in alcohol, tobacco, or firearms.
[40] See 'Administrative State' in appendix.

redistribution and envy. They have been persuaded that taxing anyone with more income than themselves disproportionately to pay the needs of government is justified, so are not disturbed with the injustice associated with it.

There are better ways. Keep in mind that the purpose of taxes is to pay for the function of governance, not to support the underclass nor the middle or the rich, and certainly not to provide income security or career mobility for politicians and bureaucrats. No civilization would tolerate a system of taxes if there were no need to administer the function of governance; it would simply not exist. Since we have need of such systems, it is solely to support that function and must not be used for any other purpose. When it is used for other purposes such as it is today, it is by fraud and abuse.

Any legitimate function of governance must fall into a classification of vital public use functions, meaning they are vital and required as functions for the maintenance of civilization in-which efficiency is gained. In other words, the vital function can only be done most efficiently by public means, so the broad civilization will benefit by the reduction of cost to them personally. However for most cases, the efficiency cost-benefit may accrue only to a narrow or specifically targeted class. Therefore revenue for such should only derive from the same class, not general.

A few principle should be applied to understand the basic building blocks of an equitable[41] revenue system. I hesitate to use the word 'fair' in any discussion involving taxes due to the fact that the use of the word has been completely distorted in this context to where it has no meaning connected to the legitimate collection and use of revenue, but only extraction of tribute from the peon class. In addition, even given its correct meaning, it would still be inappropriate for the simple fact that 'fair' implies anything but equitable precision in the

---

[41] Equal mutual benefit. Equal exchange of value.

application of collecting revenue from a population. Today the connotation of 'Fair' implies more along the way of a thumbnail estimation or sweetheart deal for a narrow interest.

Equitable precision must apply to funding governance just as much as it does in business and commerce. An *inequitable* transaction in a market would not be tolerated. When you transact business or commerce, you expect to pay the exact negotiated price and receive the full value of the object of transaction so any equivocation[42] is not tolerated by you the customer, nor the merchant making the sale. How can it be any different when it comes to paying for the legitimate benefit derived from the legitimate function of governance?

Somehow Americans have been persuaded that equity does not apply in the case of funding governance. Too many have been brought up believing the lies told by those who brought us the *'progressive tax'* system. It is the erroneous belief that there are some who's sole function is to pay the taxes, and others who may exempt themselves from this burden, viewing themselves only as the beneficiaries. If you listen to those who defend such a flawed inequitable system, they will say that a *'progressive'* tax implies that the tax is used to *'progress'* the civilization forward, while anything else is *'regressive'*, implying that we would go back to the stone-age without this particularly flawed inequitable system. The justifications are an extreme example of hubris in the art of deception. I submit that the word 'progressive' comes from the 2nd plank itself. It is from the ideals of communism. When has communism ever progressed anything other than the monopoly status of global elitists?

There are classes of interest who benefit disparately from others which break along the lines of **specific** and **general** populations; therefore, by far most revenue generated is specific and not general. Specific taxes are called *'user fees'*,

---

[42] Inequitable; bait and switch; fraud; changing the deal.

and are only paid by those who benefit directly from the services or infrastructure provided. Examples are sales tax on gasoline to pay for the upkeep of roads; Recreational licenses (hunting, fishing, hiking etc.) to pay the upkeep of wilderness, wildlife, rivers, lakes, and streams, search and rescue, etc; property tax to pay for police, fire, roads and infrastructure.

Property taxes should be assessed and accounted addressing the precise equitable benefit derived by each property owner for the fees paid. This means the current practice of assessing a tax based on the value of the property and not on the benefit and accounting of service obtained, fails the principle of precision equity. Property taxes must be targeted specifically and only toward those objects of benefit, so should only be levied on the individuals who actually benefit. For this reason, taxes to fund public education are inequitable and illegitimate for the simple fact that people with school-aged children are a specific class only.

General taxation is for the purpose of funding benefits which are common so should come from the entire population, while the vast majority of the total of revenue collected will be targeted to specific uses, so only those directly benefited will be expected to pay. For this reason, targeted revenue will exceed general by several multiples.

An example of a general class are all individuals needing protection from the military of hostile nations or foreign invasion, which includes all individuals. This tax should be the same for every person and paid out of general revenue collected through a consumption tax. Others may span both general and specific classes; examples are: General law enforcement; consumer protection enforcement; the regulation of business and commerce, etc., where benefit accrues to both.

The population at large get the benefit of a firm expectation of safety in product/service/environment, while specific producers realize the benefit of a suitable market and the potential to profit. In this case everyone pays the general class

148

portion while the producers pay for maintaining the regulation, so must be targeted. As an example, the cost of safety testing and regulation for food, drugs, medical care, products, etc, should be paid by fees charged the producers.

The best general tax is an *import tariff*, because it puts the burden on foreign producers to pay a good deal of the general revenue needed to maintain the nation. They benefit by access to the domestic market for their products, while the public benefits by offsetting the tax burden and by adding protection to their markets and jobs, while they also pay a portion in the form of higher prices on the foreign produced goods. In addition, general revenue should be collected in the form of licenses and fees for publicly owned resources such as mines, wells, etc. Producers who extract minerals profit by extraction and sale. Mineral rights of publicly owned resources belong to the individual states, and the nation as a whole so there must be an equitable exchange between them and the producers. In the case of mineral and resource license revenue, states own the public resources within their lands along with the nation at large, therefore, revenue obtained from that portion owned by the nation should come apportioned in distribution.

General populations should 'feel' the pinch of paying for the benefit derived, so must encounter taxes in daily transaction as opposed to embedded taxes which are hidden to the individual, however, that would not include any form of income or production tax, but only a separately tabulated consumer excise tax on purchases. A broad Point of Sale (POS) excise tax is equitable for many reasons, but mainly it provides revenue to support the object of the tax. In other words, any revenue collected is targeted toward the administration of whatever the benefit is, which removes redistributionist function. A consumption tax accomplishes all objectives stated. A consumption tax also affords the individual political decision maker the opportunity to understand revenue issues and vote with their wallets.

All taxes should be levied at the state level, not Supra-State and proportionately administered. Under no circumstance should any function of governance be allowed taxing or self-funding authority. All functions of governance should have budgets set strictly by the Sovereign Democratic Majority, and administered by directive of the same.

CHAPTER EIGHT

Bad Elements of Governance

Over-Burdened Civilizations

Civilizations have rules which govern them and components which make them work, but not all elements that have forced their way into modern social structures are necessary. In fact, modern civilizations are over-burdened with institutions and programs that make too many demands of the populace, burdening them with distractions. The unnecessary and burdensome elements are put in place by narrow-interests, and only serve their purposes.

Parties

We have reached the pinnacle of what can be termed *'Advocacy Government.'* Political advocacy Parties, which include the Democratic, Republican, Libertarian, and Tea parties, and the rest, are what peons and surfs use to ask favors of the king. Of course this is a tongue-in-cheek way of saying what everyone already knows, so in some sense it may not really warrant pointing out the obvious characterization but not everyone is aware that when one cuts through all the rhetoric, this characterization is what we are really left with. The owner of the house does not ask the gardener for permission to enter or construct a wall on his own property, so the owners of the nation should not ask a party, or politician, as an oligarch or king for permission for anything, because in our modern civilized era of '*We the People,*' that chain of authority is not supposed to exist.

Instead of asking for permission or favor, we should just decide the matter amongst ourselves, which can not be done by asking an advocate to intervene with the imperial government. All representative members of our government belong to a party, although there is nothing written in the constitution requiring such membership; parties do now, and have from the early part of the Republic, controlled the entire process of our governance.   Parties are special narrow-interests and in their position close to the palaces and corridors of power, they are brokers; they hold all the cards; or at least that is what you are led to believe. You are made to believe that the only way you have access to power or justice is to go through some sort of advocate.   Advocates, and those seeking favor include corporations, lobbyists, pressure groups, and parties, and various other forms. Political advocacy parties play both sides of the game while leading the charge. They are the entities who all the other groups go to when they want advocacy, and having members elected to all offices, they are also the ones who make the rules and dispense the money and favor. They almost exclusively, represent their paying patrons, and not the people that elect their members to office. The electors are told that they have no where to go but must trust their representatives who are all members of a party, to do right by them and promote their interests above that of the party. This is insanity and utter nonsense.

"*The system must be reformed, and we must elect good people*"; oh so now we hear the cry of the truly confused and desperate. For how many more decades do we need it demonstrated that the problem will not be fixed by reforming a terminally flawed and intrinsically corrupt system, or by electing 'good' people to a bad system? We elect them constantly, but they will never 'reform' their advantage away, even if they were able to. The problem is we are desperately, continuously trying to make a system which is operated by parties as an integral element, which CAN NOT WORK, perform what we think it should when it was never designed to do so and it has only gotten worse.   Parties notwithstanding, our republican form of government never worked the way people have believed it was supposed to.   It only works in the way that it was designed to at this point, which is a system allowing elitist members of society the power to rule over the rest of us and steal our right. We were told as much by one of the architects of the American republic, John Adams, who said it would fail in the short term.   He was right and it does not work now, but the lie that it does is still believed.   What must happen is for the original Americans, the SPEP, to realize their right and power to change it and do for themselves what they expect parties are supposed to do for them now; it is really not that hard, but they must understand how it works now and how it can work.

Business

Government is not an entity charged with creating jobs.   That is the sole role of the private sector and private enterprise will provide that function more than adequately if the society will give them the latitude.   This is a very good example of the duplicitous hypocritical nature of parties, in this case, the republican party is guilty of railing against the size of government, then decrying the fact that government has not created enough jobs for the population.   They have not learned or understood the moral that *"you can not have it both ways."* You cannot expect government to provide jobs for the population without the resources to do so.   Demanding the government provide jobs, or an economy conducive to job-creation only gives permission to that government to grow its size and partly justifies its spending.   Empowering a bloated public institution with this power only enlarges it's size and gives it additional power to dictate in all areas of policy. Government being the provider of jobs, whether through public sector jobs, or through those that promote incentives for the private sector to provide them is a corrupt philosophy originating through narrow-interests for their purposes. It is not in the interests of sovereign people.

Government exists solely to provide public service functions; it is not an enterprise so we do not need government involved in schemes for making money as an enterprise, nor should it be in the business of promoting business, nor favoring certain business over others. Government is a servant and not a business. We are not members of a team, nor clients or customers, and our role in society is not in paying taxes to support the *'enterprise.'* Governance is a mechanism that we in our sovereign wisdom and right, have instituted to serve classes of functions strictly on our behalf. It hardly fits the definition of business.

Social Safety Net

Modern western societies will not tolerate destitute people, especially children or helpless people starving needlessly, suffering in need of medical care, or living in depraved conditions. No decent society would tolerate that and even the most vociferous would change their minds if confronted with the reality of those conditions. To a large extent that is the reason welfare and government aid programs have grown in tolerance, but those that advocate and defend such programs are short sighted. It is not the role of government to reduce, manage, or eliminate such humanitarian need.

Welfare for the poor and destitute is better handled by voluntary community, church, and charity organizations, which are more than capable and eager to provide adequate levels of the aid required to handle the need. Government welfare programs are geared toward dependency not aid, and not designed to remove the handicapped, disadvantaged, or those merely down on their luck from being entrapped by bad lifestyle choices or circumstances outside of their control. That assertion has been proven over the decades in-which government welfare programs have been in existence; it is common knowledge and widely accepted. I have known people, in-fact, family members that are in poor, less than standard living situations, however by and large, I have concluded that many of them consciously make choices to get there and continue to make bad choices which will ensure they remain there. They are willing to take a handout from government or anyone willing to support them, but many are not really willing to do what it takes to change their lifestyle. This makes their situation a matter of choice on their part.

For the most part government welfare programs compete with genuine charity and are hostile to the private voluntary organizations that actually work for the benefit of people. Remove the welfare functions of government including medical emergency and witness the emergence of massive private aid organizations and funding from the overwhelming hearts and pocket-books of people sympathetic to those trapped by the pitfalls of life. There is a saying in christian circles, *"The poor you will have with you always."*

It may not be evident to everyone but those choosing to remain in a state of poverty perform a civic function by providing a living example and lesson of the consequence of bad choices for the youth; to take seriously the need for responsible life choices, and for work to make one-self of worth to the balance of the society. Cutting past the clutter of fluffy speaking, to clearly articulate the truth of the matter; a healthy society needs a certain number of examples of poverty and depravity to warn and instruct the young and foolish to work hard and be responsible for ones self, to avoid joining the ranks of the destitute.

Egalitarianism

There is no such thing as equality of persons. It has never been the case and it is not likely to become reality in the current socio-economic paradigm. The modern faulty notions of egalitarianism came from the morally-bankrupt, scheming, leftist freemasons that brought ruination and war to all of Europe with the French Revolution. It was part of their Utopian slogan (Liberte, Egalite, Fraternite) Liberty, Equality, Fraternity, which on the surface sounds good, however, the most charitable thing I can say about it, considering the source is that their ideas of *'Equality'* were taken to mean that there should be a recognition that the elitist intellectuals and nobles of France were *'equal'* with the king as men. It was very hypocritical though because, despite the rhetoric, they really only sought equality for their noble class and not those they considered beneath them.

That is not to say that equality before the law is a bad thing, quite the contrary, we have embraced this idea and consider it a hallmark tenet of western civilization, that all men should be treated with fairness and dignity before the law. Much of what I write about signals a disgust with the elitist favoritism that pervades much of our system now. If equality of men is taken to mean that somehow we are all the same so we should expect to have equal lives, it is at best short sighted and at worst a destructive lie straight out of the depths of hell.

It is espoused today through horrible tenets called 'social justice', which is simply theft and redistribution in the guise of justice. It is shoved down our throats courtesy of googley-eyed foreign interests and citizens alike, who, having been born and raised in Neanderdale, are fond of calling the theft of property and rights, 'justice'; but does the fact that simpletons who make up the rabid crowd, who make outrageous unprincipled assertion, actually make it so? No, of course not. There is no justice in taking from someone who has right to something and giving it to someone who has never had prior claim or right, just because you believe they should have it; or that we should all share alike. Most of the rhetoric of social-justice is designed to inflame the greed of one group, inorder to beat another over the head and weaken their resolve regarding their property and right. 'Social justice' only serves elitist, leftist, redistributionist causes. It has absolutely no value or integrity and is not worthy of any consideration, so should never be attached to any tenets of governance.

Immigration

With this issue, I see little difference whether it is legal or illegal immigration. To be sure, the difference is vast but for the sake of this discussion both are treated as what they are which amounts to foreign persons moving into our midst, sharing our lives, and our fate. First let me say that the often quoted platitude that, *"we are, or were at one time, all immigrants"*, as a way of putting us all in the same boat which landed here at the same time, from the same place, with the same mission, and giving us all the same status regarding the nation, is pure leftists nonsense. This notion tells us that Original Americans have no right in deciding for another person or group what we are afforded, as if we arrived here in Happy-land Park by the luck of the draw or a twist of fate, like it is a lottery, or favor bestowed from on-high to the lucky ones. Despite the inability of most people to articulate the reasons why this notion is bunk, they do nonetheless recognize it to be precisely that. The same could be said about China, or France, or Saudi Arabia, but no one believes that either China, France, Saudi Arabia, nor anyone else must open up and accept massive influx from the rest of the world; nor that immigrants to those places have either the right to invade there, or the same status of rights which is endowed by heritage with regard to the founding or origin of those nations; that is a ridiculous notion; so neither does it apply here.

It must also be understood that what America is and has become has very little to do with luck, but has to do with who and what we are as a people, and our European roots. The nation reflects what we are, not where we live. The same can be said of other people from other places. They cannot escape who and what they are by emigrating into America; it will only follow them here.

Even the immigrants to America realize that their status is that of an outsider and will never be that of a native. People from other countries that come here want what everyone else wants from life, and we should always recognize that, but that does not constitute the obligation of Americans to sacrifice their own right, land, culture, heritage, and identity in order to accommodate others that have absolutely no right whatsoever in the question of living, working, or occupying space in our land. Consequently their want or need of a 'better life' does not entitle them to immigrate into America. Original Americans have a heritage, status, and right bestowed as founders of the nation and the republic. They are conquerers, founders, pilgrims, frontiersmen, explorers, adventurers, discoverers, planners, architects, engineers, builders of cities and states, mappers and carvers of the wilderness; all architects of the civilization. Although many have immigrants in their background, the last thing they should be considered are immigrants.

Original Americans do not see a problem with the status of a majority of their ranks in terms of the current euro-centric racial and ethnic makeup and see no need to change that. In fact that is really a galvanizing issue that will move them to become politically active more-so than any other single issue, why? Because any purge or changing of that status is against them and theirs and everything they represent, and the country and heritage they have built and been brought up with. Simply put, *it is our country and we will never be moved or put out of it. We will die if necessary to preserve our birthright. Those that come against us or attempt to move us risk an unprecedented backlash, which is just in the early stages of forming. Those that do so, wake a sleeping giant at their peril.*

Immigration favors corporate and business interests, political parties, and ethnic pressure groups and no one else, period. It is clear how immigration is disadvantageous to natural Americans. Natural Americans are the original European Americans who founded and built the country. They are still the largest ethnic population by a long way, despite decades of effort by groups that do not like that fact. Immigration is used in a very scurrilous and divisive way. Immigrants are used by elitists through the media as a ram to pound down the identity and resolve of natural Americans. The effort is aimed at diluting their numbers and reducing their political influence because they are an impediment and a real threat to the agenda of global statists. America, both the nation and the republic, as founded, stands in the way of their global utopian rule and they need to remove the obstacles which still pose a threat to their hegemony. If nothing else, this should get your attention if you fall into the category of Natural or Original American; American v1.0.

To consider if immigration is good for the country, or whether it should be increased, decreased, or eliminated altogether, many questions must be asked and answered, but one in particular must pass the acid test. If an individual person or an entire tribe wants to immigrate to our country, there are many reasons they will give which almost always add up to an advantage for them. The only relevant question is what advantage is there to the SPEP made up of natural Americans, who are the owners of the nation? If the answer for entering the country from the immigrant nets out because the immigrant wants a better life for their family, this makes them an economic refugee and does not pass the test, so should not be a consideration. No one in the world has some imagined fundamental right to emigrate into America. America is owned by people so immigration must represent a real tangible demonstrable advantage to the owners of the nation, not just those seeking entry, and absolutely no advantage or opportunity for the myriad narrow-interests.

We are told that we need immigrants to do the jobs Americans are not willing to do. The obvious answer to this asinine assertion is that what those who say such things really mean is they do not want to pay the rates Americans are willing or need to receive in exchange for their labor; a situation made more onerous by the entry of the immigrants willing and able to undercut the rate demanded by Americans. Immigrants undercutting the wages of Americans are exploited and also victims, although willingly, of a system driven by the clout and dictates of narrow-interests to advantage themselves, just as are the Americans being undercut.

The issue of immigration is in the category of **Bad Elements of Governance**, because if there were never one more immigrant to set foot in the country again, we, the bulk of the nation would never feel it nor even realize it, but would carry on the same as before. For that matter, at some point we would realize the advantage of not having gone down that path and hastened having to endure and suffer the net loss of so many things brought about by immigration, mostly from the 3rd world. If we import 3rd world immigrants, we become the 3rd world, and sadly it does not work the other way around whatsoever. We end up like so many of these countries that are full of masses of poor, uneducated, desperate people who live amongst and serve the elitists oligarchs, living in palaces, who daily pluck the meager substance of their pigeons.

Third Wish

This section bookends the prior section by the same title. Despite the observation and firm belief that history repeats itself, it is seldom that an opportunity to correct the mistakes of the past comes to one or in this case a whole nation, but that is exactly what we have at this time. The 3rd wish means the opportunity to recreate a functioning and responsive civilized structure that operates more according to sound principles of governance and within a correct chain of authority. If not done, the opportunity will soon depart and will probably not appear again in the foreseeable future.

A lot of the reason the window for this change is short is that what little sovereign clout the people comprising the nation still have is diminishing at an alarming rate while the self-perpetuating abomination in Washington and their benefactors are attempting to further dilute the rights of Americans, by flooding the land with 3rd world asylum seeking, economic refugee immigrants, who care nothing of, nor understand the principles of sovereignty or liberty as we once had, but more respond to government graft, favor, and dependence. These people are also victims of the same regime; they do not have the political rights of those of heritage, but are quickly commandeered for the vote anyway.

This situation has created a backlash and economic stress which has caused the government much disfavor among the people. This type of disfavor tends to unify people toward change. But, change for the sake of change, a recent popular political campaign slogan, is very dangerous. Indeed our government, in all three branches has never had lower approval than right now and it is not going to get any better, only worse. That being said, it has been observed that the communist party in Soviet Russia enjoyed similar disdain, but still maintained absolute power for generations and then only disbanded on orders from the west.

We are not that far from tyranny here. And anyone tempted to believe in the popular misconception that, *"It could never happen here!"*, should wake up and observe the current unprecedented destruction of our rights and the looming economic disaster, both of which were thought of as impossible not long ago. A window of opportunity is opening and getting even wider as things worsen, and indeed there is power in that to be harnessed as a catalyst in bringing about the necessary change, but that window will snap shut soon just as assuredly as the sun will rise tomorrow. Correcting the situation must be accomplished starting now!!!

Where Do We Go From Here?

The bad elements of governance listed in this section are not exhaustive by any measure but only cursory. All ideas presented in the previous sections have inspirational and probably theoretical value but are not tremendously useful beyond that unless they find some real application in the lives of people. A plan for affecting real change is outlined in the next several chapters titled *'Sovereign Body'*, *'Structure'*, and *'Movement.'* They, and subsequent sections that follow lay out the necessary steps and outline a theoretical structure embodying the principles described in much of the text.

CHAPTER NINE

A Message to Conservatives

Ideological Relocation

I stated earlier[43] that the message in this book is targeted at 3 groups: 1) Anti New-World-Order / Anti-Globalists; 2) Conservatives; and 3) Everyone else, and I would include Tea Party followers with conservatives. The reason I have chosen to speak to American conservatives in this section is because the ideology of conservatism encompasses the vast majority of the middle-class (what is left of it). By and large, conservatives come from the recent mainstream history of American identity with a sense of who they are, what they have, and what is at stake. Conservatives epitomize much of traditional American values. They sense that currently the nation faces very large problems; things are not right. They also have the power and energy necessary for advancing our civilization along traditional lines, and better, they feel they have been denied their own right, and are willing to work to put things right. Conservatives feel they have been betrayed by the republican party who is moving hard to the left, leaving them in the gap. My feeling is, conservatives would like to move elsewhere but are not convinced of where their home should be. Some admire the Tea Party, others feel they should join with Libertarians. Conservatives are much more attuned and

---

[43] See Chapter 1: About the Book

receptive to the ideas presented here, whereas liberals are composed of much smaller fringe elements of special interests and the underclass. The fringe values liberals espouse means they are not very likely to accept the message presented here.

As I mentioned, I came out of a conservative background but stopped believing in the conservative message because of what I was sold, which seemed rife with blatant hypocrisy and the fact that I was fed up with making excuses for something which I increasingly viewed as empty rhetoric, which attracts many folks by appealing to their own sense of right but never delivers anything beyond the promises. This section is for those readers who identify with the conservative moniker, and those who were formally of the same persuasion like me, and countless others that have decided to look elsewhere for answers to the growing uncertainty.

Many have realized that the republican party does not now, and really never has represented their views despite duplicitous rhetoric to the contrary. The views of the anti-globalists are the closest to my own political philosophy, however the philosophy which I call the **Sovereign Democratic Majority** differers because I do not recognize that the current form of government can or should be reformed or remade. Where I differ from the anti-globalists who some affectionately refer to as conspiracy-theorists or nuts, is, I do not believe we can salvage or continue down the road of the republican form of *'Constitutional Government'*, but I believe we must rebuild in a SDM form through a sovereign-body which determines our policies without a so called ruling class, elected or otherwise, nor the structure to support that prison.

The anti-globalist movement is a political ideology gaining tremendous ground with overlap and roots in the Tea Party and anarchists alike, but originating way before the Tea Party. It will continue to grow in popularity as the nation stares down the path of intractable malaise culminating is some measure of collapse, then rebuilding in the near term. It is my belief that this group will inevitably realize the inadequacy of their current philosophy and move down the path toward the SDM philosophy or some variation on it.

If you are reading this and hold conservative views, this is an open invitation with my sincere hope that you will study and absorb the material and ideas discussed, withhold judgement, and allow the times and events unfolding at present to demonstrate the importance of what is presented. Read and learn. It should be apparent that the republican party is failing and being abandoned by many that can no longer stomach the compromised views; while the Tea Party really has no where to go with no viable solutions or ideas. What should also become evident is that the fastest rising political ideology is from those calling themselves Anti-NWO and anti-globalists who were at one time conservatives, with a small number from the ranks of radical anarchists. Conservatives are leaving for the reasons stated. It is a much more workable ideology and a natural home for conservatives. The following section has some anecdotal criticism and perspective on conservative philosophy.

Liberal vs Conservative

On the political spectrum, seekers of truth should realize that you were initially put in the middle between the Liberal and Conservative positions by education and media conditioning. Seekers of truth initially start to examine both sides, then proceed to the right because it speaks a more systemic, or holistic-philosophy[44] for civilization. These are the things that identify with the human heart, and a persons relationship to the civilized whole. Those that go toward the liberal side are usually drawn by single to multiple issue, and less by holistic-philosophy. They may be drawn by preference for those things that personally benefit them or their particular sphere of

---

[44] Encompassing and considering all aspects, and all consequences of a philosophic or operational system.

influence and acquaintance. This is a considerably self-centered view and philosophy, which renders considerable damage to the political body. Conservatism, in a pure form, is less destructive, and as a philosophy it is probably benign. As a practice, it is less destructive to the body.

Young people in particular, when attempting to determine in which direction the truth lays, more often than not, set up camp in either the liberal or conservative positions, not realizing that these political positions define and occupy a very narrow band of thought. Most never explore anything beyond either of these 2 flawed and very limited philosophy. It is imperative that they move beyond the bankrupt liberal and conservative philosophies, and begin to explore much of the thought that moves to the right of there, meaning, toward the philosophy of Libertarianism, and the Tea Party. However, one should not stop here either, but only wave to these very narrow and inadequate philosophies as they continue to seek the truth. You will know you are entering into a more utilitarian and useful area of thought when you begin to read about the evils of the Federal Reserve, Secret Societies, The New World Order, and so forth. However, the closer you get to the meat of political reality and world order the more rocky the road gets. The journey forward is not comfortable and not convenient, but fraught with mis-information, mis-direction, and lies, which are there to dissuade the student or truth seeker from continuing down the road of discovery. The road must be taken with caution, and discretion must be carefully exercised. It is not a quick journey but many assertions must be carefully weighed to discern the truth from the garbage.

The chasm between Conservative and Liberalism goes back into the late middle ages, into the renaissance to the age of 'enlightenment' with the emergence of humanist thought, which moved away from the authoritarian influence of the Catholic Church in everyday life of people. Like other things that emerged such as science and even Protestantism, there was a need to re-evaluate the human condition, human ruling institutions, and the reigning philosophies of western civilization. Conservatism sought to preserve the old order and authority while liberalism sought to throw off or abolish it outright and institute new ways. Both philosophies hold pretty much the same today. Conservatism has been dragged along kicking and screaming as civilizations over time have consistently favored liberal movements. It is characteristic that conservative thought will duplicitously resist and condemn liberal ideas and initiatives only to embrace them and attempt to define them as their own ideas at a later time.

Conservatism is generally benign and harmless but in-effective, while liberal ideas since the beginning have consistently produced disasters and are more often than not, responsible for human tragedy on a large scale. Liberalism has mostly been responsible for moving western civilization down the path it has trodden by upsetting the existing order. Usually after the damage is done, things settle down where a synthesis of old and new paradigm exists, then conservatives move in to take ownership. Examples of liberalism at its finest are:

- The genocidal operations of the architects of the French Revolution.

- Communist and socialist movements and power grabs.

- The era of big government. The welfare state.

- The Nazi Regime.

- Virtually all financial crises in the US and Europe for the last 300 years.

- Feminism & the Abortion industry.

- The push back of Christianity from public life and the rise of paganism and the occult.

- The destruction of the family unit and the neglect of the rearing of children.

- The bankrupt counter culture of the 1950s/60s and the drug culture of today.

- Co-opting the education of the young. Public education.

- The dumbing down of the intellect of children and the populace.

- Globalism, global trade, and dictatorial world government. The New World Order.

- Advancement of the homosexual agenda.

- Most of the wars in the western hemisphere in the last 300 years.

- Many of the wars in Asia in the last 150 years, which have been instigated through actions of western powers.

The most familiar compendium of ideas from the liberal philosophy have run their course at this point whether enacted or forced or not, and it is believed they will continue to suffer significant decline in acceptance. Those advancing liberal philosophy have recently brought considerable ruination and the world is getting tired of it.

Many of the ideas originally advanced by liberals but tempered by conservative views have brought some 'good' such as the ideas of democracy which moved civilization away from the autocratic rule of kings, but most of it has been disastrous for those living through the enactment. Enactment is generally reckless with great disregard for the populations effected. 'Good' is relative, and is shown in quotes above because it may be considered only better than the state during the disastrous period in which it is put into place. It is also 'good' because the upheaval it created during enactment, facilitated better policies gained by the populous, which are seldom congruous with the aims of liberalism. This means it only afforded the populace the opportunity to advance good new ideas, however, not the adoption of liberal ideas.

It is my sincere hope and belief that we will enter into a new era of thought, and away from the excesses of liberalism and return to many of the philosophies embodied in conservative ideals as we transition to a new century and the challenges of the future. Having said that I must confess that the thesis which I am presenting is more in fitting with the definition of liberal than conservative, because it specifies a radical change from the existing order. That change however, could also be considered a response to a status which will force itself upon the nation and the world, and stemming from the collapse of the existing order which has been ravaged by liberalism.

Conservative

ORIGIN late Middle English (in the sense [aiming to preserve]): from late Latin **conservativus**, from **conservat-** **'conserved,'** from the verb **conservare**. Current senses date from the mid 19th century onward.

Conserve - verb

protect (something, esp. an environmentally or culturally important place or thing) from harm or destruction *: the funds raised will help conserve endangered meadowlands.*

Concierge - noun

1 (esp. in France) a caretaker of an apartment complex or a small hotel, typically one living on the premises.

2 a hotel employee whose job is to assist guests by arranging tours, making theater and restaurant reservations, etc.

ORIGIN mid 16th cent. (denoting the warden of a house, castle, prison, or royal palace): French, probably based on Latin **conservus 'fellow slave.'**

Liberal - adjective

1 open to new behavior or opinions and willing to discard traditional values : *they have more liberal views toward marriage and divorce than some people.*

ORIGIN Middle English : via Old French from Latin *liberalis*, from *liber 'free (man).'*

The original sense was [suitable for a free man,] hence [suitable for a gentleman] (one not tied to a trade), surviving in *liberal arts*.

Another early sense [generous] gave rise to an obsolete meaning [free from restraint,] leading to sense 1.

From the definitions given, the word *'Conservative'* stems from the designation of a *'caretaker'*, while *'Liberal'* stems from the description of a Nobleman mover-shaker.

Note: Conservus means *'fellow slave'*, while liberal means *'free man.'*

American Republicratism

So says the title of this section, or maybe it should be Democlicanism. However it is imagined or described, everyone understands what is meant but not all agree on what it is. I would like to give a perspective on a few aspects to illustrate the failure of the dominant set of political ideologies which the nation has adopted. Illustrating the point to which they are ingrained into our identities, people will say such things as, *"My parents were democrats, so I am a democrat,"* and *"The republican party is the only party that can hold back the tide of socialism."*

Although I would like to deal equally with the liberal as well as the conservative view, I believe the liberals are more a lost cause than those that hold the republican views. Persons embracing American Republicanism personally believe: *"I am represented by people that I and my peers and neighbors elect and approve to make decisions for my life, based on the republican system in which 'we the people' elect them to speak for me, and enact policies that are in alignment with my interests. It 'works', therefore I have an incentive to vote for candidates who share my particular values and outlook, who are likely to enact things to preserve and protect my right and my interests."*

The reality is American Democracy works differently. Even though you would never ever consider electing people known to be predators on society, who come from much different ethnic, cultural, and political traditions and outlook, who are likely from a different part of the country which may as well be the other side of the world; and whereas people who are not your neighbors and do not share your values or outlook but have values, interests, and outlook completely at odds with your own, do elect them. Further, whereas you would condemn those who they elect as an abomination to all that is decent, nonetheless, those who elected them have tremendous respect for them and embrace their policies, so they have tremendous influence over your life. This means others choose for you, not you. I will never accept that, nor should you.

The system does not represent my interests, and it does not represent yours. I would never, ever consider voting for either representative Barney Frank or senator Charles Schumer and many others (John McCain comes to mind), both from New York who's north-eastern, big government values and attitudes are completely at odds with my southern values, yet both sit-on or head committees in congress that enact policies which greatly effect me, extracting tribute to enrich those who elected them. I consider virtually all of their policies stifling and robbing me of my interests and rights and I would never agree to virtually any of them. This is the flaw in so called American 'Democracy', it just does not work as represented.

I live in Florida, so I nor any of my neighbors elected Frank, Schumer, or McCain, nor the parade of leftists clowns who preceded these for the last 150 years, yet they have tremendous influence over my life and yours. That is American democracy in all its glory.

Conservative Recipe For Salvation?

I have little faith in, and no misplaced confidence in the so called conservative leadership and voices that are today claiming to have all the answer to the nations problems. In my estimation, they have completely missed the boat. They continuously cite the problems ad naseam, over and over again with no solutions offered while most of their followers loose confidence that they ever had even an inkling of understanding what the problems are. It is my opinion they are shills for the Republican party and are tasked with leading the troops of Republican faithful down one blind alley after another, always with the same old tired sorry excuses for why things continue to go from rotten to disastrous. In my estimation they have ZERO credibility, as does the narrow interest Republican party and most of its leadership which are as duplicitous as any in word and deed.

Metaphorically, the conservatives are *'lost in the weeds;'* fearing their message rings hollow; increasingly falling on deaf ears with only run-of-the-mill liberals to blame, they have finally sought to search a little more broad afield to find more suitable bogey-men to blame and have stumbled across the pup-tent encampment of Cloward-Piven and Saul Alinsky. They have spied them out and are now in the process of surrounding them and putting a siege-work plan of attack in place, while loudly sounding the hero alarm. What they have failed to realize is that Alinsky, Cloward, and Piven are derelict outcasts from the great fortress of betrayal, full of thousands of considerably more powerful actors and the architects of destruction which lies just around the bend and where there is already forming an array of battlement to wage a considerably more effective war by those with considerably more power and ability to beat back the menace.

The conservative pretenders are not likely to see or acknowledge the real evil until it is too late even for them. They have proclaimed themselves to be the embodiment and fount of all truth and knowledge concerning the American civilization for too long, but now the mask is slowly coming off to reveal a conservative face of duplicitous treachery and the betrayal of those they pretend to speak for.

Having cited the problem endlessly, their latest and only 'solution', or as I view it, their latest *fund raising scheme* is to tell us they have finally figured out a workable solution and the way to '*save the nation*' is to amend the broken and defunct constitution. Ignoring the fact that it has been completely shredded at this point. But if we were to amend it through the states, this will somehow convince the imperial government and central-planning to start obeying the decimated constitution and all of the new amendments. This is pure pucky-smudge.[45] They really have no answer or solution, and they are really only interested in getting your attention to continue their charade. So then lets look at their proposed amendments.[46]

1) **Term Limits**. A tired canard. Limit the terms so the staffers and bureaucracy can take a more active role than what they already do which is to draft nearly the entire deluge of crap swirling about there already. *"Hello congressman Noobie I am your staff manager. There's your desk and phone. Please answer the calls that come in and try to get them right if you can. I will try to get answers for you if you get a stumper. In the mean time do not bother us because we are busy planning your re-election by creating the image that*

---

[45] Use your imagination.
[46] Called the 'Liberty Amendments' from the book by the same name. By Author Mark Levin. Not verbatim. Listed here but summarized with comments.

you actually know what you're doing, and that you are actually doing something."

2) **Giving the states the power to elect senators.** Wow that would simply change nothing. The entire system would suddenly not straighten out and not start firing on all cylinders once again. How simple it is to achieve nothing; states electing their own senators. How novel! By the way in case you missed it, there is considerable sarcasm in the comments.

3) **Limiting The power of the Judiciary.** I thought they were already limited by the constitution. Hmm, that one must not have taken. Better do it a few more times for good measure.

4) **A balanced budget amendment.** A tired old canard. Imagine the taxes if this one is implemented. We are much better off without that.

5) **Limiting bureaucracy.** Like the way it is done by the letter of the word already. Ever hear the phrase 'Enumerated power?'

6) *Defining the limits on the Commerce Clause.* For this one I give partial credit and '*e*' for effort. It is a step which, although does not repeal the misguided and sorely abused act (regardless of intent), it does demonstrate some understanding of the foothold from where much abuse originates.

7) *Limiting Federal power to take private property.* A simple 'finding' by the court and a workaround renders this with less value than the paper it is printed on.

8) *Allowing State Legislature to Amend the Constitution.* Great, the parties and narrow interests simply move part of the machine from the federal level to the 34 already identified states needed to pass whatever amendment they wish to shove down our throats. State operatives and bureaucrats are easier to extract favors from and cheaper to buy off. It may come as a shock to some to learn that most of

the trouble we're in today came about by the narrow interests enacting and shoving amendments to the constitution down our throats. They can enact them at will just as easily as they skirt and ignore them. I would instead wish to reserve whatever little integrity there is still left in the various statehouses than to infect them anymore.

9) ***State Authority to Override Congress***. See comment for 8 above.

10) ***Protecting the Vote***. By requiring photo ID for all federal elections and limiting the early vote. Although the idea has some merit, it still leaves the narrow interests firmly in control and operating unbroken.

In my estimation, there are 2 amendments really worthy of consideration, which if enacted could make a difference, creating a significant barrier for elitists to continue with most of their schemes, while empowering us, *the people*, with some say in our own affairs and that of the nation, but strangely these are not even mentioned by the conservatives that 'speak' for us. Somehow this makes it hard to believe in the sincerity of such notions and gestures. To be fair, one of them is almost mentioned and I gave some credit for effort.

They are:

1) **Article I, Section 8, Clause 1**, *The Congress shall have Power To lay and collect Taxes, Duties, Imposts and Excises, to pay the Debts and provide for the common Defense and general Welfare of the United States; but all Duties, Imposts and Excises shall be uniform throughout the United States;*

A reasonable amendment would be to repeal this clause in its entirety and move the power to collect all revenues, set all budgets, and fund all federal activities to the states, putting the power of the purse closer to the sovereign people, closer to the proper chain of authority. Further, it must be moved to eliminate any collusion between party operatives in state offices and the feds, to make sure the people have the power to oversee the entire process.

But while we're at it, if we go to this length, why not recognize the truth and the proper order and go the rest of the way so that the people take all of their sovereign right back. Repealing the power for government to self-fund through any means leads ultimately to that place, does it not? By the way, the natural outcome of the repeal of the power to tax would be that the income tax amendment, number 16, and the enforcement agency it summoned from the netherworld,[47] would likewise be extinguished.

2) **Article I, Section 8, Clause 3**, *The Congress shall have Power… To regulate Commerce with foreign Nations, and among the several States, and with the Indian tribes;*

Repeal or severely restrict (not just clarify) the power associated with this monstrosity which currently gives the imperial government the power to peer right up the altogether; to insert deep and ream hard; to give America an anal probe. They use this one to justify their intrusion into every aspect of our personal private lives and the sovereign affairs of states.

We do not need new amendments which would not be observed anyway, but if enacted, I could see these 2 important measures as putting the establishment on notice of what is coming and nothing more. Isn't is curious though that the *'conservative'* stalwarts do not even suggest a move in this direction? Why do you suppose that is?

One more school of rhetoric worthy of mention is the class of conservative canards such as cutting taxes, drilling more oil wells, creating more jobs, and the entire litany of measures from those that benefit by their enactment; all of which are supposed to foster healing by increasing revenue to the government. Understand that whenever conservatives

---

[47] The Internal Revenue 'Service'

advocate cutting taxes, a fair recommendation indeed amongst many others, they usually accompany it by promising that it has been proven in the past, and will again result in increased revenue to the government. ***How hypocritical to ostensibly rail against the monstrous size of the growing federal bureaucracy while advocating measures to further that growth!***

Our problems do not stem from not having enough of our blood flowing into the offering bowl at the alter in Washington. That will only make it larger and more oppressive than it already is. These assertions are based on faulty thinking; that our problems stem from the government not having enough money to burn on worthless projects or the US government's own irresponsible deficit and debt putting a stranglehold on the nation. The strangling effect of debt may be a fact but throwing more tax revenue onto the pyre will not solve anything, only make it worse.

In actuality, the fact that we feed the beast can be directly shown to be the root of all of our trouble. We should wake up and realize we must stop feeding the monster. This is a case where the real solution lays in the exact opposite direction of the prescriptions we are assured will solve our problems. Consider the source and follow the money. Those that advocate such things usually have their fingers in the pie.

Some reading this will argue that cutting taxes, creating more jobs, and drilling more wells are generally positive things. My response is that those things are indeed good but they are incidental to what is prescribed and only offered as fodder by the advocates offering the faux solutions. The debt problem can be more easily solved than most people even know and does not require feeding the beast. That solution will be discussed later.

Because I criticize conservatives does not mean I agree with the more leftist views of liberals. I single out the conservative view because the people that embrace these views are the ones constituting the vastness of the middle-class of the nation; people with the power to make the necessary changes if they will only see past the mist of lies and realize there are better ways. I believe they embrace these false views due to the fact that there is some truth amongst the lies in what is espoused, in harmony with their own life experience and conservative upbringing, so they identify with them.

Holding-fast and signing-on to the entire conservative package, the corrupt along with the good, is done for many reasons including the lack of knowing viable alternatives. It must be understood, the conservative package taken as a whole dead-ends with the demise of the nation just as assuredly as does the liberal package. I vehemently loath these false views and recommendations by both sides which are in reality, 2 sides of the same coin, with the same narrow interests driving them, and all are considerably to the left of the natural views of most people which are more harmonizing with the lessons of history and the laws of God and nature.

Conservatism as practiced is at best fickle, wishy-washy, duplicitous, and hypocritical, with very little of substance and only making a mockery of the age-old sound principals of civilization, and that is a generous assessment. It can be characterized by a past history of correctly, vehemently opposing the corrupt and bankrupt socialist proposals of liberalism, only to heartily embrace and defend the same later after they have been enacted and have accomplished the planned and anticipated destruction. Examples of this are: The civil rights movement and the resulting laws of the 1950/60s; the social welfare programs such as social security, medicaid, and medicare; etc. These were all vehemently opposed by conservative ideology and the republican party when introduced and shoved down the throat of the American public, but they are now embraced and defended as if they are their own by the same. Pure double-spoken hypocrisy!

CHAPTER TEN
Sovereign Body

Automatic World

An idea occurred to me when I happened to notice that on occasion when I went into the kitchen at our house, there were times when many dirty dishes were piled up and other times when none were seen but the place was spotless. I noticed that it happened when I was not there to witness it being done. Everyone knows the dishes did not just put themselves into the dishwasher, run it, then put themselves into the cupboards; a person did those things.

My wife was very relieved when I explained that I really did grasp that deep concept because mostly it was done by her when she cleaned the kitchen. However, her doing so voluntarily engendered in me and my teenage son an attitude of expectation. All we need do is walk in and set the dirty dish on the counter, and mysteriously the problems associated with too many dirty dishes never became unmanageable for either of us because someone else would take care of it, and frankly, neither of us cared who or how it was done. All we care about is that it is not a problem for us. The observation led to an idea of how to express a foggy concept bouncing around in the minds of many people.

To a large extent, this is how the unwashed masses view the world and the nation; it is *'Automatic World'*. There is always someone that will take care of whatever little problem or malfunction occurs which might inconvenience, worry, or burden us, so there is no need to be concerned about anything as long as we live in *Automatic-World* because it will take care of itself..., somehow, and we do not really care about the details. This is a great example of how our population has been trained to think; somewhat by flawed education and media conditioning, and somewhat by the mental diseases brought about by unmerited prosperity. The problem is, *Automatic-World* does not really exist; it is a fake-out, removing the person from having to think or act for himself.

A powerful effect of having a nation of persons infected with this flawed thinking, having never witnessed or understood the bloody details of the inner-working of the real world, is, they are not aware, and have no baseline appreciation for the scope or cost involved in what it takes to operate a civilization as complex as ours is. Its easier to ignore the problems instead of taking responsibility for our own situation and fate.

Organized criminals are picking over our bones, operating massive fraud in our midst in partnership with government, which threatens the integrity of the nation's infrastructure and the freedom of the population on a daily basis, but the population refuses to believe problems really exist, because if it were really true and we were actually threatened, we would know it and someone in the government would simply pass a law to fix the problem. If there were really problems threatening our civilization, the news media would be on top of it and they would tell us. We refuse to see the truth of it even as it consumes us. Its called the ostrich syndrome; hide your head in the sand.

There really are no rules, and there are no guys in white hats. *Automatic-World* does not exist. Criminals and politicians are really free to exploit us at will, and they are doing just that and have been for a very long time. They are emboldened to continue to do so unless we stand up individually and as a powerful group with a firm and loud voice. No one is going to swoop in and save us from the bad guys. We are on our own and it is completely up to us.

It is an unfortunate fact of human nature which consequently is reflected in our civilizations, that humans will not take responsibility for their lot in life until it is too late to save themselves without significant compromise. We at this juncture, are on the precipice of disaster and people are finally starting to wake up and realize the gravity of the predicament, but at least we are awakening.

Each individual is responsible for his or her own safety, security, wealth and happiness, and *we the people* as a nation are responsible for the same to the degree that it applies to our civilization. In a world where it is necessary to exploit the division of labor, meaning we as individuals and groups must rely on others to do some of the things we can not do for ourselves, it is imperative to understand and embrace the many vital things which we simply must be directly involved in. We absolutely can not abrogate our responsibility to oversee and control the administration of our own civilization, meaning, we can not entrust it to another. It must be done by all of us.

Sovereignty

I have already expounded on the idea of sovereignty and will continue to hammer home the concept as it is vital that the people who make up our nation realize they must take the initiative to solve the problems and renew our civilization. It will not happen by the initiative of the rich and powerful, nor with politicians, no matter how much they attempt to persuade you otherwise. We have at present the unworkable disaster which they will always deliver. Our task can only be accomplished by the authority which comes from our individual and group sovereignty. If you haven't already gotten sick of reading about the word, be sure that you will because I will continue to pound the idea home.

Sovereignty has to do with the will of the people endowed with the right of political participation and their ability to express, negotiate and, exercise that will. Full unhindered, undiluted, unabridged sovereignty of the people means the same rise and fall on the decisions they make, and further, this consequence illustrates that it is their right. As a civil body, they are not accountable to others, and no other has any right to supplant the sovereignty of the body. Sovereignty has nothing to do with the power to act in a manner violating the humanity of other individuals or groups that are not members of the sovereign body. It is not a license or badge of omnipotence, or oppression.

The phrase **Sovereign Democratic Majority** succinctly defines the form of deliberation and adoption proposed. An SDM is very simple. It is the outcome of any issue determined primarily by the up or down vote of a **Sovereign Body** by the simple majority **Fully Qualified Weighted Vote** (FQWV), therefore this **Democratic Majority** is not a fixed group, but changes issue to issue. A Sovereign body is not a mob or a group tasked with oppression of others who are not part of the body. The purpose is simply to provide a mechanism by which problems or policy issues can arise, be discussed and debated, solution proposed, testimony presented, language written, then policy adopted, however, it is premised upon the qualified right of those people, which eliminates others not possessed of the right. Any civilization must employ some variation of this mechanism; be it a kingdom, dictatorship, oligarchy, representative body, or a Sovereign Body.

Civil Constructs
For most of the history of civilization, the idea of property ownership has developed to become familiar so as to be taken for granted. I mean by this that individuals instinctively know

what it means to own things, but are not aware of where the idea and practice of what we commonly refer to as 'ownership' came about, or how it works. As I have already elaborated with the discussion of 'rights'[48], both ownership and rights amount to what are called a *Civil Construct*. Actually rights result from the net equilibrated balance of all forces applied, but are supported through civil constructs, whereas ownership emanates less from force and more from familiarity and tradition.

I will elaborate more on the institution of ownership later after discussing more about what Civil Constructs are, and how they find place in our world. To be simple, civil constructs are human inventions, used to provide the structures necessary to support civil order. They are conventions and institutional systems which are generally universally recognized and accepted by populations. Most people if asked what they are would recognize them immediately because they are encountered in daily life. For these institutions to be in effect, generally they must be recognized and respected by the populations who view them as vital to the function, administration, survival, and continuance of the civilization.

Examples of civil constructs are : All systems of civil and criminal law; all human economic and monetary systems; all political systems and others. The importance of the discussion about civil constructs is that by understanding what they are, how they work, and how they have come about gives us the power to see how they can be used to redefine our civilization to more suit our own purposes. In past ages, these systems developed over long periods of time and were defined through numerous proposals, actions, and decisions by many people in many lands. There are several that are extremely important to become familiar with due to their power over our outlook and attitudes. As a society, perception of civil constructs has the power to control our behavior to either our detriment, or to

---

[48] See chapter 'Gaining Perspective.'

great advantage depending on whether they are viewed properly or erroneously. Perception can affect our motivation and willingness to tolerate injustice, making us passive and accepting of corruption and theft, or instead, give us the motivation to disregard longstanding misconceptions about them, with a mind to zero out the errors, then redefine and redeploy them.

The important thing to understand is that civil constructs can all be redefined from scratch. In this process there are really only a few basic rules, and these are well respected by virtually all populations since the beginning of civil society. A society can at any time, redefine their civil constructs inorder to correct course from where it has gone off. Having said that, a wholesale redefinition of all foundational constructs imbued in western civilization is certainly not warranted, but only a little correction or clarification is needed.

I started with, and will conclude this section with the example of ownership, and I will elaborate on another very important civil construct in the next section. In high school, I along with most of my peers learned that when white europeans came to the new world, they conflicted with the natives who did not have nearly as developed a concept of owning 'things', due to a misunderstanding of the concept particularly where it applies to the ownership of land; so the ideas have had a different meaning by various people. I also elaborated on the question of ownership concerning our land, and our heritage in the chapter 'Declaration.' It is instructive and quite enlightening to apply and expand the concepts discussed in this section to the same questions brought up in that chapter.

Today the idea of what ownership is, and how it applies should be universally accepted. Having said that, there are many among members of the elitist-class in the US and other countries that do not accept the universal understanding as constituting the construct definition of *'ownership.'* Lets examine the elements which are necessary to render the effectual construct of ownership:

1) Equity.

2) Recognition and respect.

In our current republic, we have entrusted authority to persons to originate and uphold systems of law, defining a lower set of rules for maintaining the civil order ordained by the founders of the republic, which are supposed to govern our civilization. The system only works if it remain within the bounds and in-harmony with the natural order, and will fail if it strays. This civil construct may only exist and have a relevant purpose if it maintains the characteristics for which it was intended which may strictly tend only along the lines of a benefit to the population, and if the entity which commissioned it and gives it power, the sovereign people, agree and accept that it does bestow benefit, usefulness, and legitimacy.

All civil constructs are subject to equity, and must be recognized by the sovereign people. Ownership demands equity. Equity gives legitimacy to ownership, and without equity, the construct deteriorates. As an example: When the federal reserve bank and the government spend money which cost them nothing, but expect that the common people must pay in blood for the same benefit obtained by expenditure, there is no equity. The value of money is always regulated by what amounts to an auction. If it is free to one, it is free to all because equity makes it so. This is where education and perception become important. There is a glaring contradiction between the ideal and the practical in the ideas expressed above and the reality on the ground. People recognize the seeming contradiction, but many believe that it is just the way it is and can not be changed; they say things like, *"That is the way it is, and it will always be that way!"*, and, *"It takes money to make money!"*, and, *"The markets are rigged, but what can ya do?"*, and, *"We don't live in a perfect world!"* I believe these are really excuses, and a frustrated attempt for justifying why things are unfair when they do not have to be that way. Many things have changed over the last 500 years for the benefit of the common man, and that is a continuing phenomena.

In another example; whenever the government or those who use the power of government make broad claims on the productive resources of others without their consent and without equitable exchange, it cannot meet the criteria of either equity or recognition. A few more examples; the rigging of markets to cheat many from their property; sweeping declarations by those in robes concerning the confiscation of property by government; illegitimately using money from taxation to bail out the losses of banks and other powerful individuals and organizations, who carelessly make frivolous unrecoverable loans; and any number of routine acts of the collusion between wealthy individuals or corporate interests who daily collude with members of government, engineering the massive theft of property from the nation at-large.

The concept of ownership can be very fragile. *Recognition* in regard to ownership legitimizes it. This implies the voluntary acceptance or rejection of legitimacy by the broad population, transcending any declaration of legitimacy by a court, which is precisely what makes it fragile. There must be widespread acceptance for the concept of title and contract inorder for it to have the weight of legitimacy. If the population at large does not recognize or accept that those who wield the power of government to their own advantage actually 'own' what they claim, then we must examine whether that ownership claim is legitimate. If the broad population do not accept the premise, then ownership is not recognized. This is very dangerous, as the widespread practice of theft under the color of law threatens to collapse the entire system if the recognition of legitimacy fails.

There is power for the masses in understanding how and what constitutes the construct of ownership. There is tremendous power in the ability to say, *"We recognize and uphold your ownership"*, or *"We do not recognize your right or ownership."* Ownership only works for either poor and weak, or the rich and powerful as long as the broad populous from which the power of civilization emanates, accept and acknowledge the legitimate right of those who claim it.

Those who practice organized theft, whether individuals, corporations or government may only do so by masking the inequity, inorder to maintain the recognition of legitimacy and right by the broad population. They must act in secrecy and maintain a veil of deception to prevent correction and a reckoning. Again, this puts it on extremely dubious footing whenever the populous is unconvinced.

There is an accepted idea among the monied class that it is not as important to own something as much as it is only to control it. Their motto is *"Own nothing, control everything!"* Mayer Amschel Bauer Rothschild, an extremely wealthy individual, who founded a very powerful financial dynasty said, *"Give me control of a nations money and I care not who makes its laws."* He certainly understood that when one holds legal title to property, by having a personal name presented or attached to it's ownership, it will attract unwanted attention and enemies. It makes it subject to scrutiny and may require proof of legitimate title, which presents a problem when none exists.

Even today, there is a healthy trade for lawyers and financial planners in devising clever and elaborate mechanisms to hide the names and mask any paper-trail leading back to their clients. However it is inescapable, control is the same as ownership, and ownership means control. In either case, both require unquestioned legitimacy to maintain. This premise effectively means the current system of organized theft is a house of cards in a considerable state of unbalance which will inevitably correct itself. It is conceivable that within a short few years, as these unbalanced systems right themselves, that many long standing dynasties of wealth and power may find themselves attempting to justify and prove the legitimacy of their wealth going back for centuries, when it is required of them by a completely different social order than what reigns today.

Exactly the same logic should be applied to the current system of laws and the current political paradigm. If these civil constructs as defined now are not capable of adhering to the universal tenets of equity, justice, and legitimacy, they are unstable and will at some point suffer a wholesale crisis of confidence. They will be repudiated and new ones will emerge to replace them.

Power V Money

Among the most important of civil constructs to understand is a fallacious view that has developed over millennia, which is the proper relationship between money and political power. As discussed before, most common people over eons have come to believe and accept the false notion that money equals power. We have heard of the so called 'Golden Rule', which is sarcastically said to mean, *"He who has the gold makes the rules."* We have been trained through media examples that if you are wealthy, you can buy the justice you want just as easily as you buy anything else, putting those with money above the laws the rest of us must abide by. We have all seen examples of the rich and connected getting a slap on the wrist for heinous crimes whereas the not-wealthy get sentences of decades in prison for much less. We are also familiar with how the wealthy and connected, banking and corporate interests, which are irresponsible and frivolous with their investing, get their billions of losses bailed out by money taxed from the masses.

This is paradoxical because it flies in the face of the axiom that the power and right of civilizations emanate from the bottom up. In past models, there was always an equilibrated balance of power shared between the Strong-man King and the common. Our own republic was created along that model, with the king being replaced by the elected representative bureaucracy.

Many of us are aware that wealthy individuals and organizations, both foreign and domestic, hire lobbyist who daily walk the halls of power in the nation's and state capitals, dispensing money for political consideration. They buy and therefore pervert the process which is supposed to be about our interests only. What many people are not aware of is that the vast majority of activity that goes on there is by and for the special narrow interests. Their money and influence shapes our lives and our fate, mostly without us really realizing how much. Some of us are aware that recently those in robes declared that a wealthy corporation is an entity as a person is, therefore entitled to buy the process out from under us.

It may come as a surprise to learn that the notion that money and wealth is equivalent to power is really a broken civil construct because it is widely but reluctantly accepted; again by misinformation and ignorance. I discussed what civil-constructs are, and how they affect our civilization and our lives, and how a civilization may redefine them when they are found to be unbalanced in the previous section. Understanding the nature of civil-constructs gives us significant transformative power. *'Wealth is equivalent to power'* is not true in reality; but is only so if we believe it to be the case and accept it. If we fatally accept this as an immutable[49] fact of civilization then we are likely to just live with it, even as it consumes us. The fact is, not only is it not an immutable evil of civilization as is believed, but it operates that way now only because we allow it. We have been taught to conflate the equivalence of the 2, mostly through biased media conditioning and faulty education. We can easily change this faulty belief and therefore the perverse double standard reality if we know and understand that it is our choice, and if we

---

[49] Unchanging; or can not be changed.

choose to make the change. It is in recognizing the truth of this lie and acting that change can come. Keep this idea in mind, it is the essence and root of the discussion about renewing our civilization which follows.

A more healthy and prosperous view for the masses is to define, teach, and act in such a way as to enforce a wall of separation between money and political power. In my view and that of many others throughout the last few centuries, the power necessary to create and maintain a civilization, and by this I mean nationhood-identity and form of governance, emanate from the people who make up the civilization which establishes their endowment, so it is the absolute birthright of the people that they should hold and exercise that power regardless of their wealth status. The founders of our failing republic believed this when they said:

*'That to secure these rights, Governments are instituted among Men, deriving their just powers from the **consent of the governed**.'*

Why is it necessary to obtain the consent of the governed unless there is a recognition of their ownership right? *'... deriving their just power...'*, which is the power to carry out the functions of governance for which it has been commissioned. If *'the governed'* were not considered as the owners, then it would not be necessary to obtain their consent. Also note that *'...governments are instituted among men...'* Its clear, sovereign people are who create governments. Why would people create something to impact their lives the way government does, unless there is an advantage for them in doing so? Governance must be a net advantage, and can never become something that diminishes their lives. People create government for their own purposes, and only their purposes; it has no other. This is ownership, and ownership means total control.

...and further,

*'That whenever any Form of Government becomes destructive of these ends, it is the **Right of the People** to alter or to abolish it, and to institute*

new Government, laying its foundation on such principles and organizing its powers in such form, **as to them** *shall seem most likely to effect their Safety and Happiness.*[50]

Because the energy that powers civilization emanates from the masses of sovereign people who have defined it, built it, and maintain it, it belongs to them and is theirs to wield and their right shall not be distributed inequitably.[51] Political equity is by the individual; by single membership in the sovereign body, and not by false, frivolous, specious, or disproportionate measure, such as by wealth and privilege, neither by mere membership in the human family. The payment of taxes to the government cannot bestow political right, so likewise, neither can purchasing the political process. When one uses the power of money to subvert the political right of another person or an entire group or nation, they do so by the theft of right.

Even in past historical systems of civilization, for the same reason, traditionally, there was a recognition and sharing of the power between the king and his subjects, wherein the king in recognizing the power emanating from the people needed their support and favor to keep his throne and his head. Otherwise the lustful pretender and contender for his throne could gather and concentrate that power for himself then use it to overthrow the despotic monarch.

It only follows that for the proper use and distribution of power, the masses of people who are not wealthy must hold and exercise the vast bulk of the power. Restating from another angle; the wealthy may not wield political power disproportionate to their particular numbers. This is not an attack on the existence of wealth or the wealthy. Indeed it is in recognition that the proper right of political participation is not a function of wealth but proceeds from the birthright with

---

[50] Both quotes from the American Declaration of Independence.
[51] Do not mistake this to mean un-equally; the two words have very different meanings.

which people are endowed among other factors, and it is time we act upon that fact and put it into practice.

Civilization

We need to discuss civilization. Forms of civilization evolve and change over time just as culture and technology changes. This means our currently failing civilization will yield, and something hopefully better, more refined will emerge than that which is passing now. I believe that we the **SPEP**, can define and lay-out a more successful and improved prototype form for successful civilization.

I thought about what to call it and decided on the name, **Sovereign Democratic Majority** form of civilization. Note the use of the word 'civilization' and not 'government' because that is an outdated notion, as the day of oppressive rule by small elitists groups needs to end while a majority consensus of politically endowed humanity is poised to emerge to define and determine the rules for future civilization.

The following are a few dictionary descriptions of some of the characteristic components of civilization.

1. An advanced state of intellectual, cultural, and material development in human society, marked by progress in the arts and sciences, the extensive use of record-keeping, including writing, and the appearance of complex political and social institutions.

2. Cities or populated areas in general, as opposed to unpopulated or wilderness areas.

From another Dictionary[52]:

1 a : A relatively high level of cultural and technological development; specifically : the stage of cultural development at which writing and the keeping of written records is attained.

b : The culture characteristic of a particular time or place.

---

[52] Merriam-Webster Dictionary

2: The process of becoming civilized.

3 a : Refinement of thought, manners, or taste.

b : A situation of urban comfort.

From Wikipedia[53]

'Assessments of what level of civilization a polity has reached are based on comparisons of the relative importance of agricultural as opposed to trade or manufacturing capacities, the territorial extensions of its power, the complexity of its division of labor, and the carrying capacity of its urban centers. Secondary elements include a developed transportation system, writing, standardized measurement, currency, contractual and tort-based legal systems, art, architecture, mathematics, scientific understanding, metallurgy, political structures, and organized religion.'

I did not find the exact definition I wanted so these do not necessarily represent the intent I had in mind. I always thought of civilization being defined as a voluntary organized state for people when living in cities as opposed to hunting and wandering nomads, and of course in this context we are really only interested in the aspects involving a hierarchical power structure not the periphery. The english word *'civilization'* is from the Latin word *'civitas'* which means city.

The other thing to note in the definitions above are the descriptions of development and change over time; the attainment of a more advanced level than the previous state. This implies an evolutionary or developmental process. It is an easy leap to accept that this process more often takes *'quantum leap'* advances around the time of great upheaval such as war or economic failure, or shortly after some high pinnacle is reached, rather than at a more or less mundane or stable era. It also implies that we are in a continuing phase of development; in other words, we as humanity have not reached the ultimate stage yet, but will continue to see vast

---

[53] Excerpted from Wikipedia search using the keyword, civilization.

improvements in systems that more favor the common and true elite, and less favor the elitist.

Anatomy of a Bureaucracy

Bureaucracies are a fractal[54] of world order, meaning they exist as a smaller model of the overall structure. The nature of such is integral to human civilization in that it is intrenched and endemic, and cannot be avoided. We can understand how a bureaucracy is formed and its structure by understanding the overall, which gives insight into the nature of politics and world order.

Let us deconstruct bureaucracy for examination by using 2 examples for analogy. The first is an onion. Spherical in shape with a core in the center and many levels of onion meat of increasingly larger radius layered one on top of the next which reach all the way to the outside. The bureaucracy is the layers that are built on top of the core.

The second analogy is to think of a marionette of marionettes, or a puppet-master that controls a puppet on each hand and in-turn those puppets control another layer of puppets by each of their hands, and so forth layer after layer. The bureaucracy is composed of the lower layers of puppets. Both structures are fractal in nature. A fractal has the general form such that a unit is a microcosm of the whole at any level.

Corporations; civic, state, and global organizations; public and private institutions; businesses, clubs, governments, human families and even some animal social structures have this shape, up to the entirety of world-order, which means the shape occurs naturally and is limited by the natural order thus the fractal analogy. The onion analogy is best suited to examine some aspects of government bureaucracy because some can be very much like those of secret societies in which the core is the cabal of decision makers and possessors of the

---

[54] From fractal geometry. Patterns which occur in nature.

true agenda, with each level outward operating without knowledge of the true agenda of any layer above their own. The current Obama administration and each one preceding for the past century certainly operated in this manner rather than with openness and disclosure, and they in-turn are a fractal of a larger model at work today. Not only may underlings be laboring with less than full knowledge about the agenda of their superiors but they may have been deliberately misdirected and given convincing but false information inorder for them to act in a natural way; to protect and isolate the core and their secrets from public scrutiny. This puts the core in a very powerful position with respect to the authority they are entrusted with. It explains much of the confusion regarding policy in government. We the public only get it after it has been passed through several controlled levels of filtration, all of which censor it to some extent, adding plausible 'cover stories' and spin for public consumption. Very little is truth.

This is a more insidious side of the nature of human organization. Because some variation of the insidious model will always tend to infect society, there is really no way to ever completely destroy or avoid the variation on these structures, so it is simply best to build the structure in such a way as to minimize the mischief that can be accomplished by the small but powerful secretive cabal. That is done simply by ensuring power is not entrusted or concentrated within small groups.

As an example, when there are only 2 layers of the onion as is the case when the Sovereign Democratic Majority (SDM) is the reigning or core layer and those in the political minority are the next. The SDM structure constitutes virtually the entirety of the civilization and involves virtually all of those rightfully endowed in the policies of the civilization with very little influence by intrenched monopoly interests. That may be an oversimplification of the model as it is somewhat abstract, but it serves as an ideal model. The goal of an ideal model should be to flatten the structure to a great extent and broaden the base, however, it will still have a 'piled' shape because it is part of the natural order. It is desirable to disperse as much of the political power as possible into the hands of as many of the **SPEP** as possible and away from the narrow interests. This is accomplished by the advent of a Sovereign Democratic Majority.

In past ages it has been the powerful narrow interests that have dictated the structure, always putting themselves in the position of advantage with the vast majority of people at a subordinate disadvantage. The shape of human institution will always coalesce to a piled or pyramid shape; it follows the natural order, but as civilizations advance and evolve and people gain understanding of their right and place in the natural order, there is less to decree that it must remain that way, with the very narrow elitists interests at the top dictating to the rest. Most of those that find themselves there have very little honor and have no more right to that position than anyone from the vast common.

In past eras the elites were there because they generally had the support and approval of the people, who were better off in the more or less equilibrated[55] structure than they would be otherwise. There was a kind of symbiosis between parasite and host which more or less worked, but at this point it does not work and it is my opinion that we have arrived at a time in the development of civilization when we can expect a fundamental shift in the dynamic of social order.

Social structures evolve over time as knowledge increases. Our structures have gone from organizations in primitive tribes, to Kings and kingdoms with serfs in serfdoms, peasants and peons, to Republican forms of Democratic process, to the current unworkable and failing morass, to wherever we will go next. The long term trend of advancing forms of civilization will continue, however, it may also experience degeneration

---

[55] At a state of equilibrium.

and decline as civilizations rise and fall. Ours at present is a great example of rise to a high pinnacle, followed by decline leading to failure.

What fundamental changes have occurred over the last few hundred years to bring about the conditions necessary for advancement to the next step of civilization?

1) Knowledge! Technology has brought new tools; computers, internet, vast amounts of information that allow the masses to know just as much and virtually the same information as elitists and the so called '*experts.*' The monopoly advantage for brokers of knowledge and information has already diminished greatly. History bears this out. For most of just the last millennia, those that had access to information and knowledge had the power to dominate the masses. That is no longer the case. The evidence for this assertion is that today we traditionally treat those with knowledge and skill as if they are entitled to a greater right than the average. They are regarded by themselves as well as great numbers of the masses as being ordained, or endowed with the right to decide policy for everyone, which is the very heart and definition of elitism.

They believe the civilization is better off if they are allowed to make all the decisions for the rest of us. They would monopolize that power and indeed they believe they have been endowed with the right to exercise the monopoly power of knowledge, even deciding who should live and who should die. The perception is beginning to change as people recognize that the elitist so called 'leaders' are no more capable of, nor inclined to make wise or prudent decisions in the interest of the whole, any more than a colony of ticks would exercise discretion regarding the life of the beast it feeds off. It would simply bleed it until dead then infest another.

There is nothing that elitists can decide or do better for the whole of civilization that it cannot decide or do for itself. They do not want you to know that and will lie to misdirect you, but it is absolutely true. The fact is, we, the SDM will always make a better determination about what is better for us and the civilization which we have constructed because it is everything that we are and represents the essence of our existence which can be characterized in-part by 5 Fs; **F**aith, **F**amily, **F**oundation, **F**ortune, and **F**uture. It is also represented by our heritage and our identity, and we will guard it and preserve it jealously. Elitists do not regard these things but would destroy them and are only interested in exploiting them for their own gain. You and me are only a means to an end for them so they cannot be trusted with our interests. This fact is currently being demonstrated unmistakably, and its realization by the vast majority will continue to become more evident.

2) **Survival!** The ability to sustain ourselves is the second element of advantage in the last few hundred years, derived from tremendous gains and surpassing a threshold of knowledge and technology. Indeed, despite the rhetoric and scare tactics of advancing threats to humanity, vast advances in medicine, the production of energy, housing, shelter, and agriculture have liberated us from rigid survival-based orders of civilization from the past. Food and shelter are much more robust and abundant now than in the 18th through the 20th centuries and before. This makes us less dependent on rigid social structures and strong-men leaders, who, in a bygone era had the rare ability to concentrate and focus power on a problem that might threaten a population, be-it starvation from famine or conquest. We still need political leadership but that is now better coming from those who are not mis-incentivized or intrenched monopoly interests. Leadership is better reasoned, rationalized, more sound, more aligned with the common interest; and most important of all, it is our right when it comes from the broad echelons of society.

The above discussion is the 3rd key, in 2-parts, to reclaiming and rebuilding our civilization. It is in recognition that because of advances in civilization the political profession is obsolete and we no longer need them. We may have in the past but we certainly do not need corrupt politicians to 'lead' us any longer and we are certainly much better off as this system passes into oblivion.

So it is my belief that the old order is failing and will crumble away and something new will replace it. The question is what will that replacement be? Will it be more of the super-classes of elitists in their narrow interest cabals, dictating everything to a planet of peon slaves as has been their dream for millennia; or will the nation composed of the masses of common, appalled at the sick behavior of the old group, claim their right and stand up to build a civilization better suited to survive and grow into the next century and beyond? I believe at this juncture the natural balance of things favors the latter, but it will not happen soon without the action and movement of people who understand what is theirs and what is at stake and take the necessary action to ensure that outcome.

The Man, the Dog, and the Alligator

There is a tendency for a great swath of our society to come to erroneous conclusions about political matters. However a much smaller percentage are more often highly mislead, misinformed, and mis-educated, and are predisposed to be 'true-believing'[56] in their outlook. They view the world as unfair and so they decry what they erroneously call our *'capitalist system'*, but meaning our political system as corrupt because they have been told to conflate capitalism with a corrupt and failing political system by monopolists attempting to fix blame and attention away from themselves; to shore up their capital-monopoly position. They decry that our system gives hugely disproportionate and unfair favor to the narrow interest at the

---

[56] Ready to believe, or blindly follow without question, or proof. Irrational persistence in belief.

expense of the whole, and therefore they call for wholesale destruction of the *'capitalist system'*, to be replaced by an enforced regime of rationed resources and privileges. This agenda has been created and put into play by the capital-monopolists who are shielded by the voice and actions of their 'true-believing' leftist stooges.

This all seems contradictory, or at least counter-intuitive; that those perpetrating the deception would employ gullible idiots to call for the abolishment of exactly the thing they wish to own and control, but that is exactly the nature of the game played. They can control and activate the shrill and weak minded pretty handily. This is done because they want to put limits on anyone that would pose a rivalry; to preserve their capital-monopoly status. Think about how one drug cartel will employ and help law enforcement ostensibly to eradicate the scourge of drugs. They really only seek to eradicate the drugs and profits of their rivals, not their own. This is complicated business but with a little study, familiarity is gained and it becomes easier to understand and accept.

The fact is half of the true-believers complaint has truth to it, namely, the current system allows unwarranted favor to narrow interests which is exploited for power to use against the balance. This is an age old argument and problem about how a small portion of the rich and connected use their power and connections to steal and cheat the vast portion of the population who are not members of their club. The true-believer's prescribed solution, which is really the agenda of those that control them, is to drive the failure of the flawed and failing system and replace it with something worse such as a socialist, communist, or other asinine and unworkable system. Those systems have never been embraced or accepted willingly by any population anywhere. It has only come about by Coup d'état,[57] or by precession of soft-tyranny followed by the skilled and shrewd application of Hegelian dynamics.[58]

---

[57] Revolution, or overthrowing the existing regime.

Where it has been instituted, it has always been contrived and engineered by a small cabal with the help of dedicated 'true-believing' operatives, and generally, ironically, funded by the very rich powerful interest they rail against.

I have to disclaim antagonism toward the rich. I am not anti-rich, and certainly not anti-capitalism. In-fact, I am just the opposite of those and believe that all people should reach whatever pinnacle of wealth and success they are legitimately able to accomplish. Most people of means are fine and upstanding but there are some with evil intent who's riches only empowers their hatred.

With these things in mind a series of questions arise: Is this merely the nature of civilization, for good or for bad, like it or not? Will we always have to put up with the inequity and abuses between the schemers amongst many of the rich and powerful and the rest of us? What can be done to advance our civilization to change this seeming injustice? Even if we were able, we would not want to outlaw people from becoming rich would we? No, that would only play into the capital-monopolists hands and not accomplish anything. The question itself and the solutions to this seemingly intractable societal dilemma is better understood and put in perspective by a simple analogy and an easy riddle; I live in florida where there are many alligators even in peoples back yards; the riddle is:

Who is at fault when an alligator crawls out of the swamp in the backyard and eats your chained dog?

Is it the fault of the dog or the alligator? Is it the fault of the dog for being a tempting morsel to the ravenous reptile, or is it the fault of the alligator who was just following his own nature?

The answer is neither are at fault because you cannot blame a dog for being a meal and you also cannot blame the alligator

[58] From Georg Wilhelm Friedrich. Dialectic reasoning.

for eating the dog; it is what he does to survive. Both follow what their natures dictate. Fault lays with you the dog's owner for failing to erect a proper barrier to keep the gator out and for chaining the dog up so that he cannot flee from the danger.

In case you missed the message that simple analogy holds the 4th key and answer to the seeming dilemma that plagues civilizations. Let us examine why.

So many shrill voices rail against those who through their advantage, power, and influence, gain more power and money by the blood and property of weaker members of society. They are loudly proclaimed as enemies of society, but in reality they are simply alligator members of society following their own nature. Can you blame an aggressive animal for being what he is? No! All anyone can really do is understand that nature and mitigate it. The same applies to the metaphoric canine members of the society.

Who are these alligator enemies of our society? They are normal ordinary members of our communities and often considered pillars of society. They are generally rich and successful, and as such they are admired by their peers and others alike. They may be heads of corporations or members of distinguished and respected institutions; they are fathers, mothers, sons and daughters, shareholders, and boards of directors. Politically they are across the spectrum. They come as Republicans, Libertarians, Tea Party, and Democrats; and they come in all shapes and sizes. In most cases they would defend their actions as legal and ethical. Some may have more liberal views and morals concerning the ethics of what they do. To a large extent they are in a position to take advantage of a corrupt and broken system and so they do.

Put yourself in the same position. If you found yourself in a favored time and place and had the opportunity to become rich, even if you had to engage in or embrace something that you found morally distasteful like eating the dog, might you not be tempted to take advantage of the opportunity anyway? Most of us would never engage if it required something unethical or unfair, but given the prospects of becoming rich in the process many of us would take advantage.

We can not indict the whole of humanity or even a small minority for falling into the temptation to hose-bag their fellow man, as distasteful as that may be. Most of those who would take advantage are just ordinary people that you would not think capable of unethical behavior and had the opportunity not presented itself to them, most would not be considered anything other than good citizens by the same true-believers that rail and scream about the rich and powerful while enabling their theft. This is not to justify the horrendous behavior of those who act in such a way, instead it is to express the view that our problem is not a lack of morals on the part of metaphoric alligators; the problem is one of inadequate structure on our part.

The analogy answers the question of what must be done to remedy our situation and make us mutts less vulnerable to being eaten by alligators. Just as it is up to the owner of the dog to realize what might happen and take responsibility by unchaining the dog and creating a barrier to protect him, so it is up to us to protect ourselves along with the week and vulnerable and society in general.

A civilization structured properly which includes proper barriers put-up for that protection, to restrict and limit the power of those that would act as predator is the only way this can be done. Let me say this another way. The problem is not that there are alligators among us, that will always be the case; the problem is the current system we have is structured in such a way as to not only allow, but to actually facilitate alligators eating dogs. The society must create a structure that is immune to this abuse.

If one is not aware of how such a system may be constructed it is easy to be very skeptical about the solution, but if a system that is considerably more immune to this type of abuse can be shown then it is more easily believed and supported. This chapter and the next deals with how such a political system would be created and structured.

It does no good to engage in hand-wringing or chastise and blame the alligators for doing what comes naturally. If that is all that is done, dogs will continue to be eaten by alligators. You only get predators if you allow them the opportunity to be predators. We must realize this and stop crying about the unfairness of our world; it does not have to be that way. It is simply our choice to decide otherwise then construct the proper system. In the next chapter we explore how a system with the barriers necessary to stop the alligators can be structured and put in place.

Our House Our Land

It is imperative to catch at least a glimpse if not a complete vision, to embrace the changes needed to construct a better order. However, before we can arrive at an idea of what constitutes a better structure we must first view the pecking order, or food chain if that relates better, in the idealized philosophical abstract. In order to simply understand how we the people should view our relationship to the nation and the need for governance, I have come up with another, what I hope is a simple analogy. It is simple enough that most folks should be able to relate to it and readily understand the meaning.

Paramount to understanding our relationship to the nation we are part of is the principle that we are **owners** of the nation, and it is generally accepted that owners have the right to full control. There is no more important truth or principle than that. We own the nation, therefore, everything that pertains to the nation is for us, and about us, and it is not for or about anyone or anything else. The nation exists to serve strictly at our interests and it does not exist for any other reason. The same applies to the function of governance; it may only exist to serve exclusively at our pleasure, and may not exist outside of that purpose. We need to be absolutely clear on that axiom.

We the Sovereign Politically Endowed People (SPEP) can be viewed in the abstract as a family that owns a house. When you own the house you have the freedom to do whatever you want regarding everything within it; who has the right to visit or stay in the house; what the rules are for television, Internet, and so forth. We also have responsibilities. We have to do the laundry, the dishes, clean the garage, keep up the yard, and so forth.

If we want to we can do all the chores ourselves or we can hire someone else to do it for us. It makes sense to hire someone to keep the yard up because there are many trees and bushes and it is just more efficient to hire a crew who is considerably more skilled than we are at doing all the cutting, trimming, and hauling. We do not want to clutter up the garage storing all the equipment necessary, however, the yard crew already has all the equipment needed. Financially and in terms of our time and leisure it makes sense to hire the crew. The same applies to keeping the house clean, doing the dishes, cleaning the bathrooms, and even cooking the meals; it makes sense to hire a house keeper to do all of these chores which frees the lady of the house to homeschool the kids, attend the home business, and whatever is needed.

In the analogy:

• The house and the yard represent the national boundaries and the land possessed and occupied by the nation.

• The family that owns the house represents the nation and is composed of the people, the SPEP. They own and rule the nation and the land.

• The chores represent those duties and functions necessary to maintain the house and the household. They are represented as the necessary functions of governance for keeping the nation and the land operating properly.

• The yard crew and the housekeeper are people hired to do a job for the family and cannot dictate anything, so have no power over the house, property, or the family. If they do not do the job adequately they will be fired and someone else will be put in their place. They are not 'elected' by the family so they do not need to be 'unelected' and they cannot simply assume or usurp any position or authority in this context; they are simply contract employees and have no recourse. If they are unwanted they are let go, never to be paid again, so they leave ending any further involvement.

The owners have the attitude of owners and have no reason to question their status as owners or regard any suggestion countering such status, while the hired hands will do the same and properly regard their irrelevant status in the relationship. The owners will jealously guard their property and right and teach the same ethic to their children. It is no more complicated than that simple analogy, and any collection or system of the principles of civilized governance should be structured to work in accordance with the ideas presented in this simple analogy.

In order to better detail these ideas I have attempted to outline the elements of what such a structure might look like. This, in all likelihood has been attempted by many others before and there are many good and sound ideas that have been proposed previously. I must stress that the ideas are thesis and I have not cited instances where they have been tried or proven. The notion that the idea is not worthy of consideration because it has not been proven yet is somewhat irrelevant because the critical situation we find ourselves in calls for creation of a better system, which of necessity, involves the process of considering and vetting new ideas. If a better system had already been discovered or tried it would not require the same discovery process.

It should be evident but must be mentioned; we are not attempting to improve on the political system laid out in the current defunct US constitution. In my view that system and the constitution that gave birth to it are both terminally flawed and will fail completely, never to be revived again. Now we can only learn from the advantages and the mistakes it yielded.

The ideas discussed here are simply presented as thought exercises for playing the *'what-if game'*, tempered by my solemn belief that they are well within the realm of feasible reality. Not only are they politically viable and attainable (acceptable to the masses), but practical by operational feasibility as well. I believe that if implemented, a system as described below would work considerably better than anything we know at current. The concepts are by no means comprehensive but cursory. I have outlined the concept with the expectation that should it prove to have popular appeal or garner consideration and support, it is my hope it may be further developed to emerge as more than just thesis, but taking on tangible dimensions. In the next chapter, I have outlined a discussion for what is by no means comprehensive, but only a baseline list of the necessary functions needed for a new civil system. I have attempted to list elements in order of importance which is difficult because everything seems to fit near the top.

CHAPTER ELEVEN
Structure

Constitution

It is recommended the reader review the discussion on Constitution in the chapter titled *'Elements of Stable Governance'*, where a philosophical discussion is laid out to make better sense of the following. For the case of the Sovereign Democratic Majority supra-state structure, there is no layer of trustee politicians empowered to rule over the nation through a constitution which attempts to keep their actions vis-à-vis the nation from resulting in descent into a ruling oligarchy with peon citizens, as is the case today. For this reason, a constitution should only reflect the sovereign will which the SPEP have determined, not define or limit the civilization.

The constitution will nonetheless record the negotiated social contract, which are the specifics of the relationship between the sovereign body, citizens, the civil structure, its operation of governance, and super-threshold mechanisms. Super-threshold levels of protection are in place to guard against frivolous modification to vital fundamental operating parameters and principles. It also embodies the language and text of all policies originated and adopted by the SDM at the supra-state level. The adopted policies and their specifics are used as guidelines for managing the affairs of the nation at the supra-state level. The case is similar at state levels.

The constitution specifies and gives definition to all necessary terms, functions, parameters, operations, and directives for operating and maintaining the adopted civil structure. The following is a short list including but is not limited to:

• *Parameters.* Defined terms, composition, operation, and structures of: Sovereign Democratic Majority, Sovereign-Body, Fully Qualified Weighted Vote, Citizenship, Executive Managers, Partisan Weighting Limitation, etc.

• *Specified Governance Functions.* Responsibility, authority, and prohibitions. Definition, and status of employed Executive-Managers.

• *Public Revenue Matters.* Specified acceptable methods for revenue generation and prohibitions on how it is collected. Parameters and policy regarding public debt; the use of public resources; etc.

• *Standing Directives.* Specified operational directive and methods for governance functions. Standing directives are those which have been already adopted and do not require additional language or support.

• *Political Participation.* Who may participate and how. Rules for policy language, and adoption. Rules for adoption and modification of super-threshold principles.

Political Participation

The fear among the detractors of direct or other forms of democracy is the *'free-for-all'* nature of them. These fears are not unfounded when one considers the incredibly disastrous notion of *'One man, One vote'*[59] in our own system which was never intended but was instituted after 'findings' and by declarative fiat from those in robes. The voting rights act of

---

[59] US Supreme Court Majority Opinion and Ruling, 1964.

1965[60] is a great example of this destructive and disastrous notion. The founders of the republic established in 1789 intended to use the democratic process for the policy-adoption mechanism and so included it in the constitution. They recognized the conquest rights of the nation's founders and excluded those not endowed from participation in the political process, which was their right inviolate. This was not an *'injustice'* as it has been characterized for the better part of the 20th century. Those excluded had no prior claim to the political right of participation, whereas the heirs of the conquest and founding of the nation do, and that can never change. Political and in-particular, founder's right, is more or less inherited and as founders of the nation and the republic, they intended those rights to be preserved on their heirs. They intended to pass on the birthright which has now been very muddled, wherein the heirs at present are not aware of their status as heirs.

To illustrate the principle and give an example, look at how public and private corporations are structured. Investors buy shares which gives them ownership interest. They are allowed to vote their shares so their particular vote is weighted to the amount of interest they hold to the whole. This principle is universal; it is the only way to adhere to the tenets of equity and justice. The process and principle is in recognition of the venerated right to own property. To alter or distort this process is to witness the destruction of the foundations of the civilization. The notion that all persons are born endowed with an equal number of *'humanity shares'* is an argument that could be made, but it does not translate to private enterprise and neither does it carry over to political birthright. Having said all of this, there is a method of compensation or inclusion for those not endowed with the same birthright as Original Americans, and that is the privilege of participation by the

---

[60] Signed into law by Lyndon B. Johnson.

compact of citizenship, however, this vote is also weighted based on qualifying criteria to be discussed later.

The proposed Sovereign-Body is composed strictly of individuals. As an absolute bedrock principle, there is no political weight given or recognized of organizations, corporations, or institutions, and that can not be compromised. The totality of the political weight of the body is distributed wholly between the majority and the minority of politically endowed persons on a per issue, per policy basis. Individual weighting is used to qualify the voter's right. Original Americans are weighted up to 100% but each issue will require additional levels of qualification. Original Americans are natural or DeJure[61] citizens along with others and with many policy issues citizens are eligible to participate in consideration. Indeed, many particular policy issues would be in a realm of participation encompassing all citizens. Similar structure and process should apply to the legislative process for supra-state and individual states alike.

To be eligible to participate in both state and supra-state policy initiatives, individuals must register with their state's Secretary of State office. They will be required to give and verify information which will qualify them based on several criteria, some of which is the outcome of competency testing. The outcome of established founder's right status will determine their particular level of weighting, while the outcome of competency determines qualification for participation in areas of consideration.

The system is not designed to denigrate or disenfranchise anyone from the vitality and culture of the nation, but is designed to ensure that those who vote to decide the issues are qualified by right, and so eligible to add weight to the outcome of policy, and indeed competent to sufficiently understand and make rational and prudent decision concerning the issue and

---

[61] Rightfully endowed; Birthright.

proposed policy, at both state and supra-state levels. Several areas of policy will require different distinct areas of competence qualification. Distinct policy areas are yet to be defined but a short list of them generally lays along the lines of: Individual and corporate property rights; general corporate and individual governance; criminality, law & justice; commerce, economic, and budget issues; civic and infrastructure issues; regulation; general governance; foreign relations; trade; defense; etc.

After completion of the registration process, the voter will be issued a level of weighting and qualification and a secured account with which they may participate through the internet. The voter will need to log into his or her secured account to cast their vote or participate in debate and deliberation. In several instances before being allowed to deliberate or casting of their initial vote, they may be re-assessed as to their level of competency for the particular issue by completion of additional testing. A more comprehensive description of the policy-mechanism system follows.

Legislative

We can answer many questions with a view of how a renewed civil system might look by describing the functional building blocks needed for such. The most expeditious route to understanding this is to describe governance functions by way of the existing model that most Americans are already familiar with, which is the traditional 3 branches of government, *Legislative, Executive, and Judicial.* We start with a legislative function. As was stated earlier, the legislative process is reserved strictly to the **Sovereign-Body** of politically endowed people who comprise the nation. In the current model, there is supposed to be a balance established and maintained by distribution of power equally among the 3 branches which in-turn is supposed to provide stability and preserve the integrity of the system. The idea being that if one branch gets out of line, it is held in check (countered) by the other 2. However, this idea has utterly failed. Today, having been completely compromised and acquired starting from the mid 19th century, all 3 of these branches collude and conspire together against the nation as a whole, although through a thin charade of governance. It has failed and demonstrates the failure foretold by one of the founders of the republic:

"Our Constitution is meant for a moral and religious people. It is wholly unfit for any other"

...John Adams[62]

For the great part of American history we were a moral and a religious people up until about the last half of the last century when the seeds of corruption sewn into the fertile landscape of the American republic during the 19th century grew to yield the fruit of destruction. We have now arrived at the depths of moral depravity as a people which renders John Adams correct when he more or less said the constitution would fail. It lasted until 1861, when the groundwork for the complete compromise and looting of the nation began.

The essence of his pronouncement is that for an *'honor system'* to work it must be populated and operated by what amounts to saintly, morally upstanding, and religious people that are not tempted by money and power, but are governed by a higher power, and always motivated to act through moral restraint. Anything less than that will quickly result in a 'free-for-all' and orgy of power, greed, and theft, leading to complete failure. He was absolutely right and we have arrived exactly at that point today.

The current system absolutely cannot be reformed, or embraced, nor revived after imminent complete failure, nor should it ever be attempted again. However, we can also not go back to an inferior system but must embrace the future and

---

[62] President John Adams to the Officers of the First Brigade of the Third Division of the Militia of Massachusetts, 1798.

move forward. A new system can only work by putting all defined functions (as branches of government identified in the US constitution), under the control and authority of the sovereign body of the politically endowed. A model emerges where the SDM becomes the form of a legislative body with absolute authority over all other governance function.

Policy Elevation and Adoption

Policy issues to be determined will need to rise through a process involving the Vox Populi (voice of the people), however, this is not in the traditional sense in-which the people express their demand through an advocacy representative, or in which they are forced to accept or register disapproval as spectators of policy issues which have been delivered to policy-makers by narrow-interests. Instead, the sovereign-body themselves and only the SPEP may give rise to any and all issues. The same then draft and vote to decide policy, then give directive for execution.

Additional mechanisms may be instituted for consideration of policy issues that concern institutions, corporations, and organizations, but these must maintain a secondary status. This philosophy is intended to ensure that those policy issues which arise for consideration are primarily those that recognize the primacy of interest of individuals and the sovereign body as a whole, and do not focus or coalesce around the interests of groups and organizations, outside of their concern to the body as a whole. In this way, so called *'minority interests'* are considered within their particular scope of vitality, value, and interest to the majority. To put it another way, the only way policy issues concerning groups outside of the sovereign-body itself are to be considered is when they are of particular interest to the body.

There is no special or narrow-interests advocacy voice allowed while those who are of vital minority-interest are properly valued, considered, and heard. Some would argue this will ignore and neglect the particular policy concerns of corporations, and vital institutions. The fact is, corporations and vital institutional interests are of great interest to the body, even as private, profit driven entities, so their interests will always be considered to the extent that the interest is aligned with the interest of the sovereign body, and indeed, it creates accountability and the proper incentive for the behavior of corporations and vital institutions.

In the process there must be a clear distinction between individual state or regional issues and those concerning supra-state policy. In both cases the process is similar and should be conducted through the powerful tools afforded by Internet facilities to whatever extent possible. As an example; issues originate and are initiated in designated forums, then elevated through online discussion at a very low level to bring attention and drive the need for consideration and action. Through persuasion and petitioning of others for support on a particular issue it may rise to a level of higher consideration. That rise (or fall) is facilitated by measured favor (or disfavor) and expansion. Upon rising to the required threshold of broad support, the issue, policy, or action will be further elevated to a status of policy consideration. Policy language must be drafted and adhere to a prescribed format before general consideration. Prescribed language format for consideration and the language of the adopted policy should be the same. Proper language and format can be facilitated by website driven processing using online tools such as legal dictionary, active code references, etc. The language should be concise, brief, and easily read and understood by common people without requiring legal training. See below for the consideration process.

Policy issues and language are decided by simple up or down majority of the weighted-vote registered, however, there may be special issues such as budget and spending that may require a higher, predefined, or threshold level for alteration. Upon closure the case for adoption by plurality should never exist.

For supra-state policy issues, apportionment by Fully-Qualified Weighted Vote (FQWV) may apply in circumstance. Issues specific to states or regions may be brought up for consideration by the whole. Examples are those involving apportionment in state or regional supra-state budget contributions or sources of revenue.

It is noteworthy that variation of such online process has been recently established and is being perfected through internet participation by tens to the hundreds of millions of individuals and groups who daily engage in online discussions of issues and ideas, building consensus and adding weight to good ideas, while rejecting the bad. The ideas presented here are simply an extension of that as a natural process, and recognition of its likely continued advancement for use as a powerful tool to conduct democratic process.

Non Time-Constrained Consideration

An issue may arise for consideration at any time and season. It should not be limited to a particular day or season. The duration of the period for consideration and voting on any particular issue can be set in a number of ways. It is reasonable that the period for consideration be anywhere from 2 weeks, 6 months, or 2 years. During the consideration period the voter may change his/her vote as often as they choose, as their understanding of the issue may evolve and change, but finalized before the deadline close of consideration. All policy issues should unambiguously comply with the current adopted body of vital fundamental operating parameters and principles before consideration, and the language and prescribed executive implementation should be measured and amended before being allowed for consideration. A proposal for changing super-threshold level policy should state the intent and requirements for making the change before allowed elevation to any level for consideration.

This can be compared to a constitutional amendment in the current system.

At some point the period for consideration ends and the final running vote is tallied, registered, and certified by the Secretary of State or the Manager of State Affairs on a state by state basis for both individual state and supra-state policy issues. The legal language of policy is then entered into the body of law and does not require any further approval or process.

This process is in recognition of the ineffectiveness of forcing issues to be considered and decided by all participants in a haphazard fashion as now where we are forced to take time out of our busy day, to competently decide all issues within a 7 to 9 hour window, every 1 to 4 years. That system is antiquated, gamed by interests, and skewed to foster corruption. It is by any standard, obsolete and quite ineffective. It makes no sense for people to stand in long lines to vote on numerous complicated and mis-understood issues while ill-equipped for that consideration; not sufficiently comprehending the consequences of that which they are asked to decide, on issues they would likely never have considered necessary to consider.

Often they are not in a position to cast an informed vote to measure or consider their own interests in the matter let alone the best interests of the whole, but instead are forced to quickly toss the coin and decide by misleading, ill-defined, and fraudulent information on issues and candidates supplied by the many advocacy voices telling them to choose from among limited options which more often than not, render all possible choices in favor of the narrow-interests on issues they themselves would never consider worthy of consideration. Corruption on an industrial scale, 'legitimized' through a corrupt process.

The SDM process is also simplified by the fact that there is no voting for candidates and no campaigning for offices because there are no candidates or offices. No more unscrupulous, unsavory, sanctimonious liars making empty promises which cannot be believed nor delivered on. That corrupt era and that corrupt process, along with its corrupt result is coming to and end, never to return. However, there is the requirement that the body have a method of qualifying and affirming the hiring or appointment of a Manager of State Affairs such as a secretary of state or simply the title: Manager of State Affairs, as well as the hiring of an executive; but however it is done it should not follow the existing pattern.

Partisan Weighting Limitation

The rules for deciding policy apply differently when it comes to representation by partisan or aligned special organizational interests. In this case the entirety of the apportioned Fully Qualified Weighted Vote (FQWV) for any and all representation will share their apportionment in a pool not to exceed 20% of the total. In the case where the portion of FQWV from party, interest affiliated, or aligned representation does not equal or exceed the 20% maximum allotment, each representative FQWV may nonetheless, not exceed their respective non-aligned status apportionment of vote. In the event of aligned portion oversubscription, the FQWV will be limited and diluted by all aligned interest and cannot exceed normal weighting.

Any entity, individual or group must also disclose any aligned affiliation. Any policy issue elevating by aligned interests must also fully and openly disclose who all advocates and benefactors[63] are, giving policy details of impact and advantage when participating in policy elevation. Aligned interests will realize full dilution of their weighted vote by all other separately aligned interests sharing up to the maximum 20% limitation of total weighted vote.

---

[63] A beneficiary. Usually taken to mean whoever sponsors it. A form of lobbying.

This is a mechanism to discourage large professional and funded organizations that will otherwise dominate the entire process. It is hoped that it will generate significant disincentive for party affiliation and the corrupting influence engendered by advocacy systems. The system is designed to favor the will of unaligned individuals and the sovereign body by dispersing concentrated power and interest, and averaging the Vox Populi while discouraging the skewing toward interest groups. Aligned interests must register and declare their alignment (partisan status). Failure to do so will subject the offender to sanctions.

Funding Governance

I laid out a philosophical basis for revenue collection and general funding for the function of governance in the chapter titled, *'Elements of Stable Governance'*, which I would now recommend for review in light of the following discussion. Plainly speaking, funding for all governance at all levels is by way of tax and fee revenues. These should not be by direct individual or domestic domiciled corporate income taxes, neither at the state or supra-state level but should come from: Import tariffs; point of sales excise tax; mineral resource and land leases; tax on foreign entities (Corporations, foreign residents, and tourists); and applicable user fees (such as recreational licenses and fees; local and interstate roads and transportation, etc.). It is my belief that when the politically endowed sovereign body of individuals are determining the taxes which they will levy on themselves to pay for the level of services they determine, there is plenty of incentives for thrift in expense and for revenues to be minimal but adequate.

Some aspects of public funding for governance are necessary otherwise none would exist, so whatever governance is instituted should be strictly limited to those functions that are more efficiently accomplished by public means such as national defense, foreign relations, state and supra-state law enforcement and judiciary, consumer protection, and the regulation of industry. It should never involve anything outside of those that fit the benefit from an efficiency gained criteria. With this in mind, in my estimation it can all (city, county, state, supra-state) be managed on significantly less than the current vulgar drain on our gross domestic production of wealth.

State and supra-state budgets should be recommended by those responsible for handling and managing or overseeing the resources of governance. Recommendations may be compiled from several separate estimates from separate governance entities. Auditing the entire process should be handled by separate functions, and reports made public. Budgets are originated and approved in entirety by the FQWV of the respective sovereign body and apportioned proportionately. States will appropriate the approved supra-state budget funds from their usual revenue infrastructure and contribute to meet their apportionment of approved budgetary requirements. States should be charged with establishing and maintaining a reserve of funds equal to 1 annual plus some fraction of usual (or current) annual budget allotted to the supra-state system.

Under no circumstances can any employed function of governance at either state or supra-state level, have the power to self-fund through their explicitly sanctioned governance function, but are expressly prohibited from such. All revenue employed must originate from explicitly defined sources and all expenditures must be audited and accounted for to ensure integrity.

Point of Sale Excise Taxes or sales taxes are a significant source of revenue and create the incentive for people to keep taxes low because they impact them directly. People will vote with their wallet. Sales tax along with all other sources of revenue should be collected at the state level and never at the supra-state level because that is improper and can lead to a supra-state concentration of power and the corruption of the proper political chain of authority.

Import Tariffs are a way of making foreign producers who would like access to the American marketplace pay for that privilege while reducing the burden on the individual. There are arguments for and against import tariffs. Those against are usually involved in making profit by importing and selling into the market at a significant advantage to domestic producers. They certainly do not want tariffs to increase their costs and diminish their profit. They argue that it is protectionist and makes things more expensive for the consumer. They further argue that it makes it harder to sell into foreign markets due to reciprocal trade tariffs, thus diminishing employment at home.

These arguments have some merit, however, those that argue for tariffs point out that it does diminish the individual's burden for a foreign supplier to pay the tax instead. They will also point out that reduced tariffs should make produced goods cheaper to the consumer but rarely is that difference in cost passed on to the consumer in proportion to the loss incurred by diminished domestic business activity along with employment opportunity and wage levels. Further it is argued that the loss of opportunity for expansion into foreign markets is more than made up for by robust demand for labor at home.

I discuss the merits of import tariffs in detail along with the discussion on trade policy in general in other sections. Suffice it to say in my estimation, some level of import tariffs in the aggregate will favor the bulk of the people and so should fall that way, while recognizing that it must be balanced in order to maintain vital trade relationships with foreign nations.

User Fees are similar to sales taxes in that it derives revenue from those that are directly benefited by the public activity or facility. How is this different from paying for anything a person consumes? It is desirable to use public resources and such for the public's enjoyment, however, it is tyrannical to make those who choose not to use those facilities pay to maintain them. If the public facility cannot generate enough through user fees to sustain itself, then maybe it should not exist. This is an argument against subsidizing public facilities that are not vital and do not meet the benefit derived from efficiency criteria, while those that are, are proven to be so by the mere fact that they pay for themselves. This is how it should be. Subsidizing the operating losses of facilities for the sake of poorer patrons should never be public policy; that is an issue for charity not the public, and rightly incentivized, charity organizations will fill the need by a considerably better margin than that of public policy.

Public Mineral and Land Leases. Examples of revenue from these are license fees and revenue sharing of public resources such as oil wells, mines on publicly owned land, etc.

Taxes and customs collected on tariffs along with some revenues from mineral and land leases or other similar classes of revenue (taxes from foreign entities, etc.), in total should be considered common sources to all states, so respective revenue derived should be considered contributed as apportioned from the states in common.

Executive-Managers

Executive-Managers are the executives that manage the various segments of governance functions at both state and supra-state levels. Examples of Executive-Managers are President, Secretary of State Affairs, Judicial Executive-Managers, State Governors, etc. These are not offices per se but are employed positions of responsibility within the national structure. In general these positions are vetted and adopted by the respective sovereign-bodies through recommendations made by the respective Secretaries of State Affairs.

The Executive-Managers may be single persons who hire others to act as administrative staff or it may be adopted as an existing organization or company designed to act in that capacity. An authority of any particular executive-manager is limited to a specific narrow set of functions. Both the states and supra-state may have numerous independent employed executive-managers.

All Executive-Managers including the Secretary of State Affairs and President are expressly prohibited from any affiliation with any aligned or partisan interest. Each executive-manager serves expressly at the letter of the constitution and body of adopted policy through prescribed policy directives.

There is no popular appeal or campaigning for positions in the traditional sense, instead candidates simply submit resume and bid for service, and apply for the job with their respective Manager of State Affairs. All eligible candidates are usually qualified and vetted by the Manager. Executive-managers are adopted per contract term and likewise removed exclusively by the sovereign body. The supra-state Secretary of State is itself nominated and vetted by recommendation of the sovereign-body and adopted by Fully Qualified Weighted Vote (FQWV.) Likewise, no active public auditioning or campaigning is conducted. Individual candidates for either must be from among Original Americans. All Executive-Managers get operational directives and follow guidelines from the body of SDM adopted policy and constitution.

Executive-Manager of State Affairs

The Manager of State Affairs is an executive-manager also referred to as the *Secretary of State*. The entity is basically a manager of governance functions in service of the sovereign body and may exist above but more than likely along-side of the President and other Executive-Managers. This entity will have the broadest level of responsibility and authority including, managing numerous respective state and supra-state governance functions. Qualifying, vetting, auditing, overseeing, hiring, and firing.

This entity will be sourced, vetted, and approved by FQWV at respective levels and will need to stay in the good graces of the sovereign body in order to maintain the job. All Executive-Managers of State Affairs get operational directives and follow guidelines from the body of SDM adopted policy and constitution.

There is a very limited set of responsibility given to the Executive-Manager of State Affairs which includes:

1) Sourcing and vetting candidates for other Executive-Manager functions.

2) Managing and maintaining respective voting systems. Certifying the result of policy adoption.

3) Keeping records. Maintaining and entering newly adopted policy into the body of adopted statutes and all business pertaining to the adopted constitution.

4) Respective state and supra-state general business and maintenance.

5) Operating and maintaining respective revenue systems.

President

The title *'President'* shall apply only to the Supra-State Executive-Manager for this function. The same function for a state is called *'Governor.'* The title of *'President'* will be held for the duration of contract. The title is by tradition, however, it does not carry the traditional meaning as an authoritative master or head of state, but by contrast, instead it is one of token or figurehead. In this model, with respect to supra-state foreign affairs the title is more one of ambassador or representative rather than ruler. However, the position does encompass the function of an executive-manager, albeit very limited. There is no absolute requirement that the proposed structure need adhere to traditional hierarchy for executives, neither by state or supra-state.

The Presidential candidate is vetted and recommended by the supra-state Secretary of State and adopted by FQWV of the sovereign-body. The President is accountable to the sovereign body so can be removed by the same.

There is a more extensive but by comparison to past systems, a very limited responsibility and autonomy given to the President which includes:

1) Foreign & Diplomatic services.

2) Managing Borders. Foreign Business, Commerce, and Trade; Immigration services; and Tourism.

3) Limited and leased emergency command of fractional armed forces.

Among the purposes of the supra-state executive is to carry out functions necessary for diplomatic representation of the nation to others. In diplomatic relations, it is desirable to allow more autonomy in representing a symbolic head of state and in diplomacy, therefore the job includes authority to propose, recommend, and execute foreign policy initiatives approved and adopted by and under the directive of the sovereign-body. The function is similar to that of a corporate CEO or a business manager, however with very limited authority.

Responsibility is also given to the President to command a very limited supra-state segment of armed forces aimed at foreign threats. Very limited emergency power may be granted to the President on a lease basis involving the actions of foreign powers. The President may make recommendation for any military response to a foreign threat. Military professionals may also make recommendations based on assessment of threat. Military action must be approved by SDM. All Executive-Managers - Presidents, Governors or others get operational directives and follow guidelines from the body of SDM adopted policy and constitution. All policy initiatives or the limited executive acts of any Executive-Manager are subject to scrutiny and override by the sovereign-body.

Judiciary

All judiciary, state and supra-state, shall be managed by executive-managers. The state and supra-state judicial executive-managers shall establish and maintain courts of justice for the purpose of administering both civil and criminal justice. Where judicial matters span the jurisdiction of 2 or more states, and diplomatic negotiation between them fails to remedy the matter, it may be referred to supra-state level for adjudication. Supra-state jurisdiction, both civil and criminal is limited to areas reserved to supra-state matters and disputes between states. There is no supra-state level power that may override or supersede the jurisdiction of any state. All jurisdictions at both levels operate independently.

The judiciary is like any other function of governance and has only the limited authority to act within its job description at respective levels. Judicial authority is strictly limited to matters concerning judicial proceedings, adjudication and interpretation of law. There is no ability for the judiciary to pass or issue any law or fiat, nor authorize or empower any enforcement action as is the case today. For the most part the judiciary at any level may interpret and render legal opinion but has no legislative or executive power whatsoever. All functions of a judiciary get operational directives and follow guidelines from the body of SDM adopted policy and constitution.

Criminal incarceration, and correction are independent matters and should not reside under the umbrella of the judiciary function; It is instead more appropriately situated under Executive-Managerial functions such as a Corrections Executive-Manager.

All opinions rendered by any judiciary is subject to review and overturn by the sovereign body at the respective level.

Military Lease and Limits

It is necessary to create and maintain a standing military force for times of national emergency and security. Historically this is fraught with hazard concerning the security of people where a powerful central government can threaten their sovereignty and liberty, balanced against the need for emergency power that may provide a military response to a threat. It is necessary to maintain and balance armed forces between the sovereign states on the one hand, and the need for a supra-state deterrent to hostile foreign action against one or all states.

While the vast bulk of standing military force are created and maintained by each state, the supra-state shall maintain a small standing ready military force not to exceed 10% of total combined supra-state and state combined. Additional limited emergency powers up to 25% of total force may be granted to the President on a lease specifying mission parameters, limitations, and term, from time to time as needed and authorized by the sovereign body. Status, advice, and recommendations are to be made to the President and the sovereign body by senior military core. In times of emergency threat, the supra-state military core and associated force heads report to the President. The balance of military command and control is apportioned and maintained by states. Individual state military core heads report to state civilian Executive-Managers.

Limited Supra-State Law Enforcement

State and Supra-State levels for law enforcement and corrections fall under the authority of their respective Executive-Managers. Supra-State Law Enforcement is strictly limited to matters that would ordinarily require interstate investigation and cooperation. Supra-State police power may not routinely supplant local police authority but must obtain a lease of authority and power of investigation from the particular jurisdiction. It is desirable to maintain separation between military and domestic police power, therefore both state and supra-state law enforcement are under a chain of command headed by executive-managers which are separate from those that control military resources.

Regulation

For consumer protection and the maintenance of common vital infrastructure, state and supra-state authority is given to executive-management to regulate various aspects of business and commerce; oversee vital functions necessary to maintain infrastructure; and provide consumer protection. A very short-list of examples of these functions are: Interstate highways and transportation; food and drug safety; product safety; banking and currency; ports; immigration; etc. All areas affected by regulation are subject to review and alteration by the sovereign body.

CHAPTER TWELVE

Movement

The Road to Revolution

Many movements have been started throughout history, usually when individuals and groups are oppressed or some fundamental aspect of their humanity has been denied or threatened. At the present juncture our nation is at a crossroads and being daily moved to some sort of showdown or provocation to a massive move of people. It is my belief that we are near to some catalyst that will ignite the flames of rebellion leading to a 2nd American revolution, as they are already smoldering from most every quarter.

The current government has gotten way too big for its britches and people are becoming increasingly distressed, having every aspect of their lives determined by politicians and bureaucrats with the power of law, using force to compel them to accept continuous insult to their humanity. In this nation there are low-level signs of a disturbance just below the surface like the barely seen sub-surface rippling wave from a tsunami event on the sea-floor, the magnitude of which is not realized until it makes its approach to the shore. It rises up larger than anyone could imagine, delivering its transformative power as it sweeps miles beyond the shoreline; far inland it moves destroying everything in its path, leaving a mess but clearing the landscape, then withdrawing back into the ocean, taking the garbage with it, leaving the land bare, only suitable for rebuilding.

For many reasons I have already discussed I believe we are not entering an era of greater and greater power and control by nefarious forces of money and corruption, but instead, we are entering a different era in which the common man will rise and take his right; that is if he will realize his right and take the necessary action to engage in the struggle. It may start small, but at the slightest indication of direction and purpose, a movement will swell and take on overwhelming dimensions as it sweeps the land, and I believe it may jump across borders and oceans to knock down oppressive power structures erected elsewhere.

That is mostly the way a revolution progresses. The small power of the ruling elite will inevitably push their luck and bring about their own destruction. It is in their nature to do so. We have already seen some of this happening. Remember the soviet block that collapsed in 1989. The Union of Soviet Communists occupied Russia and numerous satellite states that were held hostage by their treacherous leaders and the communist party. When the wall fell and the first few puppet criminal heads of these satellite states fell, it unleashed tremendous energy which swept through that part of the world. When the end came and the people took their liberty back, it unleashed a powerful response which did not fare well for the likes of Nicolae Ceausescu, the communist leader of Romania, or the leader of the slavic Balkan states when Yugoslavia broke apart to become independent states again with their own governments and the renewed autonomy to make their own determination; nor was this revolution gentle with any of the despots guilty of holding these oppressive states together. Some will point out that the Yugoslav breakup, which occurred in 1992 was followed by a series of devastating regional wars, nevertheless, the old alignment was failing, destined to collapse and it eventually gave way allowing the emergence of their renewed civilization.

Despite all the rhetoric on both sides, no one can deny that all of the nation-states involved in the old Soviet-Communist system, from Russia, to Croatia, and every one in between are better off today than they were under the despotic totalitarian system of that era.   Russia now has capital markets, many emerging individual entrepreneurial enterprises which are producing goods and services, and the people have considerably greater freedom than virtually anytime in the last century. Their economy is robust and growing and they have smiles on their faces once again for the first time in at least 100 years or more.

Then lets not forget the so called *'Arab Spring'* which started late 2010 in Tunisia in North Africa, then spread through Libya to Egypt, then beyond to other Mid-Eastern states who's people rose up to throw off the oppressors dictating their lives. The world is changing as people realize their own right and place and that of the so called elitist leaders who only plunder and steal; their usefulness and necessity is fading and that fact is becoming more evident.

Sovereign Formation of States

The States that make up the current alignment called the United States are independent political entities, having been created from the beginning by sovereign bodies of men that pooled their interests and resources together to form them. They were originally fashioned from the colonies which formed via various regional settlements from Europe.

It is not necessary to go in-depth into the history of the states to understand why the existing sovereign states are the 5th key to a rebirth of our nation; suffice it to say that the current states were formed when state founders got together and created a charter spelling out the particulars of the proposal for the formation of the state. The state was then formally created and application was made to join the current union of states. That is a nutshell history of the formation of the United States.

It is desirable to preserve the current alignment of states to whatever extent possible, however at this juncture there exists 2 or more nations politically. For the sake of discussion I believe we have 2 political nations and 2 houses. The alignment remains pretty much the same as it did during the civil dissolution of the 19th century. The divide is really due to cultural and political differences between the northeastern establishment regions along with portions of the west coast, which seek to dominate the balance of the nation culturally, politically, and economically; and the south, mid-west, upper mid-west, and parts of the west, whose people are much more believing in older, more sustainable values in accordance with the dictates of human behavior, the laws of nature, and the laws of God. Some would say that means 'conservative', however, that word has come to have meanings that are antithetical to a true liberation and renewal of our civilization so I choose not to use that label; although it is clear in the minds of most what is meant when the label is used.

This segment of the nation are more likely to express religious faith and family values while adhering to views and values instilled into a society from bootstrapping oneself and one's community, without dependance on the dictates of the all powerful Oz like government. Whereas the character of the other house is more one that is fond of believing themselves as cogs in a giant machine, not prone to question the status quo but instead, stand and salute regardless of the agenda or the methods. I do not mean to imply that these people are cozy with enslavement, only that the regional governments and the people are more integrated with that view so they are less likely as the others to abandon the form of the current failing system in favor of something significantly different. That being the case, we must embrace an attitude of acceptance for all who come in good faith.

While the states still have an autonomous operating structure, and although they need no permission or authorization to secede or un-join the union then form a new alignment, a formal resolution of secession is not likely to come from any of the state legislatures nor governors who are heavily aligned with the political establishment in Washington DC. At current, both Republican and Democratic parties and all other contenders for wielding the reigns of power have a political stranglehold with considerable allegiance from the individual statehouses. Whereas this may seem to be an intractable problem, the fact is, the political infrastructure of individual states would be a considerably easier nut to crack than the intrenched federal behemoth.

Any attempt to usurp the federal system including a full frontal assault is very likely to end in humiliating failure, and as it happens it is not necessary. The federal system cannot sustain any semblance of effective operation without the approval, trust, and support of the people of the nation which is suffering significant decline. It will suffer total fiscal and financial failure in the short term which will result in the lack of resources to continue to purchase the loyalty and support of the political infrastructure of individual states. As stated before, this failure brings opportunity; a critical window of opportunity linked to an emerging financial crisis will arise, immense and global in proportion, which will provide the catalyst needed to galvanize the political will to act. It is my belief that enough people will abandon flawed ideas, focus their attention to the matter at hand and move decisively to enact something considerably better than that which is failing now.

At this point, the picture becomes very blurred due to the inability to see the outcome of the many, many events likely to occur henceforth. Many of the events are considerably more predictable than others, thus the foggy vision. A popularly disseminated and likely future series of events affecting the US government and the nation is as follows:

• At some point despite current record low interest rates which are artificial and contrived the situation will reverse and interest rates will begin a rapid aggressive move upward. As bondholders and lenders begin to doubt the credit-worthiness of Uncle Sam they will demand higher interest to lend. This will happen unless the federal reserve has the capacity to absorb all the demand for cash on retiring bonds, then continue to hold rates down while the government rolls-over the maturing debt instruments. Bond investors will invariably find more attractive deals elsewhere, so it is not likely to hold.

• The need to retire short term debt then renew it to meet obligations will necessitate the current relatively low interest debt burden be replaced by much higher interest rate bonds with much higher debt service.

• Printing more money to meet the obligations will drive inflation and interest rates up. This is an irreversible, regenerative, and spiraling situation.

• The mounting federal fiscal debt will come due in the sense that a default will figure very prominently causing a crisis of the dollar which will manifest itself in a general collapse of US government debt securities.

• The collapse of the bond market will feature globally.

• Despite the ability for the fed to print money, it cannot infinitely maintain a con-job on the world. Printing more only accelerates monetary devaluation and interest rates. The federal reserve and the US federal government systems are inseparably linked. Both are staring at imminent failure. The government will loose the ability to pay its debt and default.

• Government services and the flow of money to the states will slow to a crawl and most will cease altogether.

From this point, it is my view that this situation will put the focus on the states to pick up the slack. It will also force the current political alignment in the states, based on the corrupt and failed political establishment, to yield. Most politicians at the federal level will be forced out or recalled by the people seeking new leadership. They will not be replaced as states are repudiating representation. The state political structure will also become suspect and subject to contempt by the people. There is a probable vying for power and control by various groups. This will fail quickly as many uninformed fringe para-political (the Tea Party comes to mind), and para-military groups, are not prepared to provide any new leadership nor solutions. This is the opportunity to move forward to a new system.

It is at this point that I believe a realization will fall across a large part of the politically endowed populace that if there is to be a move toward creating a new system, it will be born of a very large move toward dissolution, or pulling away of states from the current government with a new alignment being proposed by various factions within the states. These will be made up mostly of common people who will reject the involvement of politicians and party affiliation. Indeed, having time to evaluate and assess the situation, people will start to realize that there is no advantage to remaining in a failed state, or one that is being gamed and manipulated into the global schemes of elitist statists. That is not what America is about.

Some variation on this realization is more likely than not. It will become clear that the idea of structuring another republic means pretty much going back to the immediately failed mess. It should be rejected and I believe it will.

There are recent parallels. In 1989, the Soviet Union, which was composed of 15+ states came apart mostly because the powerful communist party and the seat of government in

Moscow was unable to hold it together. As a result, the Soviet Republics and satellite nations went their own ways.

Some questions arise; *"Why create a new nation instead of fixing the old one?"* Aside from the many reasons already given, it is simply easier for us to take our marbles and leave than to wrest power from the existing intrenched interests; or to remain hitched to the main engine which is in danger of running off the track. It is amply justifiable and a natural response; the only viable option for the vast majority of Americans and the only option that makes sense.

"What about the Civil War between the states; wasn't that as a result of state secession?" No, the civil war was started, as are most wars, by the conspiracy of agitators and agent-provacoteur.[64] An already seceded South Carolina, in response to an aggressive provocative act ordered by Lincoln as a pretext for a war response by the north, ordered an artillery bombardment of Fort Sumpter[65] in Charleston Harbor which was occupied by foreign northern troops. It was a foreign military invasion of one nation by another which started the war. In the south, the war is referred to as the *'War of Northern Aggression.'*

Another thing to consider is that we are not the same nation as we were back then. All states stand to suffer the same fate, so there is equal incentive for all to seek to save themselves from fallout. The majority of other states will likely follow a move toward self-determination, detaching from the train wreck about to happen. Also it is in hopes of regaining as much of the entire roster and alignment of the original states willing to accept and comply with the requirements.

I must reiterate what I have already stated; the described scenarios are oversimplifications of the dynamics likely to

---

[64] Agents charged with sowing discord. Usually to entice rash or illegal acts surreptitiously to provoke a desired political outcome.
[65] From the diary of Senator Orville Browning and the book 'A Youth's History of the Great Civil War in the United States, from 1861-1865' by Rushmore G. Horton, 1868. See Appendix.

occur. No one can accurately predict the course of things to come so cannot determine the destination of such events. It is my sincere desire that should a situation anything like the above scenario commence, sufficient number of properly informed, intelligent, and level headed individuals will have at least had the opportunity to examine and evaluate the options and prepared. That is why it is imperative to prepare ahead of time, to educate as many people as possible into what events are likely to unfold, and the options available to mitigate the fallout, then work diligently to ensure an outcome that favors the sovereign-body of politically endowed people.

Guerilla Sovereign

Something must be done to alter the current trajectory of history. Recent tools such as the Internet and Youtube have begun to remove the veil from the face of the monster in our midst. As a result, that monster has begun to act less secretively but more overt in actions, recognizing they are being exposed, so they are beginning to show their teeth. As a result of the outpouring of information exposing the evil, creating distress amongst the people, more and more of the population is sensing something stinks with the status quo and are beginning to become agitated and frightened. This phenomenon is a signal to us that have come to know the beast; what its aims are and how it operates; to become organized and active.

We need to take advantage of the catalyst provided from the fear and pain amongst the population. We cannot let the opportunity get past us. We have the greatest opportunity forthcoming and will be much more successful garnering the support of a mass movement of people willing to get behind a leadership that will give answers, more-so than anytime in the recent past. I am not a believer or a supporter of the Tea Party per-se because they have been compromised from the beginning; neutralized as a political movement and led down a blind alley by their own leadership, however, the reality is they represent a mass movement built as a response to the treachery and failure we have witnessed in the last decade, which proves the premise that now is the time to pull together with the right knowledge and leadership. We can offer something of substance and leadership, not the failure of tired, trite, retreads from the Republican party. The Tea-Party is a rich field which can be plowed with a bumper crop of movement harvested.

We need to get past this era of hand-wringing over the fact that evil exists and is very familiar and plan how we are going to deal with it. We need to stop endlessly reciting the problems from the executed conspiratorial movements; we have established that sufficiently and it is very well documented. Now we need to organize and execute plans to deal with the threat. We must change the dialog from one of attempting to prove the existence of the real problem to the masses to one of, *"We know the evil among us, we have seen its face! What can we do to fight back? What plan may we use to deliver ourselves and our nation?"*

I do not believe that anyone has really addressed that question adequately nor formed a comprehensive starting place to deal with the question. Knowing about the evil that has been done for generations is part of the information necessary to formulate a solution, because it gives insight into the nature of the beast and how they operate, however, it does not present the solution nor even operational tactics for defense much less a strategic plan for victory. There are many ideas from many quarters but to form a comprehensive plan requires a considerable effort to organize. I have presented my thesis, but I cannot do what I have advocated alone. It must be done by consensus with the support of many others that agree on what direction solutions lay and what measures are practical and achievable, given the resources available.

We must recognize our own history and understand the real strength of the beast; what it can and can not do. It is certainly not omnipotent, but neither is it a vapor. Its power is somewhere in-between and we need to understand and measure it. We must discover then recognize its true nature; that the current evil among us is really much weaker than the image they put forward somewhat by our own hand, by painting a picture implying that it is futile to fight them as they are all-powerful and all-pervasive. In reality, they are like the little man behind the curtain in the story of the Wizard of Oz; mostly smoke and bluster but capable of advancement through extremely powerful tactics and their intrenched positions within the current structure.

They can really only operate in secrecy and when exposed they scurry off into the darkness and use their network of operatives to cover their tracks. Ask yourself; do you really believe that this problem cannot be overcome? Take away their ability to operate in secrecy, maintain a network of operatives, or cover up their deeds and they will slink back into their dark crevices. We must recognize and embrace the advantages we have; there are many changes on the horizon which are already compromising the advantage they have cultivated in the past which gives the people tools to confront and defeat their schemes including:

1) Loss of the monopoly on information, news, and opinion. People are increasingly getting their news and opinion from numerous sources on the internet and alternative media, while abandoning the New York Times, LA Times, Washington Post, NBC, ABC, CBS, CNN, Fox, ad-naseam. They are only left with the brain-washing monopoly given by the public education system, and there is considerable disgust at its dangerous infection and impact on our society; producing generations of ignorant, insolent, brain-dead zombie individuals, not capable of even minimal function in our society.

Private online education has begun to show considerable promise to Americans and is being developed and increasingly adopted for educating the young. Americans are increasingly disgusted with the insolent schools, teachers, administrative staff, and school boards that demand unlimited taxes from property owners to pay for their programs, pensions, and perks, while they are to be unquestioned and unchallenged and completely unaccountable for delivery of a consistently very poor quality result. Just like the monopolies that occupy media, and the financial and political systems, I believe this system is due a wholesale change as well and it will be forthcoming very soon.

2) The unstable global financial house of cards they have created. Many people believe this is part of their plans, but, while that may be the case that does not mean they are in control of the outcome. Indeed, I believe a collapsing financial system will put them at a tremendous disadvantage, unlike in other times when they benefitted having done the exact same thing. That is because of the fact, as I stated before, they are now very exposed so people will know who is at fault and will blame them explicitly. Their ability to garner the support of the people for much of anything will be considerably undermined. They will have overplayed their hand at that point.

Most of recent history was relatively untouched by their influence but punctuated by periods when they aggressively moved their agenda forward up to the current time when they are moving fast and with large gains, but are exposing themselves. This leads me to believe that they are only able to move when opportunity presents itself to them. Like a cancer over time, they have grown to occupy positions of power continuously which is why they are able to move to take advantage of their opportunities. After the system is shaken, they loose those positions of power and influence because they are exposed.

My premise is that they are able to move their agenda forward on us mainly because our so called Democratic-Republic form of government gives them tremendous power to act against us whenever the opportunity presents. We must change the structural dynamic given by a weak and compromised system, and craft a new civilization that is considerably more immune to their machinations and schemes.

Once we start down that road, we will have no choice but to stay the course until we have won the struggle by engineering a new civilization with a considerably more sound structure. We will then need to shore-up our new civilization and make it considerably more immune knowing how the bad guys think; designing it in such a way as to avoid their influence, the concentration of power, and exploitation vulnerabilities. We must teach our children about the reality of evil in the world, something we as a society have failed to do adequately, preferring to turn away from it and ignore the existence of such things. This era of history must be exposed and made a main tenet of education in all of its aspects. We must peal back all facades, expose all players without regard to name, ethnicity, religious or political affiliation, ideology, or any status, element, or factor that people may want to hide and protect now; there is nothing off limits. If we are vigilant, honest, and thorough, we will set them back at least 50 to 100 years.

We have a model to follow which is our own American revolution. We, the underdog Americans did not fight based on the standard and accepted practices of the world at that time which the British used, but we invented new ways to fight. We fought as guerrillas fought, meaning we fought in an unconventional way. They were bamboozled as a result because their generals and their foot soldiers could only fight using conventional warfare. We also have that advantage now.

We must decide how far we are willing to go and what we are willing to sacrifice. In my opinion, we must be willing to abandon everything we have come to believe represents America, because if we cling to any of it we may loose all of it. We cannot know or predict what our nation or civilization will look like then, but it is better that we fight to win rather than compromise to keep the temporal things we know now. It is better to put everything on the table and say our goodbyes to it now and hope it will still be ours after the smoke clears, rather than holding on now and risking the loss of everything. What am I talking about; what things must we be willing to give up? There are a number of things but a short list includes:

• The current composition of the country may change and our identity may be altered as a result.

• The US constitution does not serve us. It is obsolete and must pass inorder to allow something better to replace it.

• The form of government will change.

• Patriotic sentiment must turn to acknowledge that not everything the US government does is beyond reproach. It must embrace the fact of treachery in our midst and call for a change. It must recognized that many if not most in the leadership of government have been compromised. The entire system has been corrupted.

• We will loose the status of the guys in white hats with the right to police the world. We will become just Americans, without an agenda for the rest of the world. We will cease being used to engage in wars of foreign adventurism for globalist interests.

• We may face wrecking poverty and loss of economic security for a period. We may face the loss of property. We will loose the artificial and inequitable advantage that a global 'Reserve Currency' afforded us.

• We may face loss of the liberty and rights we now take for granted. Some involved may be ostracized. Some may loose their lives. However, it is more likely that we will gain liberty like what we have never experienced.

We must recognize that success on our part will spread to other corners of the world and many will follow and adopt our model. We have the opportunity to lead the world once again. We must catch a vision of what our nation and our world can look like after we have won our lives and our nation back. We must envision that model now then present it to others inorder to get them to join in with us. It is a political campaign, we must sell the vision.

It is not necessary that we get every single person on our side inorder to adequately fight. The revolutionary Americans were a very small group and were thought to be nut-jobs and traitors to the crown by their contemporaries. They were shunned, informed-on, harassed, and marginalized by many but at the same time they were considered heroes by many sympathetic to the cause of American independence. When they demonstrated some measure of success their support grew significantly; it will be no different with our struggle.

Opposite Reaction

There is a law in physics which states, *"For every action, there is an equal but opposite reaction.*[66]*"* This applies in social dynamics as well. It is one of the laws of nature that manifests in a variety of ways. The world in recent times, and in particular, western nations have endured many decades of abuse and theft by small but powerful nefarious interests which have dictated near a century of misery to Russia, and Central Europe. With their grip finally having loosened, the people have regained a modicum of their heritage and rights.

As I stated earlier, the same applies to many other parts of the world in recent years. This proves that the pendulum will only swing so far in one direction before it swings back again. In

---

[66] Newton's 3rd law of motion.

my view, all the utopian plans of the global lefties are just that, plans. Their ability to push those plans on humanity only extend through the time that things are relatively good in economic terms, due to the fact that people are relatively passive and are more agreeable to foolish ideas if they feel good and secure about their lives in general. That time is rapidly coming to a close. Regarding the schemers, and to paraphrase scripture, *"They have filled up the cup of wrath."* They sought to destroy the relative prosperity and liberty of the west, and to some degree they have managed just that. However, it seems that the very thing they sought to accomplish may result in their undoing. This is what is called a dilemma.

The powerful money interests who hide behind their utopian-stooge fronts will inevitably push their luck and go too far. It has happened many times in history and it will again; this time is no different. The aftermath of the French revolution was pretty brutal for the perpetrators who were guilty of the murder of tens of thousands of innocent. Their megalomania got the better of them and in the end they were pushing absolutely insane schemes on the people which they exempted themselves from. This was done in the name of improving the lives of all the sheep they used to spark the revolution. Some in their own ranks realized that it had gone too far and intervened, attempting to save their own skin. They ended it by turning on their Jacobin[67] and Girondist[68] revolutionary brethren. The man at the top who was left holding the bag when cracks started to form was Maximilian Robespierre, who, driven by extreme paranoia, directed much of the purges against rivals and set the end in motion. The purges were emulated 130 years later by a succession of tyrannical leaders of the communist Soviet Block. By some accounts, Robespierre was shot in the face by his underlings and then

---

[67] Murderous radical political group who wielded dictatorial power during the French Revolution.
[68] French Moderate Republican Party Members.

beheaded by guillotine; the very weapon of terror he wielded against his rivals and fellow conspirators. The revolution lasted for 5 horrible years and ended with the lives of most of the revolutionaries dead; killed by the guillotine or by the angry mob who turned on them.

The parallels between the French-revolution and our own current state of affairs are striking, with ideologically the same group of plotters having been emboldened to attempt another go at ushering in a utopian age of *'enlightenment.'* It may not be evident to the masses or spelled out in todays news headlines, as it manifests a different face today, but to be sure, the objective of a world of slaves ruled by an elite cabal have not changed. To most folks who bother to keep themselves aware of political matters, these things are wrapped in left vs right political party squabbles; incomprehensible executive and legislative budgetary incompetence; fiscal crisis with looming financial failure, with mind boggling wars and foreign policy initiatives tossed in; all designed to confuse, conceal, and misdirect from the truth of what is actually occurring.

Beside the French revolution, there are many other parallels with recent affairs in history including 2 world wars; the rise of elitism entering into a state of dictatorial power through the United Nations; The World Bank and IMF,[69] and complete global financial control by the international banking cartel, along with the many heads and tentacles of the global monster.

Their mistake is they miscalculate human behavior and response. They adopt a static model in which they believe they can predict how people will react to their dictates and strangling schemes, based on how docile they behave in a time of relative prosperity. They do not adequately take into account what happens, or it may be better to say, certainty is diminished when conditions worsen and people begin to look

[69] International Monetary Fund

to blame someone for destroying the relatively prosperous conditions. The situation has been aptly described by a few humorous analogous rhetorical questions such as: *"What happens when you are in a cage with a bear, feeding it raw meat, and you run out of meat?"* Or, *"What happens when they run out of other peoples money?"*

The fact is human dynamic social behavior is not as easily put under the microscope during times of distress. They behave more like a herd of cats than sheep. Its like predicting the weather out past a week; there is no good track record with that either. Elitists rely on their own flawed estimations of what predictable reaction will follow their move to put shackles on the populace. Even with a contrived crisis, it is at best, unpredictable. This stems from their view of humans as chattel[70], resources, or property like livestock. They believe they can simply herd, warehouse, and manage people like animals and they will comply with the carrot and stick measures employed. This of course is a very grave problem and a mistake. Although much of the world has been oppressed by tyrants throughout history, Americans have never known that kind of manipulation and are not likely to respond to it casually. Chattel do not have a sense of right and self-worth; nor can they use their sense of self-preservation; or with intelligence equivalent to those doing the oppressing, react to their treatment, then turn the tables; chattel simply accept their fate. The same cannot be done with humans in any significant way before disaster comes quickly back upon those who attempt such foolish moves. Americans were born free and they will not accept slavery, ever.

So then, lets examine what may happen if the US, and/or the global economy or merely the dollar were to start a slide toward collapse or merely falter and teeter on the edge, or otherwise suffer failure which sparks some level of civil

---

[70] Chattel means personal possession, but is the same root that the english word cattle stems from.

disorder in the US. There are many views on this that range from: A measured and passive response from the federal government, which then has no choice but to scale its size and authority back to survive within the confines of the original limitations given in the constitution; to; it considers the populace as an enemy of the state then initiates an oppressive move to self-preservation including: marshall law; wholesale confiscation of firearms, gold, personal property; and anything else a paranoid, out of control, rogue regime, driven by megalomania would do.

Increasing numbers of folks in various grass-roots political movements believe they are more likely to respond with the latter; a kind of authoritarian power grab, suspending the remainder of the failing constitution attempting to force some sort of socialist dictatorship with the intent of moving the US past the socialized political states in Europe, to become an integral cog-state in the *New World Order*, removing all pretenses of democratic governance. There is also everything in between.

Lets examine the extreme case. Assume the federal government responds aggressively, according to a more recent style, with the dictates and lying rhetoric about how they are here to help ensure public health and safety as they impose martial law while jack-booted thugs parachute in or move in to main street USA by armored military vehicles, then herd the helpless chattel to and fro, to occupy the landscape, just as they have recently in Iraq and Afghanistan. By the way in an incredible act of treachery, the Jacobin traitors that administrated the 'revolution' with an iron fist during the french revolution did so under the guise of what was called, *'Comité de Salut Public - [The Committee Of Public Safety].'*

If such a scenario were to take place, and at this point many believe it is more likely than not, the government would loose all moral authority, therefore in the short term there would be little to no willingness or voluntary cooperation by the public.

In my view, they will have lost all authority in the minds of the public to lead in a crisis for the simple fact that they will be blamed for having precipitated the disaster. There will be little motivation for the populace to give them moral authority. Indeed, the approval rating for all branches of government are at all time lows and that is not likely to improve in the depths of significant financial displacement or oppressive dictates let alone a collapse of the global economy. This presents a problem for the global hegemonists who must then lay claim to the situation, because government cannot advance far without the trust and cooperation of the people they claim to govern.

So the question arises; whats to prevent them from simply ignoring the opinion of the people, suspending what is left of the constitution and further imposing oppressive dictatorial mandates on the population; or creating some other false flag, Hegelian pretext to do whatever they deem necessary to preserve their positions of power, such as inflaming a war then obligating the nation to conclude it? The answer is nothing will stop them from these things and it is probable that there may be some moves along those lines. The question then becomes; How successful will any of these measures be in the long term, 2 to 5 years, for preserving the failed system or mobilizing the nation under the plans for global hegemony? What is the probability that it will remain intact beyond the short term? In my view the answer to that is **Zero**!

There is no way to determine how any party may respond; it is all a total guess, therefore, the outcome is unknown. It is not my purpose to attempt to predict the course or outcome of any future events. The discussion is simply to examine the possibilities while taking an educated guess based on supposed scenarios. This thought exercise may be informative for readers who have never heard this point of view and have never considered that such things could ever precipitate.

In my view, any outcome of a scenario where the existing government moves to suppress the population will succeed about as well as most anything else they do, which means it will fall apart pretty quickly. History supports this. This government's ability to maintain continuity with the status of legitimacy will have completely failed and they will not have the resources to continue to operate as such for reasons that have to do with the fact that it takes money and manpower to enforce a dictatorship, or a crippled 'democracy/republic', neither of which do they have at this point and that situation is not going to fix itself. In my estimation, the populace of the US, who have a heritage of freedom and democratic process are not likely to roll over and accept the authority of a completely failed regime whom they will blame completely for irresponsibly precipitating all of what has transpired. They will view them as an unwanted and illegitimate regime.

At this point, individual states will step-up and attempt to fill in the slack. State governors and legislatures are generally an extension of the federal system, but they will be called on and looked to, so they will assume the authority to:

1) Limit the inept and illegitimate role of whatever is left of the federal system. To stop meddling and interference by the broken federal system in affairs of state, they will attempt to prove that they can pick up the slack and provide moral or political leadership. In the minds of most Americans this will have been completely written off.

2) State governments will also attempt to fill in with emergency relief and coordination. Other than emergency assistance, statehouses have little leadership and no solution to offer otherwise.

In my view, state political structures will fare better than the federal system, but only marginally so and only for reasons which have to do with weighing loyalty to political parties versus the interests of the people and whatever nation is to emerge. They will attempt to determine in which direction the political winds are blowing, inorder to get in front of it. At this point, with political ineptness established and their organization marginalized, common people will find it much easier to take up their role as owners and founders of the nation once again while political organs take the backseat. Time for them to get the hell out of the way and let the people do what only they can do; build their civilization.

As I stated before, no one can accurately predict these events. We are not really sure what the starting point is, much less the steps that will transpire given any circumstances or event contingencies. Therefore as before, the preceding hypothetical sequence of events amount to little more than speculation. However, as events have unfolded in the last few decades somewhat as a predictor, some of what has been discussed will have proven to have at least moved down a near parallel path to that anticipated, if not touching actual events.

It is not the path but the ultimate outcome which matters, but that is also the most difficult to really nail down with any certainty. As stated prior, it is ultimately up to the people that comprise the nation to decide their own fate and not the narrow interests that are bent on steering it down their crooked path; therefore we should work like it depends on us and pray like it depends on God.

Morning

To quote a recent political slogan, *"It is morning in America once again!"* That is to say, if history favors us and we are successful as a nation and a people in taking hold of our own fate, we will one day wake up with a new nation and I would like to offer a glimpse as I see it.

With the failure of a dysfunctional state and the ruinous financial climate occupying the lives of the masses, traditional government will be blamed and the populace will not want to repeat the mistake; people will seek after alternatives for rebuilding the nation. That is our opportunity. Having destroyed the established republic, global hegemony is the goal of the elitists that are driving the failing US financial system. Global hegemony means that all people including Americans, loose their independent identity and their unique views on liberty, religion, wealth, humanity, and so on, then are forced to adopt views that are completely antithetical to their traditions and to what they have been brought up to embrace, and certainly considerably beyond what most every culture on earth, past and present would find acceptable.

The power of the groups driving hegemony is completely effected through a predatory domination of small groups (government) who wield the power and trust of the civilization. That is the hegemonists main focus of attack and control on a society and a nation. They have been able to so completely intrench themselves and their agenda into the very fabric of America's heart and soul by way of our flawed political system which has been erroneously entrusted to represent the interest of the civilization. We the people supply the power of civilization, and to the extent we do we have ignorantly given power to members of the government to make decisions for our nation and lives. They have removed the limitations and threaten us with our own power. We vote them in every day, month, and year. We have been raised to believe this is the only way that democratic process can work. Clearly it is not.

The adoption of the **Sovereign Democratic Majority** process will result in a completely new and effective manner for a nation and society to operate with hegemonist predatory elements falling away for the simple fact, there are no power groups entrusted to legislate on the behalf of the populace, so they have no host to infect and no focus of attack. The SPEP are now the legislature; they are the law givers. They make up a majority of the people endowed with political right from the foundation of the nation. This group will guard it jealously and are not prone to frivolous moves with global ambitions.

Hegemonists will instead find it necessary to attempt to bribe the entire population, or at least the majority of this group which will make up somewhere near 40% of the populace. This becomes a very costly undertaking with an extremely limited rate of success, due to the fact that only the dimmest members of the society can be cheaply bribed into selling their own souls for short term gain, which will not ever be enough.

Imagine what it will be like if we the people again own and operate the nation without trusting elected government:

• No political decisions that favor a very small minority at the expense of the sovereign majority and the nation. No policies enacted which counters the will of the sovereign majority.

• No more foreign wars of adventurism, hegemony, or opportunity for plunder.

• No spending money on worthless projects that profit narrow interests.

• Entire current federal registry of law is thrown out. Henceforth it has no authority, force, or effect with any state or individual.

• No wasteful self-determined federal or state budgets and no deficits that accumulate debt and obligation upon the nation. The function of governance no longer includes the ability to self-fund any aspect or authorize any form of debt.

• No central banks, but only private, competitive banks that are publicly overseen and regulated. The money for these banks originates from the wealth of the populace, not narrow financial interests.

• No politicians, campaigns, elections, or their lies.

• No more foreign persons, illegal or otherwise, invading the nation or claiming a right of asylum or to occupy space in our land. The borders will be sealed and undesirables deported en-masse.

• No more court 'rulings', and no arbitrary 'findings' by any court. Courts must render opinions based on the accepted and adopted body of laws. Corrupt or otherwise compromised opinions will not be tolerated. Court opinions are immediately subject to review and overturn by the sovereign-body. No court has any executive power whatsoever.

• No federal income tax or revenue system. All budgets and taxes are set by the sovereign-body. Total taxation will not exceed a maximum determined by the SDM (~6% of GDP), and no law-abiding individual will ever be forced to disclose personal private financial information, or ever again deal with a dictatorial bureaucratic entity. Only the revenue necessary to minimally operate the infrastructure of the nation is collected and not a penny more. Taxes are not collected directly on citizens, but through non-direct means only. Taxes for all levels of governance come solely from Point of Sale excise, import tariff, foreign entities and interests, user fees, and the lease of public resources. There is an absolute prohibition against any function of governance from self-funding. All revenues are collected at state level and below, and all funding for supra-state governance will come from the states by directive of the sovereign-body.

• No more bloated bureaucracies staffed with completely unqualified people, given outrageous salaries and pensions.

• Parents are considerably more free to teach their children whatever they deem necessary and uplifting. No more state apparatchiks[71] dictating the curriculum.

• Religious Christian observance is free again in private and public life.

• Freedom to learn and to teach respect for American heritage and culture to the young. Free to preserve and celebrate our heritage and reject diversity.

---

[71] Bureaucratic functionaries that facilitate government agenda.

Currently there is an entire alphabet soup of agencies designed to control commerce, political speech and dissension, and the express political will of the people who are the owners of the nation. Following is a short list of some of the most egregious, which would not be tolerated. With the Sovereign Politically Endowed People in-charge, only what is actually in the interest of the nation will be enacted and tolerated. The following are examples of laws, government agencies, or other institutions that would never have been adopted under the Sovereign Democratic Majority system:

• Federal Reserve system which was given monopoly operational status for the nation's monetary, banking, and currency.

• The Income tax, and the Internal Revenue Service.

• The Department of Education. Along with the teacher unions which have the power to dominate the education of children, counter to the consent of parents obligated to pay for the indoctrination of their own children.

• The Environmental Protection Agency. Bureaucratic enforcers of the globalists cabal tasked with controlling use of all private land and business activity.

• The Affordable Care Act (Obamacare). Designed to create a path toward monopolizing the American healthcare industry, diminishing quality of care, while driving costs skyward.

• Obama. Only Original-Americans are eligible to hold this level of Executive-Manager position in our civilization. Never again the nation subject to an agenda of payback, or revenge as represented by the hatred of disenfranchised malcontents and foreign interests who have no stake or appreciation of America's heritage.

• US Department of Homeland Security and the TSA (Transportation Security Agency). Intrusive agencies that interfere with the normal free flow of commerce and the movement of people, ostensibly to protect us from terrorism.

Many people would agree that we are more in need of someone to protect us from these oppressive agencies than terrorists.

We should expect a new era. With the SDM writing the laws, the power for investigating past crimes against the people and the nation, facilitated through corrupt government, will be used to correct past injustices. Examples are: Recovery and restoration of financial assets stolen through corrupt laws and rulings. See the section *'Civil Constructs'* in the chapter *'Sovereign Body.'* These will include the recent rape of the American public and other nations by large banks facilitated by government, who committed massive fraud and were the beneficiaries of massive cover-up and the 'bail-out' infusions of money guaranteed by the American public. Other examples include the structure and mechanisms of the federal reserve bank itself for the last 100 years. All distributions of assets obtained inequitably would be subject to recovery and restoration actions. It is shameful that the administration of justice has not been done prior to now; it certainly should have been; but due to corrupt laws designed to protect criminals, upheld by corrupt courts for the better part of our recent history, vast inequitable appropriation, accumulation, and distribution of wealth by criminal elements throughout the nation and the world have transpired for far too long.

Those who's assets were taken illegally by the government will have the opportunity to recover them and expect sanctions and penalty compensation from the criminal perpetrators. Criminals given cover by the corrupt institutions can expect that any and all *fruit of the poisonous tree* will be taken back and returned to those who were cheated.

CHAPTER THIRTEEN
Debt Analysis

Debt Driven Economy

The table below titled '*US government Fiscal Parameters*' illustrates some data that tell us the story of the US economy. With simple study of the data, persons not versed in government fiscal budgets and economics can see that we have some very deep problems forming on the horizon, even if experience is only limited to balancing a household budget. This is not difficult to comprehend but may require some clarification. The table lists some important figures that will be useful in the following discussion. It lists the years of interest at the top, but notice they are the beginning and ending of a transition period. The beginning is 2008 and 2009, and the ending is the most current time for which figures are available, 2013, with the 2012 figures used for averaging the numbers.

US Government Fiscal Parameters (Billions)				
	2008	**2009**	**2012**	**2013**
Total Revenue	$2,524	$2,105	$2,450	$2,774
Budget Deficit	$459	$1,413	$1,087	$680
Government Outlays (Spending)	$2,983	$3,518	$3,537	$3,454
Deficit as a Percentage of Outlay	-15.38%	-40.16%	-30.73%	-19.69%
Public Debt	$9,986	$11,876	$16,051	$17,548
Gross Domestic Product	$14,292	$13,974	$15,685	$16,203
Spending as a Percent of GDP	21%	25%	23%	21%

Table 1

It is easy to notice right away that the Public Debt is mounting much quicker than the Gross Domestic Product (GDP), and there is really little else needed to tell the story. However, I shall proceed with a premise for what has been forming; a fundamental shift in the economic vitality and viability of the United States, which is rapidly deteriorating and the recessions of 2001 and 2008 have revealed the shift. In particular, the super-recession of 2008/09 was very severe and required extraordinary measures to avoid complete collapse, and to drive the economy out of the abyss it was plunging down into. These measures included extraordinary amounts of stimulus capital poured into the economy, through a federal reserve policy called quantitative-easing[72] which continues today, several years past the official end of the recession, accompanied by interest rates that reached negative levels in real terms. These levels have not been seen in the last several decades, but were characteristic of the last 2 recessions, with the most recent one requiring more 'juice' than the previous, which also suggests that the next one, slated to start mid to late 2016, may be a killer of the current economic world order.

As stated, the premise is that there is a fundamental change that unquestionably revealed itself with the recession of 2008 in-which GDP growth, is virtually completely Keynesian at this point, meaning there is no organic growth without massive monetary stimulus intervention by the federal reserve, facilitating massive fiscal deficit spending, and the transference of faltering private bank loan losses to public debt. With these measures, GDP growth has reached a point of diminishing returns. The apex probably occurred sometime in the previous 2 decades, but has only recently become very evident. It is generally accepted that the US economy since 2008 will realize a '*new normal*' in terms of growth and employment. The

---

[72] Central Bank buying of specified amounts of worthless financial assets from faltering government, commercial banks, and other private institutions, to absorb their losses from frivolous investments, thus driving lower the yield on financial assets.

'*new normal*' means we have to get used to unemployment figures in the mid to upper single digit range for full employment, and these figures will most certainly exceed the range. It also means us designated as '*tax payers*' by the elitist powers that will have been, can expect to bend over and take a more frequent reaming in terms of taxes, while government continues to grow wildly out of control, unabated.

Economies are usually composed of markets where private individuals and companies sell goods and services between themselves, to produce the what is necessary to maintain the civilization.   Instead, ours is increasingly composed of unproductive speculation, and wasteful government enterprise. What more needs to be said about our economy other than observing the events of the current days?   Until 2008, The US federal government spent about 3% of **Gross Domestic Product**[73] more than it collected from all sources of revenues. In 2009 that went to about 10% of GDP, and the current president has said that this level of deficit spending would continue indefinitely into the future. We will now look at this in terms of real figures which are easily understood. This can best be done by examples.   The following tables of figures titled '*Gross Domestic Product Growth*', examines GDP growth for the years 2008 through 2013:

---

[73] The total monetary sum of goods and services produced domestically.

Gross Domestic Product (GDP) Growth		
Pre 2009 (Decade)		
	2008	
Current GDP	$14,291,500,000,000	
	$14 Trillion	
Non Recession Growth Rate (good year)	6.00%	
Recession Year Growth Rate	-1.50%	
Ratio of good to bad Years (5/3)	1.67	
Real (Avg) Growth (current cycle)	3.19%	
Real (Avg) Inc/Dec in GDP	$455,541,562,500	
	$455 Billion	
New Revenue. Assume 50% tax	$227,770,781,250	
	$278 Billion	
Post 2009 Into the Indefinite Future		
	2009/13	**2012/13**
Current GDP (Averaged)	$15,088,200,000,000	$15,943,750,000,000
	$15 Trillion	$16 Trillion
Non Recession Growth Rate (good year)	2.50%	2.50%
Recession Year Growth Rate (bad Year)	-4.50%	-4.50%
Ratio of good to bad Years (5/3)	1.67	1.67
Real (Avg) Growth (current cycle)	-0.13%	-0.13%
Real (Avg) Inc/Dec in GDP	-$18,860,250,000	-$19,929,687,500
	-$18.6 Billion	-$20.0 Billion
New Revenue. No new revenue so not taxed.	$0	$0

Table 2

2008 represents typical growth (increase) in GDP for that year during the previous era of around 3.2%, which is $455 billion. The tax revenue generated from it is $278 billion which is added to government coffers. Note in the post 2009 era, if you average the years 2009 with 2013, and 2012 with 2013, all of which are years in the *'new era'*, there is no net increase in GDP, but it is negative (~-$20 billion) in each instance, while 2008 shows normal (for the previous era) growth. Also note that 2008, while a recession had started, was nonetheless a somewhat robust year in economic terms; 2009 suffered significant decline, and 2012 was weak, while 2013 was robust for the *'new normal.'* Note the table indicates as part of the calculations, the previous era peak growth rates of +6% for good (non-recession) years, and −1.5% peak declines for recession years, with an approximation of 5 growth years to 3 recession years to yield an average of 3.2% for an 8 year period. The 5/3 estimate is the same in the post 2009 era, but the peek rates have changed to +2.5% and −4.5% respectively to yield a of −0.13% average in GDP growth.

Referring to the current GDP, which is the sum total in dollars of all goods and services produced domestically, for 2008 was about $14,300,000,000,000 or $14.3 Trillion. Before 2009, the federal government borrowed or printed about 4% of this amount on average, each year, which is $560,000,000,000 ($560 billion). This is termed the *'fiscal deficit.'* An additional $560 billion was needed that year to close the gap between what it brought in through taxes and fees and what it spent. Referring to the table below titled *'US Government Fiscal Deficit'* reveals government fiscal shortfalls, and the rate at which the debt is accumulating. Most of the deficit was borrowed from nations, banks, and individuals, which increased the national debt. Note that although in 2008 there was positive GDP growth, it was mostly eaten up by government deficit.

US Government Fiscal Deficit

Pre 2009 (Decade)

	2008
Non Recession Year Deficit (good year) % of Spending	-15.38%
Real (Average) Deficit	-$458,600,000,000
	-$459 Billion
Difference (deficit + growth tax revenue)	-$230,829,218,750
	-$231 Billion

Post 2009 Into the Indefinite Future

Years Averaged	2009/12	2012/13
Non-Recession Year Deficit (good year) % of Spending		-25.28%
Recession Year Deficit (bad year) % of Spending	-35.43%	
Ratio of good to bad Years (good/bad)	1.67	1.67
Real (Average) Deficit	-$1,235,180,898,112	-$883,650,000,000
	-$1.2 Trillion	-$.9 Trillion
Difference (deficit + growth tax revenue)	-$1,235,180,898,112	-$883,650,000,000
	-$1.2 Trillion	-$.9 Trillion

Table 3

The deficit, if borrowed from the federal reserve is new money which is simply printed. New money put into circulation this way hits every household with inflation, which eats at savings, and the ability to pay the cost of living. If it is borrowed elsewhere, it is debt and accumulates every year that the federal government spends more than it brings in. It is laid on the backs of taxpayers now and for future generations to pay back.

Pre-2009 debt burden

Before 2009 each and every person's tax burden increased by $459 billion or $1500 per year. If we use the accepted figure of 116 million households in the country, the burden is an approximate $4000 additionally laid upon each family's debt obligation, for each year in that era. Keep in mind, this is above and beyond the taxes that are already paid each year by that family. These are in the form of deferred or future taxes to be levied, for the repayment of obligations the US government will borrow each year from banks, investors, and suckers from around the world.

Post 2009 debt burden

Now looking at the table below titled *'Public Debt Obligation'*, which shows debt obligation for each person in the country. For 2009 and into the indefinite future, we are told that the deficit has more than doubled because the government now needs to borrow and spend considerably more than it did before. So whereas before we had yearly increases of $1500 per individual, and $4000 per household, now we have the debt burden increasing each year by $4,000 for individuals and $11,000 per household. The annual debt obligation increase figures are calculated by taking the respective yearly deficit figures and dividing it by the population. The increases shown are 170% between 2008 and 2009 alone, which fell to an increase of 86% over 2008 levels per year by 2013. Averaging the increase figures we get 178%. Ask yourself if your wages and household income are going to be able to keep pace? Do you see a 200% increase in your yearly discretionary income to pay just the increase, which will not even touch the principle?

Public Debt Obligation		
Population		
	2008	**2013**
Number of Individuals	307,000,000	316,000,000
	307 Million	316 Million
Number of Households	115226802	115226802
	115 Million	115 Million
Gross Public Debt		
Government (GAO)	$9,986,100,000,000	$17,547,900,000,000
	$10.0 Trillion	$17.6 Trillion
High Estimate (Include UO)	$63,000,000,000,000	$220,000,000,000,000
	$63 Trillion	$220 Trillion
Pre 2009: Yearly Obligation Increase (2008)		
Individual	$1,494	
Household	$3,980	
2009-On: Yearly Obligation Increase		
Individual	$4,023	$2,796
Household	$10,720	$7,669
Total Current Debt Obligation		
Government (GAO)		
Individual	$32,528	$55,531
Household	$86,665	$152,290
High Estimate (Include UO)		
Individual	$205,212	$696,203
Household	$546,748	$1,909,278

Table 4

The annual accumulating deficit has been accruing for many years, and the total accumulation is called the Public Debt. Apparently there are no actual figures on the number of American citizens, but only the population present in the country, which is shown in the table. It can be approximated by using a figure of around 40 million for illegal aliens, and another 5 million legal aliens, which leaves 271 million citizens that are presumed responsible for paying the debt. However, that is not a reliable method, so I will just use the current US Census figures of 316 million with the caveat that there is about 50 million that will not contribute to paying the burden, so the actual debt per person is higher.

Examining the total national debt, various figures have been proposed for this ranging from $17 to $63 Trillion. Breaking it down, the $17.5 trillion figure is the official tally, it does not include *Unfunded Obligations*. Unfunded Obligations are mandatory payments for programs such as Medicare, Medicaid and Social Security. A news report in the early 2000's, based on government GAO[74] figures combined with figures from the *US Comptroller of the Currency*, put the total figure (public debt + unfunded obligations) at $53 trillion, while a more recently updated figure put it at $63 trillion, and other recent updates from other sources put the estimate as high as $220 trillion. It is probably safe to assume the real figure is currently somewhere in between the latter 2.

Using the 2008 population figures of 307,000,000 (307 million) presumably responsible for the debt; to use an outrageous liberal implication, we can determine each *'tax payer citizen's fair share'*. Taking the $63 trillion figure as a moderate estimate would put each individual's current total tax obligation at $205,000 and each family's current total tax obligation at $547,000. If one cannot accept these figures because they seem unreasonably high, then cut them in half or by ¾ and see if that really makes it any more acceptable.

Using only the official GAO tally for debt, and comparing the debt pre and post 2009, you can see each individual's burden has gone from $32,500 to $55,500 in just 5 years. This equates to a 72% increase over this period for both individual and household. That is, the national public debt has increased 72% in the last 5 years. This should alarm everyone. At this rate, how long will it be before the interest on this debt

---

[74] Government Accountability Office

consumes everything. There are some who will say that we have seen similar levels of debt and greater as a percentage of GDP before, which were paid down, which is true. However, they were not paid down fully, and these were during times of very heavy warfare and reconstruction of the aftermath, where all productive resources of the the entire nations, from large to small, was virtually mobilized and put on a war footing. We are not experiencing that now, and have not in the lifetime of most living persons. The 2 recent wars in the mid-east, although a contributing factor, did not weigh nearly as heavy as the second world war. The cause of the current accumulation of debt runs much deeper than war alone, and will have a much greater impact.

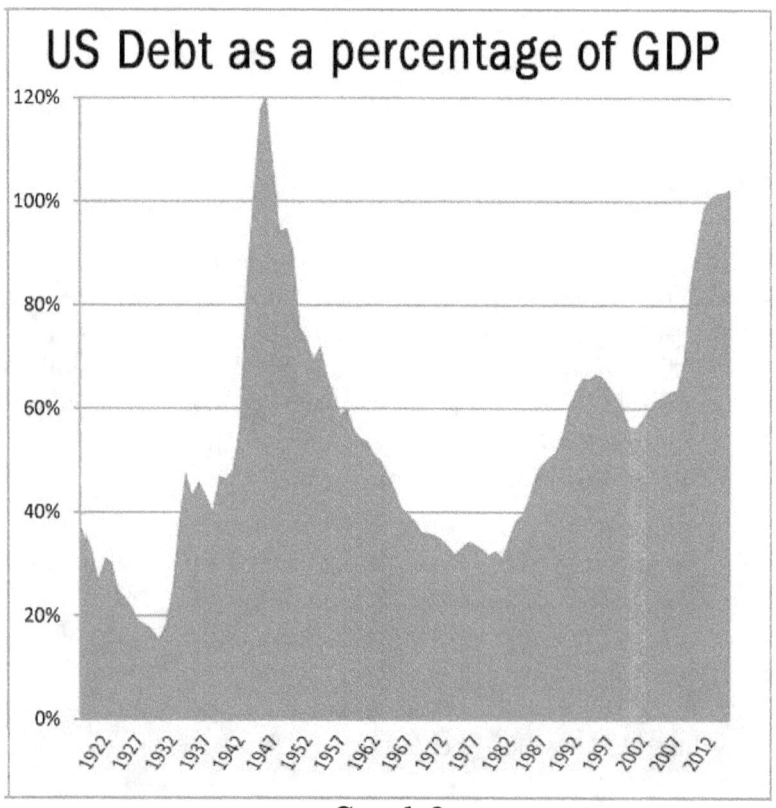

Graph 2

The debt as a percentage of GDP tells an unambiguous story. Referring to the graph titled '*US debt as a percentage of GDP*', observe the trough periods when the debt/GDP levels fell after having risen. Notice the 3 periods around 1932, 1982, and 2002. Note that the levels do not return to the previous low, but continue on to higher lows from the previous. This is the trend, and it is unmistakable. The implication is that debt-service will continue to consume more and more of the wealth the nation produces, until a set of catalyzing, and cascading events brings the house of cards down. I believe that to be a near term event.

To put the individual and household burden in perspective, imagine that your family has financed a house for a principle sum of $547,000 in-which that figure is increasing at 14.4% per annum; with varying annual interest, ranging from 3% to 15% accruing; to be paid over yours and your families lifetimes; while you have received nothing in exchange for the burden, and your children are born indebted. You do not get the advantage of living in the house or discharging the obligation if you can not pay for it. That is your families debt, courtesy of the United States government, like it or not. Then assuming it possible to make some headway, the question becomes what will the debt burden be by the time you have already paid whatever the actual current outstanding balance is, because the unpaid principle and interest do not stop, but continues to accumulate? With the current political paradigm continually intact, this debt burden will not be paid in one or two generations, but will greatly burden the many to come, and if the truth be told, it can never be discharged. It is a perpetual burden on the current generation and those to come. There is absolutely no embellishment in this discussion. The debt-burden and the expectation to accept and pay it are very real.

Examining the ratio of the increase in GDP to the annual budget deficit, we see a troubling trend. The deficit that is spent each year is justified by an erroneous assertion, based on a drum-beating media mantra, that deficit spending is not really the wasteful bloating of an out of control bureaucracy, but is actually investment and will cause growth which will enrich us, and the additional revenue generated by the growth will more than offset the deficit. This is clearly not the case. Any growth in wealth is consumed by the debt trend, and it is not likely to improve any time soon because the wealth producing capacity of the United States, by which it could pay down the debt and deficit, is rapidly being depleted by the globalization of the economies of the world.

Globalization has been sold as an appeal to a kind of fairness morality, more prone to be accepted and believed by inexperienced and amiable people, as a kind of *'economic equilibrium'* or uniformity in which there must be a process toward the equilibrium of economic strength around the world, where the only means in which the poor nations can become less poor is for the richer nations to supply the deficit, by giving up their markets and industrial capacity. A parity of the wealth of nations is ostensibly the desired outcome of globalization. All of it is folly and a con-job on all nations.

Debt Service

Debt service, which is interest payments on the debt is a mixed bag. Currently it is the 4th largest budget item behind the Department of Defense, Medicare, and Medicaid. A significant portion of the official public debt, currently at about $17.5 trillion, is held in short term bonds of about 2 years, which need to be rolled over as they mature. They are currently at historically low interest rates due to the recent deflationary environment, quantitative easing, and a severe economic recession. These combined have given us artificially low rates averaging about 2%, so the general debt-service (interest payment) on all instruments held by foreign and domestic investors amounts to no more than about 6.5% of spending, and about 1.4% of GDP, which is currently about $220 billion in annual outlay.

In 2013, the total debt service was $421 billion, or about double what the public was led to believe. That amounts to about 12.2% of outlays, or 2.6% of GDP. This includes payments on some or all of the unfunded obligations which are generally left out of publicly stated budget figures, but are serviced from the general budget nonetheless. We have seen the percentage of outlays for debt service in the 15% range recently during the 1990's, as confidence in, and demand for US government debt instruments was greater, so interest rates were commensurate.

Interest rates have fallen to historic levels, which has contributed to the debt problem by creating less of an incentive for the government to spend with its means, instead of massively borrowing at cheap rates. What will happen when we see bonds needing to be rolled over at rates of 6%, 8%, 10% or 15%, the likelihood of which is very high within the next decade? What will the debt service be as we need to roll over $20 to $25 trillion at 8% or 12% in order to finance it?

At 8% an official publicly held debt of $22 trillion will require interest payment of $1.76 trillion, to become the single largest budget item. Estimating the growth rate of public debt to continue to significantly outpace GDP growth, I will estimate at that time, GDP might be in the range of ~$18.5 trillion, so debt-service payment would be ~ 9.5% of GDP, and this does not include unfunded obligations. Project the trend out for another decade, and see what happens. There is significant sleight of hand at work. We will not outrun the debt bomb. It is easy to see that debt service could become the single largest US government budget item, squeezing out all other. There is the possibility of debt-service growing to consume 25% or more of GDP, which would nearly double current federal revenue from all sources. That is a very real near-term possibility.

Any person with a modicum of sense can see the writing on the wall. This means the US Government and the nation as a whole are insolvent, and the situation unchanged, is not likely to ever recover balance or solvency. It is my belief that at some point in the last 50 years, the nation as a whole has gone past the point of no return. As the Caesar declared, *'the die has been cast,'* and total collapse is an inevitability.

Even if we were able to reform and make the hard choices to spend within our means, or were to be forced by circumstance to spend less, still the service on the debt exceeds our ability to ever repay. Modern Keynesian economic theory which in-part drives the politic of the profligate spending today dictates that whenever an economy produces at less than optimum capacity, the government should make up the difference by spending, which usually means considerable inefficient and wasteful busy-work spending. This 'theory' was developed by the Fabian socialist John Maynard Keynes in the early 20th century and is widely and erroneously credited with helping end the great depression of the 1930s. However, back then, the country was hardly massively in debt as today, while the industrial base was on a significant upward trajectory, with little foreign competition domestically, and had not recently been decimated by globalization, which is the sad reality today.

Left to flounder as it is, the prospect for the nation to rise from the economic decline it suffers today is not a good one. Having said that, there is still tremendous potential for recovery in our future, with significant growth, if we successfully change the fundamental structure of our civilization. All hope is not lost, but the needed change will require significant restructuring of our monetary system, and not a mere refinancing or simple reform, which is akin to rearranging the deck chairs on the Titanic.

In the following chapters, I lay out a very sound idea and method based on sound economic principles for taming and eliminating the debt burden from the nation. It is very simple as it employs the basic fundamentals of capitalism, and when understood, it becomes quite clear that the problem is much easier dealt with than common wisdom would suggest.

CHAPTER FOURTEEN
Debt Solution

The Debt is Only as Good as the Money

So what are the popular prescriptions for the solution to the looming debt crisis? If you listen to the popular media, talking-head pundits, economists, and politicians, you are told on the one hand by the Democratic Party prescription, that we can only solve the problem by more of the same; government must massively increase wasteful spending on social programs, with massive raising of taxes on the diminishing rich and the diminishing middle class, as sort of steal and pilfer more from the sheeple to give it to the free-booters approach; A Keynesian-Steroidal solution, the logic of how this accomplishes anything being lost on all rational thinking persons. Indeed the end of the Keynesian con-job, has most assuredly finally come.

And on the other side, the view of the Republican party, that we can only solve the problem by massively cutting the graft and profligate spending, and massively cut the crippling taxes which so burden the business class, so as to allow the economy to grow greater than the rate of debt accumulation and debt service. Theirs is a sort of cut back, scrimp, and earn our way out of it approach. However, political realities being what they are, neither of these are viable or realistic at this point. While in years past, the Republican Party prescription was the most popular and responsible with the masses, and probably had the greatest chance of success in forestalling the inevitable crisis, the democratic approach is the clear choice for those who favor, and are reliant on socialist graft for sustaining their lifestyle. The fact is, neither party has ever been able to get a handle on the massive irresponsible spending, which is by far the most distinguishing characteristic of both parties, which in my view, means that we have at this time and probably at some point in the past 25 years, passed the point of no return; meaning the problem is not really solvable by conventional thinking, but will require some measure of 'dissipation'[75] and pain before the natural forces that govern the universe once again set things right.

The financial economy we have created, like electricity or gravity, is governed by the laws of nature, and when harnessed, it may yield a system useful and beneficial to mankind, or one that has the potential to destroy us. We must recognize that the financial economy, just as any other phenomena that interacts in our lives, is governed by natural forces, and with neglect it will at times act just as other powerful forces of nature; like hurricanes, floods, earthquakes, etc., and so it is not hopeless, but with the correct application of some simple and sound economic principles in harmony with the natural order, the inevitable decline which must occur, will accelerate so that healing may occur.

Debt acts as a drag on the economic machine which becomes very inefficient. Debt destroys profit by forcing higher interest rates and taxes thus making growth much more expensive, greatly restricting credit and the necessary capital. Without the prospect of making a profit, growth and prosperity are not possible. In time past, restructuring the debt (digging the hole deeper by refinancing), may well have been the simplest and most direct way to deal with it, but it will not solve anything at

---

[75] Absorbing or dispelling the energy from a traumatic impact or occurrence.

this point. At best, that would only give a very short reprieve by kicking the can down the road once again.

If a new national entity (nation) and identity is to be established, or if we are only able to achieve the preservation of the existing one for a while longer, it is paramount that the service of the debt not be a priority nor interfere in the slightest with the renewed progress of the nation. Because of this, the only way it makes sense is if the real burden of debt is massively reduced in real terms through a massive debasing of the dollar to the point that it is effectively worthless, and we are well along that path now. This may just be the likely outcome of attempting to fix or preserve the old system, or likewise of a new nation being carved from the old, and is certain to be the result of doing nothing.

The debt is only as good as the currency in which it is denominated. Allow the dollar to assume its real nominal value near zero and the debt will effectively disappear. The question becomes, how we accomplish that? In short, we have a monumental problem, and it appears, no solution, only a few very bad options. The first is default or repudiation, and the better one which is referred to below as an alternative to repudiation is called 'substitution', or replacement. We replace something that is essentially worthless, the dollar, with something worth a whole lot more, a new sound currency; then let the two (or more), compete. There is no default with this one, and it accomplishes much more.

Repudiation

One of the likely bad options would be the repudiation of the debt, but with some degree of mitigation for the severe consequences that are sure to follow.

From: http://www.merriam-webster.com/dictionary/repudiating

re pu di ate

Function:

transitive verb

Etymology:

Latin *repudiatus,* past participle of *repudiare,* from *repudium* rejection of a prospective spouse, divorce, probably from *re-* + *pudēre* to shame

Date: 1545

1: to divorce or separate formally from (a woman)

2: to refuse to have anything to do with : disown

3 a: to refuse to accept ; *especially* : to reject as unauthorized or as having no binding force <*repudiate* a contract> b: to reject as untrue or unjust <*repudiate* a charge>

4: to refuse to acknowledge or pay <*repudiate* a debt>

*(Notice that the dictionary definition makes it clear that the word is derived from the Latin for **shame**).* The definition **3** above fits our current situation best and really describes the reality of how the debt came about.

It is clear, to repudiate is to walk away and refuse to accept responsibility for the debt. This is not the same as bankruptcy where the country as a whole would be in receivership and under the control of some governing authority, with the power to impose austerity measures, and the wholesale seizure of assets without recourse or compensation. Nor is it under eminent domain by foreign debt holders. Eminent domain is the case with small countries when they cannot pay back their loans and the **IMF** (International Monetary Fund - the globalist loan-shark enforcer organization), under the auspices of the global banking cartel, steps in to give a few very painful choices.

In this case, repudiation means that we, the people, and sovereign states, simply refuse to pay it. We walk completely away from the debt while we maintain our integrity, and sovereignty. This is as cognizant and as solemn an act on our part as was the purposeful accumulation that put it upon us. Although it does mean default, so it will require an extraordinary structure. Because the bulk of the public debt is held by the Federal government, and not the states or the people, the debt is not valid. It simply becomes un-collectable if the government that holds the debt itself no longer exists. A new alignment or union of states would not be obligated by the debt even though many would argue otherwise. Even if a case could be made that the states or the people could be held liable for repayment, there is really no ability to enforce the debt or force payment on a new entity that will not accept it, and has the power to enforce that repudiation. Does this mean we hand over an equivalent in our wealth and resources? The answer is unambiguously, NO. That is what is meant by un-collectable. The debt is not valid, so it is unenforceable.

A very powerful argument can be made, and it can be credibly demonstrated, that the people and thus the nation are not liable for this debt because at some point in our history, the federal government had been co-opted by interests that drove that debt and engineered a campaign of complete destruction of the wealth and economy of the country, contrary to the interests of the nation. At no time did the people, meaning those endowed with legitimate political right, the SPEP, as a whole nor a majority, approve nor condone such reckless accumulation of debt on their behalf. Attempting to force the existing reckless debt on a new entity which will not accept it, would accomplish nothing.

On the other hand, a new structure emerging coincidently with repudiation would not be burdened to operate under the current corrupt global banking cartel system, nor the exceedingly small number of individuals and narrow interests which comprise the power network that has dominated the global financial system for more than 150 years, at the expense of the masses. If properly structured, a new entity could operate on probably 1/16th (6%) or less of the previous arrangement for a given population and GDP equal to that of the old. That would mean the average person would not have to pay an estimated 50% of his working wage now consumed by the cartel. The newfound freedom from debt burden could instead be used to fund productive and meaningful purposes that would benefit our civilization as a whole, not just the all consuming federal and state bureaucracies serving hegemonist schemes. However, given that it would constitute a default, repudiation may bring about a severe restriction on the acquisition of credit from abroad, and even among our own people. It may also affect trade, and the ability to obtain some materials needed for longer term planning.

Alternative to Repudiation

There is a better option to absolute repudiation of the national debt that will replace the old failing monopoly Federal Reserve monetary system, and the monopoly debt it has created, which can be done in a specific way while mitigating fallout and the pain to the nation at large, and would certainly be acceptable to a new national entity, although it may involve more than one option depending on pathology and progress. The process is to develop a second competing currency to the dollar that will reflect the real value of the wealth of the nation, and gradually exchange this currency for the old as it declines. Indeed, there are many significant economic advantages that will accrue to the nation and the people by this process which will be discussed below. A prerequisite for this process is that the new currency must be sound;[76] backed by real assets; not monopoly chartered but competitive; and it must be absolutely accountable. It is also desirable that it be

---

[76] In good-standing: in quality, and reputation.

somewhat immune to inflation or debasement by the whims of politicians, bankers, and the churners of money. It absolutely can not be considered as 'fiat', meaning it can not have any legal tender mandate of face value; instead its value and integrity must be regulated, certified, and guaranteed.

Understanding the necessity of the second competing currency is simple. Consider that if you hold securities such as stocks and bonds, you are told to diversify to mitigate against the possibility of total failure if you hold too much of any one issue; the *"don't put all your eggs in one basket"* strategy. The more diversified your portfolio, in theory, the more you are immune to a total failure if any one security goes bad. We have at present that exact scenario and so based on fear of a possible failure of the dollar, and the rest of the world economy with it, people are instinctively attempting to diversify by holding some substitute for the dollar. When that inevitable failure becomes pronounced and it is evident that we can not continue the same as before, the economy of the nation at large, and other nations, will still continue, although dramatically diminished; because people will continue to transact business using barter and substitutes for the worthless paper currency, although at a greatly diminished rate.

That being said, the new condition can not be closely compared to the old because of the scope of the losses, shortages, ruination, destitution, and despair that will dominate the economy. The closest substitutes for paper currency that are accumulated as a hedge against that day, and such that fit the purpose, are commodity metals such as gold and silver, followed by stocks in companies that are financially sound and positioned to survive and even do well when the economy fails, such as producers of food and basic necessities, with a shedding of the stocks from more discretionary goods and services producers. Again, these are a good hedge for the individual against the day of reckoning, but for the nation as a whole, they lack some very desirable characteristics which paper currencies have, especially when attempting to rebuild and restore a nation's economy and functions, and those are portability and liquidity, among others. The dollar, as is the case with all paper currencies, is very portable, denominable, and can be represented electronically thus it can be held by individuals in virtually any amount or denomination and so used in instant exchange for very minute amounts in the transaction, or transmitted instantaneously anywhere in the world. In contrast, try getting change in gold for a 1oz gold coin from the grocer. This just makes the case for the indispensability of paper currency as the lubricant of modern economies.

It is without question, that a reduction in the real burden of debt would usher in a new age of prosperity and entrepreneurial vigor similar to a much earlier time in the history of the United States before the people were convinced of their status as mere 'tax payers' who's function vis-à-vis the government, is to furnish money and power to further the schemes of those who co-opted the government, who have harnessed its power to their own purposes. Indeed, a renewed financial era, if combined with sound monetary, banking, and proper governance, would create condition for sustained and meaningful growth rates equal with or greater than the annual 10% to 15% that was seen in the nation during most of the 17th through the 19th centuries.

A Hypothetical Standard

The following outlines the hypothetical in which a new political paradigm reins in the significantly reformed nation, or a preferably brand new one derived from the old. A revolutionary monetary system is also needed at this juncture. A new century is upon us and it calls for a new monetary system more able to serve the need, while old systems designed for the state of the world economy and the US a century ago, can not adequately serve.

The following hypothesis is strictly for the purpose of discussion, and not intended to be taken as an actual proposed measure. That being said, it is with hopes that something like the discussion is borne, and an actual proposal and plan be adopted, while the alternative of doing little or nothing is unthinkable. Consider if such a quality new currency (discussed above) could be created and adopted by a new national entity, and an exchange rate could be established between the new currency standard, and the dollar; where the value of one unit of the new is initially, arbitrarily set at one thousand dollars ($1000); a convenient number for the sake of illustration, which coincidently also roughly reflects the current cost of production for an ounce of 0.999 pure (24-karat) gold, but not the market price of the metal. In actuality, the current average cost of production is about $1,100 in inflation adjusted terms. This is to establish a standard.

I considered several names for the new coin, which really only serves as a limited intrinsically valuable physical token of the paper version. I immediately decided against using the name *'dollar'* due to the obvious confusion with the current original, and federal laws that prevent that name from being co-opted. Several names seemed worthy of consideration: like the *'Dram'*, which is derived from the greek word *'drachma'*; a unit of mass, but already named for Armenian currency. If you think you have already heard the word *Dram'* used, ironically it is because the word is used in Scotland and elsewhere to refer to drinking alcoholic beverages such as scotch whiskey, as in *"I'm having a wee dram."* All double-meaning confusion aside, the name is less important than what it represents. The name should be something that conveys confidence and describes the object.

I have also considered the *'Tresor'*, which is a greek root word for the english word *'Treasure.'* The word *'Trove'* or maybe *'Troven'*, is also associated with treasure; and the word 'Bull', which is derived from *'bullion'*, the name for refined gold and other metals, and also the bovine-*bull*, a favored word used to describe people who are generally optimistic about markets, business, and economic matters. However, the *'Bull'* is unfortunately also negatively associated as an ancient and historic symbol of paganism and the occult, something with an already negative connotation when associated with money. I would eliminate the name *'bull'* for that reason. Not to create confusion, I would also eliminate any derivative of the words *'karat'* or *'carat'*, both of which derive from a greek word for a unit of weight. Regardless of the name chosen, the principle to which it applies is more important, so we will choose to use a variation of the name *'Dram'*, calling it the *'Dramen.'*

Now let's make the *'Dramen'* a standard coin composed of one full ounce of 0.999 pure (24-karat) gold, which puts the dollar at about one-one thousandth $(1/1000^{th})$ of a Dramen. If we then give a designation of its $1/1000^{th}$ denomination, we can call that the Mili-Dramen, since $1/1000^{th}$ is designated by the greek *'mili'*, but lets call it the *'Minidram'* instead since that rolls off better. Back to the notion of the coin representing a standard. Ideally a standard is something fixed over long lengths of time for reliability, like a unit of weight is fixed and does not change. The difficulty is in attempting to establish a baseline or standard of value. A standard unit of value, composed of a commodity metal like gold may vary considerably due to several factors, but mainly due to scarcity of supply with high demand which can be summed up as market conditions. For this reason, I have chosen to base the value on the average cost of production over a number of years rather than the market price, which will fluctuate considerably more. I believe gold is the best suited for this purpose, but I am not an expert on this subject, so it is conceivable that there may be something better suited, with a considerably more stable cost of production, and other more attractive qualities. The case for gold being the best suited is based on a few factors:

1) It has historically been used as a standard due to it having some intrinsic value, and the fact that it will not corrode.

2) It has a very high industrial use so no matter what happens to market conditions, it will always retain some value.

The advantage of establishing a baseline standard of value is that it can be used as a cornerstone, or point of reference when imputing value to any other economic object. From manufactured products, commodities, services, real property, along with everything else; all need to have their appraised value derived from a baseline of reference.

So summing up we have a new hypothetical currency standard coin called the Dramen worth approximately 1000 US dollars, with one Minidram (1 mĐ) worth about 1 US dollar.

1 Đ (Dramen) = 1oz. 24k gold

1 Đ (Dramen) ~ $1000 USD (initial exchange rate)

1 mĐ (Minidram) ~ $1.00 (US Dollar)

Gold Coin as General Currency

The reasons stated above for the preference of gold as a standard has a history which happens to overlap its suitability and preference as currency, however, the case for gold as currency no longer holds. Gold along with silver have been the preferred substance for making coins for use in general commerce because of its positive attributes, such as the fact that it guarantees its own baseline value intrinsically, it does not rust or tarnish, and because its portability and liquidity were suitable for the more primitive economies of the recent past which were not nearly as sensitive to issues of convertibility, portability, liquidity, and denominability,[77] which is the ability to be represented in fractions or denominations. Although, for a modern economy, the problems associated with using gold or silver coin as a

---

[77] How easily it can be divided by smaller amounts or other forms.

currency for general circulation are many, and some of those problems are as follows:

• For an entity to issue currency against a reserve, it must first own or obtain the assets stored in the reserve. This is the main argument, and repudiation against those that hold to the notion of US congressional monopoly of issuance being cited in the constitution. The government can only issue enough to cover what is needed if it possesses the gold, which it currently does not. It currently has only 261 million ounces, worth about $350 billion. What is needed under the current hypothesis for maintaining sound money (or virtually any other substitution scenario) is an asset base of value representing all currency (USD), in circulation and debt. This would require and astronomical amount of gold which our current government, does not possess, nor does any country or bank.

• There is a limited supply of gold and silver in the world, and most of it not in the US, so there is little prospect of achieving the substitution scenario using gold or silver alone.

• It would put limits on other uses for these metals, which are significantly industrial and commercial, because they must be reserved for capital. Gold has varied commercial use that would be discouraged if it was to become a general currency.

• A currency composed of a commodity such as gold is subject to the problems of the fluctuating supply and price of that commodity which can destabilize the value of the currency in relation to other markets and commodities. As an example, if the currency of the realm is made of gold, then any new supply of the currency which is needed to expand the economy must be limited proportionately to that of any new supply of gold that can be acquired and converted into the currency. Because gold is scarce it chokes the supply of capital necessary which significantly limits economic growth, and would render the country to 3rd world status.

• Precious metal coin is not as portable or as liquid as is necessary for a flexible and fluid modern economy.

Backing by Gold or Oil

A paper currency representing units of a single commodity such as gold or oil would have considerable advantage regarding flexibility, and portability, over the commodity itself serving as the currency, however, just like the commodity itself, it is subject to the problems of the fluctuating price and supply of the backing commodity which can destabilize the value. As an example, barring the practice of extreme leverage from fractional reserve banking, if the currency is only backed by gold at a unitary[78] reserve rate, then any new supply of the currency must be limited proportionately to that of any new supply of the commodity acquired and vaulted by the issuing entity. That price is of course also subject to world supply and demand forces which would likewise create an undesirable instability. Problems range below:

• Limits on the other usage of the backing commodity. As has already been discussed, the backing commodity must be mostly reserved for capital formation. Gold's varied industrial and commercial uses would be discouraged if it was to become a sole wholesale backing for a general currency.

• A paper currency with a de-facto backing commodity such as crude oil suffers the eventual decline and failure of the oil producing sources. It is believed by many economists, historians and the like, that the decline in the supply of easily obtained crude oil is at least a contributing factor to the current eminent failure of the US dollar.

These reasons alone are sufficient to eliminate both gold and crude oil, or for that matter, any other single or limited group of commodities as singularly suitable for use as currency or even as the major backing for paper currencies.

---

[78] 1 for 1

So while discussing the need for a new currency, and outlining an example of a new currency construction, what is the purpose of discussing the attributes of gold or other commodities as above in such a manner that would conclude with reasons why they are not suitable as a currency, or for backing one? The answer is firstly that even with a brand new currency constructed completely outside of the usual parameters, and all of the flaws and failure associated with attempting to instill intrinsic value, it is still an effort in the correct direction and better than relying on a complete fiat solution, therefore it may be done in a limited way. Secondly, there is always the need for a standard or baseline of value, and there must be some limited production of this standard in physical form available as discussed above in the context of the treatment of 'coin' as laid out in the US constitution. The founders of the republic also recognized the necessity for a standard and that is why it was done. In this case, just as in the past, the standard defines in physical form what money is and it's worth.

So summing up to this point, we have a new hypothetical monetary standard in Bullion form called the Dramen (Đ) made of 1oz. of 24K pure gold, and its fractional thousandth denomination, the MiliDram (mĐ), or MiniDram, which rolls off the tongue better. The Dramen serving as a standard, and the MiniDram, in paper form, serving as an initial probable substitute, in competition with, and in exchange for the US Dollar, and as a utility currency issue, meaning it and other derivative denominations would be used in everyday commercial/retail exchange, printed, and issued by banks. We have also established the need for the currency be paper in terms of flexibility and other qualities, or composed of something which gives the same utility as paper. We also have established that it can not be backed by a singular commodity due to supply and demand issues. I might also throw in that it must have the quality that it may be represented electronically as is the dollar today.

We have not really outlined anything extraordinary yet. Some aspects of this discussion are somewhat similar to what many other proposals have called for during times of financial crisis and in relatively prosperous times as well. Although these proposals generally call for a complete replacement of all dollars with gold coins, or a new fiat money such as an index composed of a basket of other fiat currencies (Euros, Dollars, Pounds, etc), or else backed by limited commodities as discussed above. Hopefully we have given ample good reasons why these will not work in the debt-substitution scenario under discussion.

Summarizing what we have proposed:

• A limited discussion of the need for a new currency and not an attempt to fix the old one. In our opinion, the old one must end, or diminish significantly for reasons to be discussed below.

• The new issue (currency) must be sound, meaning it must carry intrinsic value, or be represented (backed) by hard assets. It can not have a fiat legal-tender mandate for face value; it must be consistent in its worth long term, not subject to inflating; be resistant to debasement; and able to be supplied in sufficient quantity to meet economic demand which eliminates or redefines certain value backing parameters.

• It must be sufficiently portable, liquid, and denominable, which requires that it be available in paper form as well as a limited precious metal issue.

• We have a hypothetically proposed example, the Dramen and MiliDram; a new currency standard that fits the requirements above, and its derivative for commercial and retail use.

• What has not been discussed is how the new currency achieves the qualities as described for soundness and integrity inorder to insure it is able to replace the failing dollar, and zero out the debt. That discussion follows in the chapter titled

'Competitive Self-Leveraging Monetary System', after some background details.

• In addition, what is not yet discussed is how it will be introduced for general use, and what the likely economic effect will be. That discussion also follows.

What happens as the new currency is introduced is dependent to a large extent on what the political paradigm is at the time. Consider that at the present time, the Federal Reserve is a monopoly banking and monetary system, and the US dollar has no legal domestic competition within the country. It presently has a monopoly charter from the US Federal Government to originate all the currency used by the government, all individuals and corporations, and all issued by US banks. This means that a new currency issue may not circulate in competition with it. The fact that the currency being issued by the federal reserve is fiat and in its death-throws due to debt, globalization, and the other fatal flaws which afflict all fiat currencies, and it is denominated in the form of US government debt instruments sold around the world, and the fact that the US dollar is the largest designated reserve currency held by investors, banks, and institutions around the world, means that not only is the American financial system destined to suffer the same fate as the currency, but it is likely to severely damage a great deal of the economies of the world while in the process of collapse. We are all caught up in its death-throws.

In any case, if we assume we are able to introduce a new sound currency, banking, and monetary system into the US or a new political derivative of the US, in a way that will allow it to take its natural course, goods things will ensue. The objective is to mitigate the inevitable fallout that will happen when the US dollar fails altogether. The same type of system can be adopted by other economies as well with likely similar results.

Inverse Application of Gresham's Law

Gresham's law is named after Sir Thomas Gresham, a 16th century English financier during the Tudor dynasty. The law basically observes that *'Bad money drives out good'* or more specifically, *'Bad money drives out good under legal tender laws'*, which is a way to say that the introduction of new 'bad' or debased currency will drive the old 'good' or un-debased currency out of circulation because patrons will horde the good and pass the bad on in transaction. This is because legal-tender laws mandate that both be used and treated at the face value, despite one having a much less intrinsic value than the other. Now why would anyone want to do that? During this period of history, it was common for a cash strapped kingdom to issue debased currency into the realm because the treasury was depleted as is the case today, but the currency of the realm itself generally was made of gold or silver so it was intrinsically valuable, but it may have been the case that not enough was vaulted in the kings treasury. The king would therefore issue a legal tender law for the new issue of coin which was made of something inferior (debased) to the old, and thus worth much less than its face-value would indicate. This was done in an attempt to gain by cheating the peasants. In order to get the intended effect from the issuance of new currency, there had to be a royal decree that mandated both the old and the new were equal and must be taken at face value, even though it was evident in the minds of those that used the coin, that they were not equal in value. History, and the wiles and schemes of men are not without a sense of irony, as the peasants invariably chose to almost exclusively pay their taxes to the king with the debased coin.

If we were to introduce the new hypothetically sound or 'good' currency (mÐ - Minidram) into general circulation in sufficient quantities along side of the US dollar, but disregard the legal tender mandate as stated above in Gresham's law, the effect would be exactly the inverse. Keep in mind the minidram does not have a fiat face value mandate like the dollar does, but its face value is real and guaranteed by asset backing. Instead of the old 'bad' currency (US dollar) driving the new good currency (minidram) out of circulation, people would instinctively instead start to refuse to take the old bad dollar in transactions, in favor of the minidram, thus ensuring, and hastening the dollar's quick demise. Massive dumping of the US dollars, and all dollar denominated instruments would ensue, the dollar would then deflate to its nominal real (near zero) value. It would finally be laid to rest along with the corrupt entity that spawned it. The rate of displacement of the old would depend on the rate that the new was introduced into circulation. Extraordinary planning and systems would have to be constructed and put into place to support the new; we outline that later.

Impact of New Monetary System

As the new currency progressed in the process of monetization, distribution, and acceptance, the exchange rate between the MiliDram (mĐ), and the Dollar, initially set at about 1 for 1 (mĐ/$USD), would quickly begin to change to some intermediate rate of probably 1 for 1000 to 10,000, and eventually in a few months to years, reach some level that could approach 1 for 1 million. This means that 1 mĐ could buy $1,000,000 as the dollar approached its real value near zero. Thus the dollar, being a fiat currency, and having no intrinsic value other than that of paper and ink, it would suffer a 1 millionth depreciation in a short period, a truly Weimar Republic, or Argentine level event, but the economy of the region would still remain intact, more or less operational and be very much on a significantly more healthy path to recovery than any time in recent history. The trillions of fiscal, foreign, and other dollar denominated debt would suffer the same fate, and be reduced proportionately in real terms.

All dollar denominated instruments would then also revert to their real value with respect to the real economy and as a result, the holders of these instruments would suffer that adjustment in real terms, but the counter-parties to these would realize a benefit in real terms. Those with mortgages, notes, loans, etc. would see the balance owed disappear and they would quickly become the sole owners of their property. The national debt would quickly disappear and the account could then be balanced out; the greatest payoff of debt that the world has ever seen. Those debtors with home mortgages, business loans, or anybody owing anything in dollars would be the tremendous beneficiaries, while those debt holders with cash, bonds, bills, notes, annuities and pensions, etc. would see their holdings adjusted to reflect the real near zero value. To be fair, if this process were to happen, it would need to be publicized well in advance to give those that are likely to be disadvantaged a chance to mitigate their circumstances beforehand.

This is in no-way a perfect solution or scenario. It may or may not execute predictably, or without fallout. Remember the objective was to mitigate an inevitable failure that would otherwise be much more devastating. This can be compared to having airbags in your car, or not, during a severe accident. Either way there is likely going to be a traumatic and devastating event in which many people may be killed or injured, but having airbags is way preferable to not. To be sure, there will still be serious disruptions, displacements, shortages and situations that may render millions of individuals and families in hopeless situations, but the outcome will be much less devastating than would be the case had individuals not preplanned, prepared, and acted in advance. Further, simply taking no alternative action to mitigate the looming disaster will result in significantly greater financial displacement than under this scenario.

Assuming we are able to muster the political will needed to once again take our destiny into our hands, and override the political strength of those that gave us the monopoly Federal Reserve system, and introduce a competing currency as described, means we are on a much better footing than before, but we have yet to discover how we get such a fantastic currency. We will examine that later, but suffice it for the time being that, that is not a problem with which we as a people have not any expertise. Indeed, obtaining such a quality currency is in-reality, a throwback to the past when western civilization really began to understand the power of capital and capitalism.

The question may arise, *"What about those individuals who are financially helpless or dependent on federal aid or pensions now; what will happen with them? Wouldn't it be better to leave the current system in place as it is, instead of hastening its collapse?"* The answer is that the collapse is a virtual certainty within a short period anyway, and to leave those failed systems in place that have so much contributed to and hastened the collapse till now, without any attempt to mitigate, is indefensible. It is much better to mitigate fallout now even though that may mean the most vulnerable are at the greatest risk, and stand to suffer disproportionately; that is already the case. Care must be taken as a society to ensure that everyone is taken care of to whatever measure possible and that we can learn again how to live within our means without the heavy hand of mindless utopian redistributionists, as we have in the past where each generation takes care of its own and does not steal and consume that which belongs to the next. If this is done, even the fallout amongst the most vulnerable will be mitigated to a large degree.

What about the morality of fact that this was an engineered action, like a controlled demolition, and some may suffer massive loss of their holdings as a result, while others may benefit to the same degree? Again, one must ask, what choice do we have? Consider that in my view, the collapse is an inevitability; history will support this. If these were shares of stock in a publicly held company, would the same question even be given consideration? Who would question it? It would be viewed as the risks associated with investing. The holders of shares, bonds, bills, notes etc. carry an intrinsic risk of total loss; the difference is minimal in this situation. There is always risk, regardless of circumstance. Also keep in mind that what happens is not a default on these obligations, but every holder is able to negotiate their disposal, so are remunerated in full.

The elimination of public debt would unleash the entrepreneurial vigor in the nation like it has never been before, because in the interim years since the last time the nation enjoyed very low levels of debt, we have gained significantly in assets that enhance productivity, such as a more literate and educated population, advance in computer and communications technology, infrastructure, tools, markets and so on. The greatest challenge is how to avoid falling back into corrupt patterns once again, and we believe that if those steps outlined above regarding the integrity of the currency and the monetary system work, it itself will resist the tendency toward the frivolous accumulation of debt.

CHAPTER FIFTEEN

Old Monetary System

Monetary Systems

Modern monetary and banking systems require a stable and sound currency that will serve the needs of the population who use it for daily transaction. The ideal currency must be non or low inflating, meaning that it must be of quality issue and carry an intrinsic (self contained) value or be bonded to something of constant, reliable, and predictable value. Then, the supply in and out of circulation must remain proportionally fixed to the economic-output[79] created by the issue, and it should not be limited by the supply of whatever underlying collateral commodity is bonded in reserve to establish the value. It must also be flexible enough to allow moderately unrestricted economic growth while maintaining proportionality. It must be available in sufficient quantity to meet arbitrary demand by whatever bank issues it to avoid a bank run scenario. These requirements bear upon the practice of fractional reserve.[80]

---

[79] Monetary sum of all goods and services.
[80] The practice of vaulting only a fraction of what is loaned, thus creating monetary expansion in-which there is more representing the true value in circulation than what is held.

Capitalism and Monetary systems

What is capital, and capitalism? Capitalism is a system for using valuable assets which are at the disposal of organizations and individuals, employed by leverage to enhance the living status. It is essential in providing margin against the elements of decay which threaten the survival of the civilization.

Capitalism is not a political system as has been erroneously taught and believed for generations. The falsehood has been propagated as a conflation of the capital economic system with that of a political system. There are no human systems of political organization existing today, or that have ever existed, which operate absent the practice of capitalism. This is important in understanding the error of those who conflate the two. The 2 systems are separate and distinct and serve different purposes. Capitalism transcends time and the political schemes of men. Throughout time, good and bad political systems have come and gone while capitalism remains. It is universal and enables political systems.

Capitalism is a process whereby capital assets are leveraged inorder to produce more of the same, thus enriching the process. In the process resulting in the creation of more capital, the increase or gain is called profit.

Capitalism is a natural tool, meaning its practice comes somewhat as a natural outcome of the human need for survival and survival could not occur without its practice. Like any tool, it is intended to be used for the survival, prosperity, enhancement, liberty, and advancement of civilization, but it can also be used to control and suppress the same elements.

It may be lost upon some that there is more than one way capitalism is practiced. Modern societies have been swayed to practice a pure form of large scale group capitalism at the extreme, meaning, the individual is forced to surrender his own right to practice individual capitalism except to a very limited small scale inorder to allow for the creation of large monopoly pools of capital to be concentrated and controlled by a limited number of the members of a society that purportedly represent the interests of the whole; they are the narrow-interests.

The reality is, the narrow-interests who have garnered the power to monopolize the control of capital only represent their own interests and use power through the political system to secure their monopoly. The individual is more or less forced to abdicate his right to profit and create capital, or to so limit his involvement that it fails to adequately serve his need, and by this the practice of the production of capital has largely transferred to the group. This is a corruption and diminishing of advantage of the individual and thereby, the greater portion of the society as a whole. Instead the advantage only accrues to, and disproportionately benefits the narrow-interests.

This in contrast to what most have come to believe; that there is only one basic form or way to practice capitalism and that we in the west practice it in the optimum form; and further, that form of practice is emulated in much of the rest of the world. So as for example, here in the US, capitalism is practiced in such a way as to concentrate the control and formation of capital by virtual, but not complete, monopoly; by concentrating virtually all, but not all, capital in the hands of a small cabal[81] of organizations and individuals. The difference between the capitalism of the west and that practiced by communists and socialists is mostly that the latter group dominate and monopolize all, or virtually all of it, while in the west a very small amount, created and utilized by the common people is allowed. With current Chinese so-called communism, they temporarily allow capital to be utilized by members of Chinese society rather than restricting all of it to members of the communist party; a phenomenon which has

---

[81] Mostly the Federal Reserve banking monopoly, Global Corporations, and wealthy individuals.

been practiced on occasion by communist regimes inorder to build up their capital reserves.

The difference in these systems is illustrated by a continuum line, or spectrum, with communism on the far left, socialism in the middle-left, and the western form of limited individual monopoly-capitalism on the near left.

Spectrum of Political Systems

Far Left	Right		Non Aligned

Communism

Socialism (Europe)

Western Democracy/Republic (US)

SDM (US - Proposed)

Make no mistake, all capitalism practiced today is monopolized by small groups of globalist bankers, in contrast to the mistaken belief that the west has a free, unfettered capital marketplace where all parties are free to compete on an equal footing. Or that the Federal Reserve Central Bank is an unbiased, innocent, innocuous entity without interest in sides, and devoid of any political agenda. Nothing could be further from the truth. The American banking cartel play the part of a disinterested servant of the nation well, but in reality they dictate everything. The term *'Central Bank'* enters into the

American lexicon being interpreted by way of Marx and Engels as the 5th plank[82] in the *Communist Manifesto* with the exception that Marx called for the bank to be controlled by the state, while ours is in private hands. The difference means very little. The 5th plank states: *"Centralization of credit in the hands of the State, by means of a national bank with State capital and an exclusive monopoly."*

In the communist and socialist systems, all, or nearly all capital has been confiscated, and is 100% controlled by the party or those that maintain the structure. In past Russian and current Chinese communist systems, those in control were/are the communist party. In the west, a small limited practice is allowed by small unorganized or unaligned groups in the society. Anything above a threshold is confiscated by graduated taxes, interest, or other mechanisms designed to limit it.

The most extreme example is that of communism where the production of capital was transferred entirely to the narrow interest and not just a limitation put on the individual. In far leftists systems, generally all of the capital is appropriated by the party who divvy it out as favor to friends and deny it to enemies; as a result very little new capital is ever created. What little is left is owned and controlled by those who leverage the scarcity of capital to buy the power to maintain their monopoly control. They effectively outlaw the formation of capital at any level.

In the west the formation of capital is more free flowing and legally protected, but in practice it is also very limited by many mechanisms. The result is a total shift of all the power of production to control by the narrow-interests. To shore-up and maintain their concentrated advantage, they employ the political power given by their advantage, making it permanent by making it a law, then hiding behind the 'Rule of Law.'

---

[82] Karl Marx and Friedrich Engels, 1848

This is not an indictment of capital nor capitalism, but instead it is a reckoning of the evil side of human behavior and a corruption of law.

What Money Is

A discussion of exactly what money is, is needed in order to understand what makes the economy work. It is instructive to understand what money is not. Money is not currency, and currency is not money. Money is more closely tied to what wealth is. Wealth is composed of assets, titles, and other substantive things. Assets are often physical in form such as the property one might own. Assets can also be in the form of capacity, like the capacity to produce something useful and desirable when one owns a factory. Most individuals have wealth or money in the combination of capacity... the capacity to perform physical work, or a negotiable skill, and physical assets such as real estate, jewelry, automobiles, life insurance, stocks and bonds, etc. Nations hold wealth in reserves of minerals, lands, military assets, foreign trade contracts, educated populace, production capacity, and infrastructure, etc. It should be understood that if all of the dollars should suddenly disappear from the face of the earth, our money would still be with us.

What Currency Is

Likewise A discussion of exactly what currency is, is equally instructive for the simple fact that virtually everybody interacts with it on a daily basis. Just as with money, currency is not money, and money is not currency. Currency can be thought of as the vehicle or container with which money is transported, exchanged, and put to work making the economy operate. How well it performs that function though is very much dependent on how that currency came about, what guarantees its value and integrity, and what mechanisms are in place to regulate and enhance its performance. It can be thought of as distilled or concentrated wealth in a portable form. It also has the characteristic quality of 'liquidity' meaning that it flows through the economy just as blood must flow through all parts of the body, thus the word 'currency' which is from 'current' meaning to run or to flow. For it to 'flow' efficiently, it must be present in sufficient quantity, so the lack of abundant currency will diminish liquidity.

Creation of Banks

There are many good books,[83] and other resources available which outline the real and unwhitewashed history of banking in the US. So it is not necessary to go too deeply into the subject except to give an overview of a small aspect which makes a relevant point. The history of the accumulation and formation of pools of capital is instructive to understand the relevance of how banks were capitalized, who formed them, and who the beneficiaries are. In the US, banks largely came about by groups of wealthy people pooling their capital together to start a banking enterprise. Assets such as reserves of gold were accumulated then made convertible and liquid inorder to create and issue paper for the purposes of financial services, such as loans to creditworthy customers. This process led to all of the commercial and retail banks in the US. This seems to have been a sound and necessary process, creating the infrastructure and the capital necessary to build and expand the nation which certainly is the case, however, the same process also gave many of them the clout and position to put severe limitations on their competition.

It created the conditions necessary for monopolizing all capital into their hands, supercharging the return on the original investment into the enterprise. Today all banking in the US is insular or reserved in the sense that it is regulated through laws written by the same individuals who have garnered the

---

[83] The Creature From Jekyll Island, by GE Griffin.

formation and control of all capital. This refers to the Federal Reserve banking system under which all commercial and retail banks are required to operate. Even small individual capital formation cannot escape the monopoly, but is restricted under the Federal Reserve system. It is a legal requirement that all banks in the nation must use the 'product' of the central bank because they operate within the system controlled by the Fed banking cartel, and the international banking cartel around the rest of the world. The balance of western civilization works pretty much the same way. Despite all the power of their monopoly for the past 100 or so years, their systems are left terminally flawed and weakened by greed and the hubris brought about by their success.

Inflation, Deflation and the Business Cycle

In any monetary system, inflation is defined as the increase in the ratio of an increase in the money supply to the corresponding increase in production that occurs. As and example, if the money supply increases 8% but there is only a 5% increase in production (the result of productivity), then there is an approximate 3% (the difference) inflation. It is often exhibited by rising prices which are in reality a dilution of the existing currency being circulated without a proportional corresponding increase in goods, thus altering the supply/demand curve. If the increase in currency produces a proportional increase in output then there is no inflation. Monetary inflation of fiat currencies is thought to measure the efficiency of the monetary stimulus during an *'inflation-cycle.'* When issued at the early part of an economic cycle, currency will yield significant increase in productive output, while later in the same cycle it produces much less output for a proportionate amount of new issue. This decline in the increased output (growth) phenomenon is inflation, and usually requires a scaling back of the monetary stimulus. Recession, or the decline of the rate of economic expansion usually follows. This is a simple illustration of the mechanism that drives the business cycle; recession/recovery or boom/bust cycles that traditionally occur every 8 to 9 years in the US. A more appropriate designation would be to call it the 'Inflation Cycle', with which most Americans have become aware of through direct experience. Recessions have lasted around 18 to 24 months in the recent past, with expansion recoveries lasting from 5 to 6.5 years.

$$F = \frac{\Delta M}{\Delta G}$$

Inflation for F > 1, Deflation for F > 0 < 1
F = 'Flation' (Inflation/ Deflation)
M = Money Supply , G = Growth

Deflation is part of the same phenomenon and not the opposite of inflation. Both deflation and inflation are on the same continuum curve. On the 'flation' curve (F) of change in money supply versus change in production output, if the ratio is greater than one it is inflation and deflation if between zero and one. With deflation, there is an overabundance of goods and services produced in the absence of a corresponding increase of currency dumped into circulation. This is characterized as a glut or overproduction. Deflation creates a positive feedback (regenerative) cycle that feeds upon the result it creates. Prices of goods and services fall because of the way humans interact by delaying purchases while under the assumption that prices will continue falling, which in-turn creates less demand generating pressure for greater price reductions, thus renewing the cycle. This is referred to as a *'spiraling down'* effect and is very difficult to break. In the US at the time this is written, it is believed by many that deflation may be the predominant aggregate economic condition.

Many things may trigger deflation especially in a global economy where currency exchange rates may change and where one country runs a large trade deficit with another. As an example, when the Chinese produce so much of what the US consumes, if its currency in relation to the dollar is cheap then an abundance of these goods will flow into the US even in the absence of monetary stimulus from the Federal Reserve, the banks, or the Treasury. If the exchange rate between the Chinese currency and the dollar change again making Chinese goods even cheaper, then significant deflation may ensue. Another driver is the recent strangling of consumer credit brought about by the housing crisis and bank failures which has significantly reduced demand for housing thus causing a rapid decline in prices. This is really only the result of deflating the housing market bubble created by cheap credit overstimulation.

Fiat Currency

The name Fiat Currency comes from the latin word *'fiat'* meaning to Decree. Fiat currencies are characterized usually by their lack of a stable or marketable value because they lack intrinsic value and are not backed by sufficient tangible assets, or any at all. They are usually paper. Fiat currencies are more prone to cause high levels of inflation/deflation and suffer the diminishment of output phenomenon because for a large part they are usually only backed by a very intangible and fickle commodity called CONFIDENCE. Unfortunately when confidence diminishes, so does the value of the currency. This devaluation inspires more loss of confidence and a terminal death-spiral ensues requiring massive intervention by the issuing institution (central bank), and the government (taxpayers) unfortunate enough to labor under this very flawed monetary system. When a crisis of failing confidence ensues, the aim of the intervening institutions becomes one of injecting that elusive commodity back into the system which is a not so easy task. Adding to the problem is that fiat systems very quickly tend toward overburden by inflation and leveraging which creates a highly unstable environment in which crises tend to become more and more frequent and severe until a final collapse occurs.

Consider what the name refers to. Fiat, meaning *"I Decree"*, as if it was possible to imbue some sort of miracle of real wealth by decreeing it. It is what it implies. It is called fiat because there is an attempt to decree or legislate that it be accepted in exchange as if it has a value equivalent to what is written on the face of it, when it clearly does not. As was discussed before, this is accomplished though legal tender laws. It seems to be motivated in-part by some sort of God complex by those that believe they have the power to attain to supernatural feats. If it was possible to decree paper and ink to have intrinsic value sufficient for sound commerce, then it would follow that fiats could be issued and applied to world hunger, poverty, the laws of physics, natural disasters and any of the other laws of nature that tend to gum up the utopian schemes of men, in which case, the use of intrinsically worthless paper and ink as a means of commerce and the evil it perpetrates could be overlooked and forgiven in exchange for the beneficial acts of the 'gods.' Fortunately, people of experience and the sense that life teaches, when educated, recognize this as snake oil.

To illustrate why it is called a Fiat system, consider that our government is not concerned about the hardship of earning associated with the money of ours they spend, something that virtually every American is intimately aware of, and which they freely appropriate and spend at their whim in whatever amount they like just by passing a resolution. Budget deficits and national debt are not a concern. Never is there a concern about if there is or is not money available or where it will come from. They just decree it theirs to spend. This conjures up the idea that they believe that all the money belongs to them and is available without cost from some eternal wellspring which they alone have access to, and to a large extent that is exactly what the situation is. They spend it because it is there for them to spend. We the American people have ignorantly given them that power. Many Americans labor under the false belief that the government only spends the money they take in from taxes and fees or what is borrowed from other sources (the budget deficit). The fact is that the government could continue to spend at the exact rate as now without collecting one penny in taxes or borrowing a dime because they can order the mint to print it and deliver it to the treasury. They just create it from paper, ink, and thin air.

Fiat Banking

The first observation that should be noted about what are called *'Fiat Banking Systems'* is that they are characterized by numerous negative attributes that are generally viewed as corrupt, unstable, false, unjust, unsustainable, favoring one at the expense of another, and virtually any other negative adjective imaginable and it is not by accident but by design. Having noted this, in order to understand how we got here we must understand the system in which we are trapped at present. Now that we have clarified any ambiguity about our position regarding these corrupt institutions, we can proceed to describe them.

Modern banking systems are formed around a single monopoly central bank (the Federal Reserve in the US), and affiliate retail and commercial member banks used to distribute the money throughout the economy. In the fiat system, banks practice the fractional reserve system which allows them to lend out many times more than they reserve in the vault. This is predicated on the principle that not every one is going to withdraw all their money at the same time, so the bank does not need to keep all of the depositor's money in the bank at the same time but may make loans with some of it to finance the needs of the community.

If one remembers the scene in the film called *'It's a wonderful life'* where all the depositor's at the 'Bailey Savings and Loan' came and demanded their money at the same time, and George Bailey had to explain that he did not have all of their money now because one depositor's money was loaned to another depositor to build a house, and his intern was lent to a 3rd person and so on, but he guaranteed that they would get all of their money at some point. That was a depiction of what is called a bank run. While a good portion of the depositor's money was collateralized in loan notes which probably had the right to foreclose on the property in case of default, nonetheless, the cash on hand was insufficient to satisfy the demand.

Now consider what happens to the value of the depositor's money when there is a wholesale mass devaluation of the asset holdings that underlie the loans and ultimately the integrity of the banks; does that sound familiar? The whole system is way over-leveraged because the bank loans out more money than it really has thus inflating the value of the assets it loans against? When a contraction of the value of the assets occurs, suddenly the bank does not have enough to cover the depositors and a deflation spiral ensues and a margin-call may result, making the institution insolvent. There is currently in the US federal reserve system somewhere near 33 times as much lent out in loans (credit), than was issued and initially deposited into banks. This is due to fractional reserve monetary expansion in which the first dollar of hard value is deposited then a multiple of it in non-backed currency is loaned out and redeposited over and over again, thus creating a tremendous inflated bubble of credit. The supply of money in and out of circulation is 'controlled' by setting the 'reserve rate' of money that must be left in the vault to cover demand, and by setting the interest rates of the M1 and M2.[84]

Now consider that in a fiat system like our Federal Reserve, not only is the currency not secured or backed by tangible

---

[84] M1- Measure of new money created through monetary expansion. M2-Broad measure of money on deposit and in circulation. Includes M1.

assets, but the banks that distribute it use the fiat currency itself to back the loans they give against a run. Given a crisis of confidence in the currency, the government, the national debt, or the money held by the banks, would it not be more effectual in mitigating the risk of crisis if banks possessed in the vault, something more substantial that could used to reassure depositors, creditors, and the public at large, such as tangible hard stable assets like gold or other materials of unimpeachable integrity, instead of the un-collateralized inflated paper cash that has created the leveraged inflated bubble in the first place. So understand that as the currency is devalued by numerous mechanisms, the only thing the banks have on hand to guarantee the value of their depositor's money is more of the same rapidly depreciating paper currency. Despite depositor insurance and/or the massive intervention and injection of depreciating cash into the system, this is a highly leveraged, highly volatile system that will ultimately fail. The financial recession and crisis of 2000 and 2009 revealed the weakness and nearly resulted in the total unwinding of the flawed system. More about this later.

Limited Upside for Fiat Systems

The current version of this flawed system, having been adopted and instituted in the US at the turn of the 20th century, has endured for the long term to date by virtue of the fact that the negative effects of fiat systems are somewhat offset by increased productivity as technology advances and infrastructures increase. Global Free Trade is also a temporary stabilizing factor for a very short time, but ultimately adds to the instability. Global Free trade allows the US to import cheaply produced products from developing countries like China which would be more expensive to produce in the US, thus importing deflation to offset the inflationary effects of the cheap money stimulation that the government and the nation desire on a continuous basis. This only lasts for so long before it runs its course. These 'free' trade policies are also consequently, mostly responsible for the recent gutting of our productive industrial capacity.

The United States, Western Europe, Russia, Asia and virtually the entire developed and developing world have instituted these terminally flawed systems and are suffering some aspects of their effects. Some countries such as the US and those in Europe are presently suffering the more advanced negative effects such as unmanageable debt; the lack of ability to stimulate their economies; and the destruction of their productive capacity (jobs) which is being gutted and moved wholesale to the underdeveloped world, while China, Asia, and the developing countries of South America which are the beneficial recipients of the economic dismantling of the developed world are in the early more advantageous stages.

Additional infrastructure and increased technology created by the availability of cheap fiat money is a temporal positive for the world because it increases the capacity for nations to produce, something which underdeveloped, undercapitalized countries struggle with. However the tradeoff is not equitable, and the overall effects are nonetheless disastrous in the long run for all.

To Coin Money

The problems with worthless fiat currencies can be mitigated to a limited degree with backing (bonding) the paper currency to something of tangible value such as gold or some other eternally intrinsically valuable substance. For millennia the valuable material itself was made into coins, which is why old coins are virtually always gold or silver. Paper currency was introduced for common use as a more portable and liquid means for transporting and transacting when it was discovered that a paper certificate could be issued instead of the gold it represented. It was a better system, but with a devious side; it was also discovered that it could be counterfeited and inflated (diluted) by unscrupulous bankers and criminals, thus elaborate designs and measures were devised to counter the counterfeiters and cheats. Nonetheless, many shady persons and groups set about devising ways of perfecting elaborate systems by which they could cheat the average person or even a nation by use of paper currency, thus initially earning it a reputation of not being legitimate.

Creative ways of certifying the value of paper and its significant advantage of better greasing of the wheels of commerce became enough to overcome the objections so it was adopted for general use. One of the ways sought to secure the value of a paper note was to certify its value by using a certifying authority to guaranty that it represented the value of the gold or other assets in the vault that issued it. Amongst many of these ways were for instance, in the US, gold and silver certificates issued for this purpose.

On this point, there are several so called 'Patriot' groups and other self-appointed guardians and preservers of the American republic who many politically conservative patriotic minded persons admire for their vigilance and attitude, but who are nonetheless misguided on many fronts. Some of these make unsubstantiated and ignorant statements such as the US constitution exclusively authorizes the government the sole power to issue coin, and then only gold or silver coin and other such drivel. This implies that any other source or form of currency is forbidden. The fact is that the US founders knew better than to condemn the US economic future to the considerable restraint that this would impose on the country.

US Constitution Section 8, Paragraph 5 says: **The US Congress shall have the power....**"*To coin money, regulate the value thereof, and of foreign coin, and fix the standard of weights and measures:*"

Now the most noteworthy thing that should be inferred from this is that the US congress has the power to "*regulate the value thereof*" which means to determine and certify whether any and all particular coin (meaning money), is legitimate or not. Also note that foreign coins are mentioned and included. Now how does the congress do that? What does it mean to *"regulate the value thereof?"* Do they have the power to fix or regulate the price of gold or its supply? How would they do the same regarding foreign coin? Obviously it can not mean any of those, but instead it means to simply VERIFY and even CERTIFY by putting a stamp of approval on the coin by making sure no one has their thumb on the scale. This is simply consumer protection which is a legitimate function of government by *'fixing'*, meaning, setting and validating the *"standard of weights and measures."*

At the time it was written, paper currency was not widely adopted by the masses so gold and silver coin were the most common form of currency and the way coin or money was bonafide was to weigh it to make sure it met the standard for the weight represented, and use other tests to determine its purity and content. For this to be done accurately there must exist a standard for weight, size, purity, etc. What can be inferred from the section 8 paragraph 5 above is that the role of the government was to simply provide accurate standards which all parties could rely on to legitimize all forms of money. Inferences can also be made that the government had other roles in the regulation thereof such as specifying how and where it must be stored, distributed, allocated, represented, etc.

This section of the constitution means that even today the government has the mandate to apply this same concept to the certifying (regulating) paper currency as well as all paper securities as is evidenced by the role set for the SEC (Securities and Exchange Commission) which is to perform legitimacy regulation on all forms of securities. Many may argue as to whether the government is actually doing this competently or not, but it is certainly within the purview of the government to do so, and I would even argue that it is a critical and indispensable function of government. I would also argue that there is no prohibition, in the constitution, on entities outside of the US government from issuing coin or paper currency for general use in commerce, as long as the value of it is preserved, certified, and regulated by government oversight.

Now certainly this has failed with regard to the US Federal Reserve which is an entity that has garnered enough influence amongst the members of congress to allow it to avoid the necessary requirements for sound money. It has also unjustly deprived the people of the benefits that a competitive banking and currency system would provide by influencing the congress into giving this corrupt institution a monopoly charter, and in my opinion that is a violation of the word and spirit of the constitution.

It was pointed out earlier that for a government to be the sole issuer of money, it must possess that money or the backing for the money otherwise it must obtain it. Most would not like the methods the government would need to employ to obtain even a fraction of the tens to hundreds of trillions in assets for collateral to back a currency. Then where would that leave us except the bureaucrats would still control the purse not the people, and I think we have had enough of that.

So as for the power ***"To coin money"***, this allows the government to issue coin, which it does, but just as it is not with a private bank, one must not interpret this to mean it gives an exclusive monopoly to the government either, nor that the only currency allowed must be restricted in the form of coin or constructed from gold or silver. That is not what was intended and not what is said.

Vapor Banking

In the 1930s' under the FD Roosevelt administration, the US Federal Reserve Dollar was partially removed from the initial gold standard (certification of underlying value) and in the 1970s' under President R Nixon it was removed completely from the gold standard at which time it was also changed from a dollar to a note. Taking the Fed dollar completely off of the gold standard meant that the government was free to appropriate and spend money without limit while having no asset backing in the treasury or the Federal Reserve bank. In terms of accounting, when it was devised it must have seemed like a nightmare sleight of hand to those forced to reckon how this 'magic' could be accomplished.

On the balance sheet of the bank, one side showed X dollars are loaned out and the other side showed the same dollars to be printed, or simply a debt entry and promise to repay by the borrower. Think about this, when there is money borrowed from the Federal Reserve the only asset shown to balance this out is an entry showing a future promise to repay the debt with interest by the borrower, which in the case of the US government, it can be paid back with paper directly from the mint. Never is there anything in terms of hard assets required anywhere in the balance sheet of the Fed. Most banks need to show some hard asset at the very least; such as an automobile of equal value to the amount loaned, balancing the transaction. If you or I, or any corporation in this country or any other attempted this, we would be tossed in jail and the key forgotten.

Now changing it from a dollar or a precious metal certificate to a note implies insolvency was reached at some point, meaning there was not enough gold in the vaults of the fed banks to cover the paper and contracts in circulation. The federal reserve notes which we call dollars are in reality closer to the junk stocks of defunct corporations. It is now nothing more than a promise to pay the bearer, the value of the note with the same worthless paper the note represents. Upon demand for redemption of the note, the bearer is entitled to receive only the same notes in an equivalent amount and nothing more. If there is a total destruction of the perceived value of these notes or a collapse of the general economy, the bearers of the notes are not going to be able to redeem gold or anything of value from the Federal Reserve Bank or its affiliates. This along with it's monopoly status means that the US Federal Reserve Note, which Americans refer to as the dollar is in reality a worthless instrument which functions as a mechanism to continuously siphon off the entirety of the real wealth of the nation, to put it in the hands of bankers, large money interests, politicians and bureaucrats, and special political interests. Here is a question to contemplate: We have acknowledged and verified that the US Federal Reserve is a monopoly. In the board game monopoly, what is the worth of the game's money in the real world?

Like in the discussion concerning all civil constructs, the manner in which the common people discover and view capital and monetary system civil constructs will greatly effect their future standing. The value of money and it's underlying asset is determined by supply and demand, which is played out through an auction. If it is free to one then it is free to all. The status of no cost to the fed and the government, while at high cost to everyone else is a charade which cannot last forever.

The Federal Reserve Bank,
Affiliates, & all Fiat systems,

Are created and run by

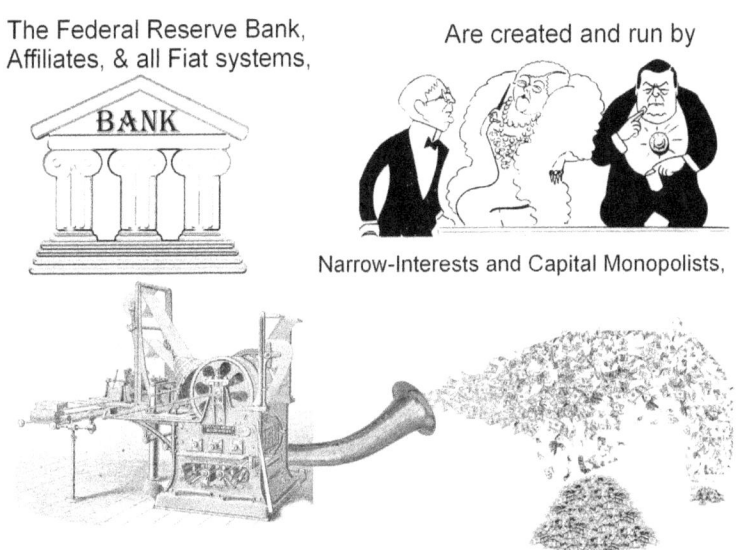

Narrow-Interests and Capital Monopolists,

Who use extreme & reckless methods to create mountains of currency of dubious worth from paper, ink & thin air; which eventually leads to total failure & collapse,

While limiting or excluding competition
from participating in capitalism.

To serve nefarious, globalist,
hegemonic ambitions.

Petro-Dollar - Reserve Currency

As has already been discussed, the requirement for non-inflating systems creates a problem for currencies in that the substance (like gold or crude oil) to which it's value is pegged is limited in supply or cannot be produced at the rate needed to avoid strangling the supply of currency and thus economic growth. Or, if the value is pegged to something that is readily available and easily obtained at present, but has a limited supply such as crude oil, it will fail at some point when that substance becomes scarce, thus resulting in a sudden devaluation and an eventual failure.

The reserve currency status of the dollar is due to it being made so by international agreement[85] and thus the only currency that can be used for trading crude oil at any bourse[86] in the world. Being that at present the US military has since the agreement, had the power to enforce the Bretton Woods accord anywhere in the world oil is produced, it stands to reason that the dollar is propped up or backed by crude oil. This is called the Petro-Dollar view of the world. The status and policy effectively backs the dollar with crude oil, but it does so by attempting to prop up the value through demand not asset backing.

To prop up the value of a sagging dollar, all that is needed is for a crisis to cause the price of crude to shoot up. Any country that wants to buy crude oil then must have a supply of dollars to do so, creating demand which supports the 'value' of the fiat dollar against other fiat currencies and various commodities. Of course those nations that subscribe to this arrangement and are party to the agreement can then peg an exchange of their currencies to the dollar. This arrangement has given the dollar and the US an economic advantage for the past several decades.

In the opinion of many, for all intents and purposes, Bretton Woods created a currency cartel in which the 'rogue' or non compliant nations of the world are not allowed in. Picture most of the nations of the world hitching their cars to the lead engine of the dollar as it careens and goes over a cliff; or picture a giant game of dominoes where the central banks of

---

[85] Bretton Woods Agreement, 1947
[86] Non English financial exchange. From French meaning purse.

the nations are the domino pieces placed strategically to fall and knock over the next in line just after the leader does.

Now it just so happens that a lot of those non compliant countries who are not allowed into the club are also the biggest producers of oil for the consuming world. Is it not predictable that fate and history are intertwined with a sense of irony or maybe humor depending on one's perspective, because many of these so called 'rogue' nations such as Iran and Iraq which are very large producers of oil are also the ones that the US and 'western allies' have deemed as pariahs.[87] The very nations that produce what is needed to keep the modern economic engine running are the ones that we have deemed to be our very enemies.

Recent news reports have headlined the peak of oil production giving the impression that we are running out of oil. Now this should not have a particular problem for the strength of the dollar except that the political power of other nations has exceeded US gunboat diplomacy and the credible threat of a military invasion by the US seems to be waning around the world despite 2 recent wars. The massive debt, waning political clout in the face of military action, and the fact that some mid-eastern suppliers along with Russia have recently announced that they will trade other currencies as well as dollars for oil, is thought to explain much of the sudden and continuing decline of the dollar and the aligned nation's currencies which are pegged to the dollar such as the Euro, British Pound, etc, and their respective economies along with it. The profligate spending of the old whores must come to an end because with a dead dollar there is no more credit.

One more note on the subject of a 'Reserve Currency.' This concept came about by centuries in-which empires (British and American) ruled the Oceans and sought to dominate all trade around the world through the power of their military.

---

[87] Outcast.

The idea is old and outdated, and certainly not necessary. Many nations are not happy with the inequity that this system burdens them with, forcing them to sell their resources to the powerful maintainers of the system at a significant discount. Many Americans fear the dollar loosing the advantage of the worlds reserve currency, but it is a corrupt and unjust system in-which that advantage really only accrues to very narrow-interests anyway. Its days are numbered, and better, non-monopolized systems will soon emerge. We preview a new monetary system for North America which fits the requirements for the previously discussed debt substitution scenario in the next and final chapter.

CHAPTER SIXTEEN

Competitive Self-Leveraging Monetary System

Disclaimer

Some of what follows is theoretical and subject to scrutiny. It falls into the category of that which is unproven, but is mostly based on sound principles. It is presented as a basis for discussion and to the extent it has not been tested nor vetted, it is not intended as representing a proposed system. In the event that it may be tested, improved upon, or found to have soundness of principle in-whole or in-part, or may function adequately and improve upon existing systems, it may be considered as constituting no more than portions of a system proposal.

The following is based upon my understanding of past historical mechanisms for the accumulation of capital, for converting assets to serve as general currency, and for distribution.

Roots Money

As with the above, I must also disclaim the following: I am not a trained economist and I have no formal experience or training in the banking industry, so the outline is intended for discussion only. However, I am an engineer and have been trained in system dynamics and problem solving. I have attempted to abstractly apply dynamic system principles to the model wherever possible. The outlined system which follows has not been created, dynamically modeled, or previously used anywhere as far as I am aware. Nonetheless, from a macro level the principles in which the concept is based are sound and I believe a successful and stable system based on the concept could be implemented.

Keep in mind, the goal is not to re-invent all aspects of modern banking systems in general but quite simply to begin exploring a better system, which could be developed and adopted; the capital of which and thus the benefit, both emanate from and accrue to the roots of our civilization. Such a system could yield sound, accountable, liquid paper money, sufficient to use in substitution for the massive dollar based debt which has accrued as outlined, and to better serve the continuing capital needs of a renewed nation. In addition, it is my intention to hopefully clear away some of the mystery about the possibility of improving on the existing monetary systems and shed light on alternative thinking which may instill hope in renewed movement for a considerably better future devoid of the aggravation the average American experiences, wrought by a corrupt and outdated system.

The solution for much of the problems discussed in the chapter called *'Debt Solution'* calls for a completely new monetary system which is radically different from what is in service now. The main characterizing features to the new system are that the currency created is sound, stable, and predictable, and created from the wealth of the nation at large and not exclusively from narrow monopoly interests. This makes it *'Roots Money.'* The system has 4 major aspects to it that render the desirable elements:

1) It employs the essence of capitalism. It is a somewhat self regulating, self-leveraging system, where the capital wealth that it enables is used to leverage the creation of more of the same.

2) The diversified investment principle, or mitigating against total failure by the practice of not putting all of one's eggs in the same basket. It gains from the stability that diversification of supply brings.

3) The forces of competition are at work. It gains from the efficiency that competitive forces bring.

4) The system borrows from far back in history, returning to old fashioned methods for capitalization with accumulation and conversion of the hard assets which emanate from the wealth and productivity of the masses of people and not exclusive monopoly capital. In addition, it utilizes and is greatly facilitated by new methods made available by the advent of modern technological tools which were absent from the advent of previous systems. The goal is a sound monetary system for the 21st century.

A Better Model for a Capital System

A better model would be for a new nation to establish liberal (in the traditional meaning of the word) laws regarding capitalism, allowing individuals and unaligned groups to pool their resources inorder to constitute a capital system which emanates from the grass roots so the benefit accrues to, and is maintained by them. The capital to operate the nation should come from the wealth of the vast majority of people and be open for participation by all people, not just the few. What do I mean by this? I am certainly not talking about depositing money into existing bank savings and checking accounts, nor am I talking about using the existing system to borrow money at interest.

In an open capital system (western style), the sources and issue of capital is very profitable for those participating. This is obvious for anyone that bothers to examine how it works. Therefore, the vast broad swath of people should be the creators, originators, maintainers, and participants in the capital of the nation and not allow it to be monopolized by a small cabal of wealthy individuals. This does not mean to preclude wealthy individuals from participating, it only puts restrictions on capital being monopolized by them.

Non Inflating Currency

It is a system in which the work-product (tangible output) enabled by a currency stimulus can also be used to shore-up the value of the currency instead of highly leveraged and inflated paper and ink, or a single commodity limited by supply and production, because the new wealth created as a result of currency stimulus is not limited by production rates of rare material and/or scarcity, so the value derived may be well established. The rate of economic growth drives the money supply and is proportional to it. Most durable manufactured goods, proven mineral reserves, new infrastructure, valuable rarities and so forth can be depreciated and leveraged for the purpose of creating new capital thus generating the facility of continued growth. This method when critically tuned will allow self-leveraging of the economy to levels that are sustainable with very moderate to zero inflation. With proper calibration and tuning a feedback loop of correction is established which regulates the money supply as it follows the lead of growth demand.

Using the output product of capital to shore up and bolster the value of the money is not a new thing but it differs from wide current practice because it is simple and strictly based on the effect and advantage of tangible input used to gain tangible output. The tangible input is real and comes up from the roots of the civilization so the tangible output is directed to, and enriches the same.

$$F = \frac{\Delta M}{\Delta G}$$

To keep 'flation'[88] within a reasonable level and guarantee its own integrity, the new system primarily relies on a correcting feedback mechanism and to a lesser degree, the power of the regulating entity. The new system rejects the 'free-lunch' schemes, recognizing the laws governing sound economic principles.

Whereas, the Federal Reserve and affiliate banks inject little real capital and consequently produce relatively little real tangible output. It is subject to: global agreements and the cooperation of fickle foreign banks and economies; is sensitive to the supply fluctuations of a limited commodity, crude oil; is totally dependent on fiat monopoly status, which means fed dollars cannot survive competitive forces; and is primarily, and substantially backed by its own dubious highly-leveraged worth. On-top of all that, it is subjected to the risk extreme leverage brings, and the reckless spending habits of those who believe the universe will always smile on inequitable arrangements; who erroneously believe they are somehow exempt from the same cost the rest of the world must pay. It will suffer the inevitable result of a corrupt system, which is absolute and complete failure.

Capitalization

Launching a new monetary system requires concentrating many forms of wealth to capitalize new banks. It is converted to currency for limited circulation. The pure currency issued by individual banks is termed Tier-1. Most tier-1 currency will be limited to commercial circulation not general. The amount of any particular certified Tier-1 issue in circulation is based on the base-line value (gold or standard equivalent) of reserve asset deposit. Capital assets may take the form of material wealth that is unencumbered (clear-title) or in-which the equity can be split-out and used as collateral for underlying

---

[88] Inflation/Deflation

the issue. This is accomplished via carefully written contract and regulations which allow negotiation, tracking, and transfer. In general, assets are evaluated and a contract engaged which will allow for restricted, or unrestricted use by the owner. Some asset classes may require physical vaulting, but in general it is intended that the owner is allowed unrestricted use of his/her property.

Tier-1 Private Bank

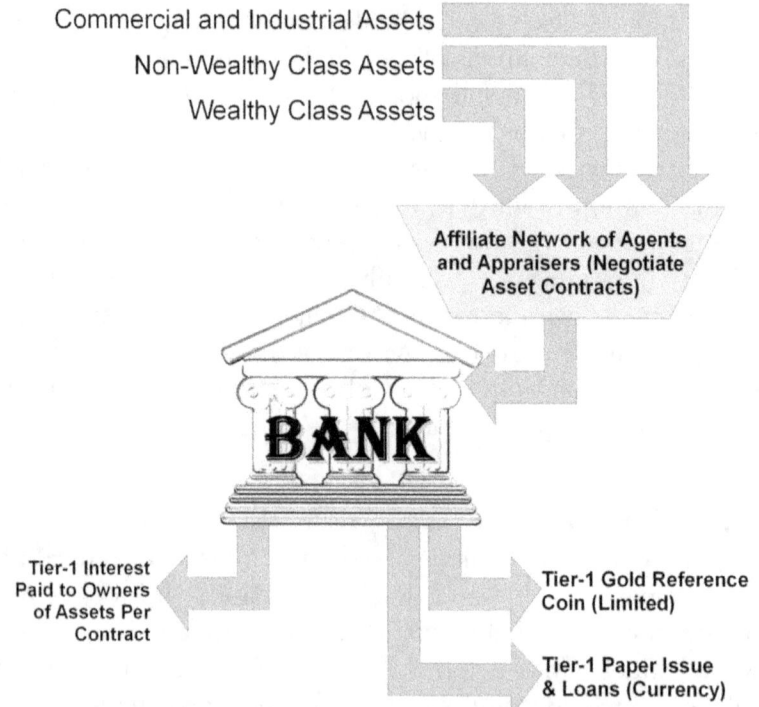

Commercial and Industrial Assets

Non-Wealthy Class Assets

Wealthy Class Assets

Affiliate Network of Agents and Appraisers (Negotiate Asset Contracts)

BANK

Tier-1 Interest Paid to Owners of Assets Per Contract

Tier-1 Gold Reference Coin (Limited)

Tier-1 Paper Issue & Loans (Currency)

As with any collateral, the contract will give the bank the right to foreclose under specified risk conditions. The contract specifies the risk-class for the asset, so it is anticipated that if a bank is over-allocated and needs to raise capital in order to meet regulatory or market requirements, it may foreclose on assets and distribute loss uniformly by risk-class. It may also transfer contracts to or from other Tier-1 banks to offset deficiencies and meet compliance.

Capital assets may take any suitable form as outlined by the regulatory body and come from various demographic groups and industry; Low and middle class, wealthy, commercial and industrial. Suitable assets are generally long term and durable.

Examples of suitable Not-wealthy deposit assets are: Real Estate; personal residences; art; gold and jewelry; qualifying vehicles; etc.

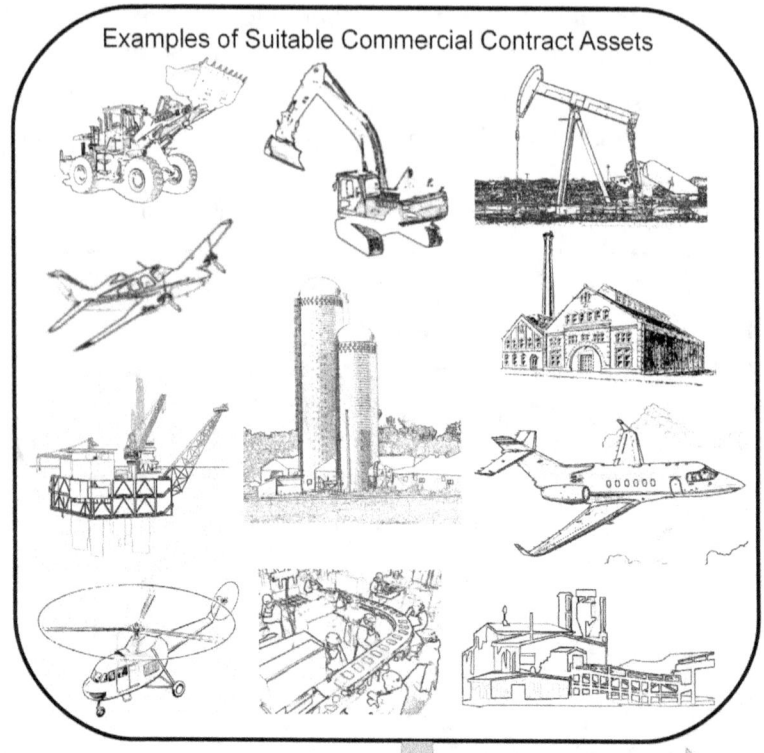

Examples of Suitable Commercial Contract Assets

To Tier-1 Private Bank

Examples of suitable commercial deposit assets are: Capital equipment; proven mineral reserves; qualifying financial instruments; inventory of goods; mines and wells; factories; precious metals, even goods in transit; etc.

Examples of Suitable Contract Assets for the Wealthy

To Tier-1 Private Bank

Examples of suitable wealthy deposit assets are: Real Estate; personal residences; antiques; qualifying financial instruments; collectible items; valuable art; etc.

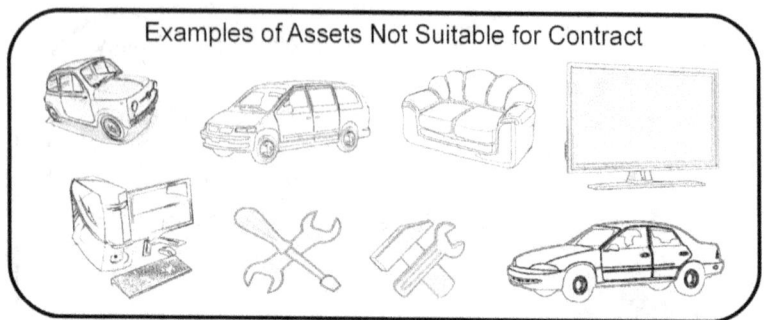

Examples of Assets Not Suitable for Contract

Examples of low and non qualifying or unacceptable assets are: Personal consumable items such as tools, appliances, automobiles; consumable manufactured goods; risky financial instruments; etc.

Numerous hard goods are not acceptable due to rapid depreciation. They are generally consumer goods with a very short usable life. Nonetheless, there may be specialists able to assess and inventory these assets similar to pawn or consignment and issue instruments against them, however, it is not likely to attain Tier-1 status.

No Monopoly Central Bank

The monetary system is composed of a system of banks at the wholesale and retail levels. These banks are located nationwide and serve local communities and the nation as a whole in business, industrial, and consumer needs. It is expressly forbidden for any state, supra-state, or other charter be granted any institution for the purpose of establishing a monopoly or central bank. **There is no central bank and no singular monopoly issue of currency**, although all issues of currency should be referred to by a variation on the accepted designation for money: example - *The Dramen*. The Banks mark or name on it is what distinguishes the issue from others. Certified licensed currency is issued by certified licensed private banks.

Competing Banks

A further mechanism for regulation of the value and supply is the competition created by fostering the issuance of more than one currency operating by the same mechanism in the same economy. The expansion of choice and the competition it enables will drive a great deal of the in-efficiencies out of the system and allow consumers and business the lowest cost of capital while the diversification buffers against catastrophic failure of the system as a whole if one or more fail.

Tier-1 Bank Competition

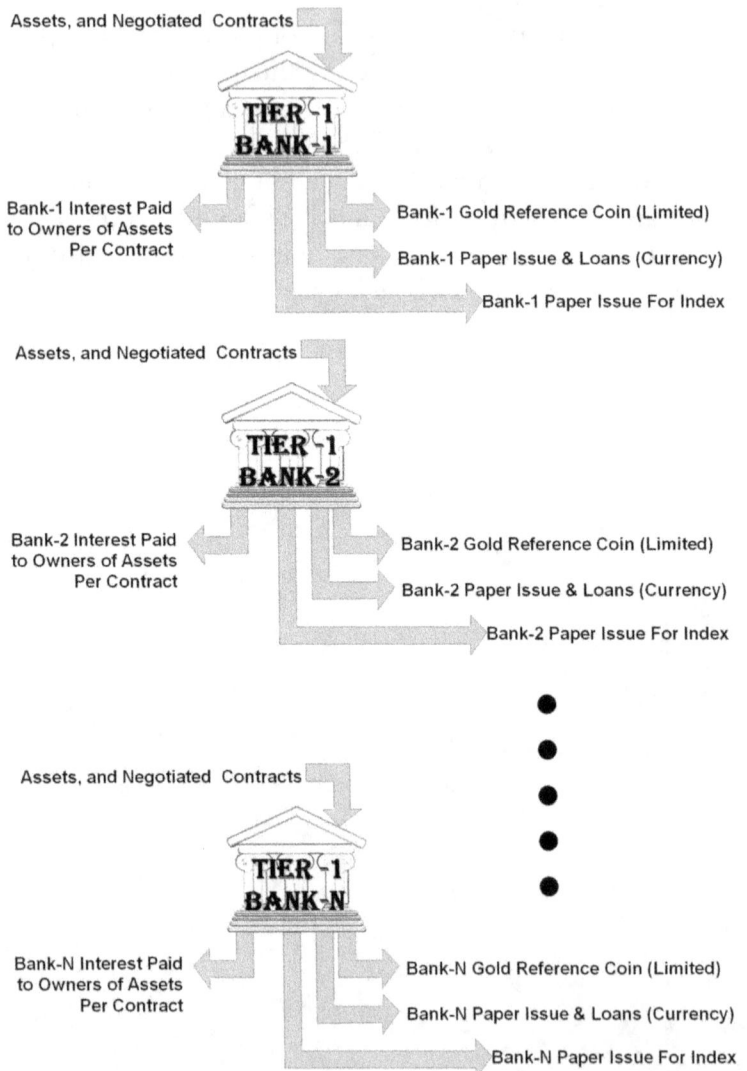

Understand, even though more than one currency is issued by more than one bank, just as there are numerous stocks in the market, there are <u>not</u> numerous currencies at retail level circulation. Instead, all are indexed together producing a single issue based on the underlying integrity of all others meeting regulation and qualifying criteria. The index currency is used in general service at commercial and retail level.

Leverage

In common financial or banking parlance, leveraging is traditionally the process of gaining financial advantage by borrowing and employing the full negotiable power of an asset but only exposing a portion to risk, usually owning or controlling a small amount employed as if the full amount of the asset was owned or controlled. It can also mean exposing more than the entire asset to risk to obtain financial advantage. In the present case we can discuss leverage in the context of expanding the economy by fractional reserve, employing more than is available in the vault. This means issuing paper that on its face represents more than the actual asset value underlying the paper. This introduces a large element of risk, and must be mitigated by other means such as modulating interest rates or insurance. Reviewing, fractional-reserve is the practice of only vaulting a fraction of what is loaned out; it is discussed above. In the practice of fractional-reserve, there is a multiplying effect of the money by the reciprocal of the reserve requirement, R:

$m = 1/R$

This effectively puts m X original-deposit amount into the system between the central bank and affiliate commercial banks. It happens because the non-reserve portion of the original deposit is loaned back out to others who then deposit that portion to be loaned against. Repeating the process again and again, yields the total m multiplied by the original-deposit, as a total circulation because there is no requirement that real or hard assets must balance the amount deposited into the system.

Leverage has a common problem which is extreme risk and should never be done improperly. The US Federal Reserve sets the reserve rates (margins) for the banks to adhere to. It is one of the mechanisms that the Fed uses to control the money supply along with setting the primary interest rates. In times of correction, the reserve levels are set higher (more in reserve), than in more prosperous times. Currently the Fed sets reserve level, R, at near 3%, so $m=33$, meaning that at any one time there is near 33 times (33:1 leverage) in loans outstanding as hard assets or cash in the vault to cover against a potential demand deposit run. This is excessive and extremely risky. Understand what this means. In the Federal Reserve system, the negotiable asset has many times its value exposed to risk which multiplies the risk by the amount of overexposure. This is akin to selling the same house many times over to different buyers. Anyone experienced with trading stocks, options, or forex (trading on currency spreads) should be familiar with trading on margin and using high leverage. With leverage there is always risk of margin calls which when triggered wipes out all principle. The greater the leverage the greater the risk.

In our discussion we do not have to adhere strictly to the negative side and common understanding of the word leverage which means operating on margin with risk. The process of investing capital to create a return on investment, or gain a profit and expand wealth is in fact also leveraging. This brings up a necessary discussion about the allowance of a reserve less than 100%. In general, it is not an ideal situation due to the fact that the essence of a good system should be to never allow overlap of collateralized assets for capital, and fractional reserve (less than 100%) is an attempt to use a contract asset to collateralize more than its value, increasing risk. Instead of attempting to answer the question about the safety, efficacy, or stability of fractional reserve banking it is better to just advocate for putting reasonable limits on it.

It should also be clear that exposure to less than the full value of an asset can be considered on the same continuum for leverage. In the Fed system, reserve levels limit the amount of money that can be loaned as a multiple of cash on deposit. The reserve requirement can also be set at over 100%. In the new system, a reserve is based on the baseline-standard value, which is the total value of all contract assets on deposit, and not based on expanded cash as in the Fed system. These levels should be limited to range between 50% and about 150%. At 150% the total amount of money created is 67% of the baseline-value of contract assets, and at 50%, it is as much as 200%. The objective should be to calibrate the system to keep the economic operating point around the mid-range $(1/R=1)$ for **reserve-level vs lending rate** curve; see illustration below. This will ensure adequate but stable monetary expansion with the level at unitary $(m=1)$ while allowing the system to adapt to changing conditions, and maintain a stable 'flation' level, $(F=1)$.

Operating Point

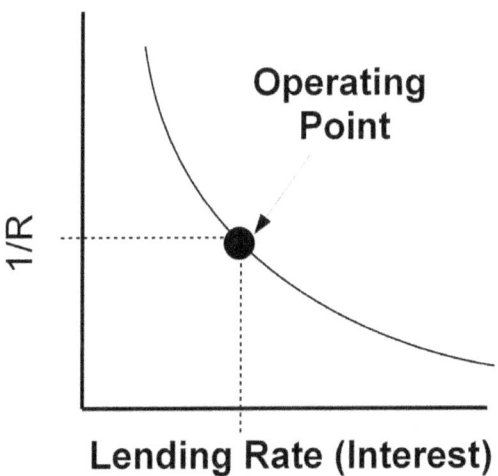

Lending Rate (Interest)

Understand the use of the word *'leverage'* here, and thus the moniker 'self-leveraging' merely describes a system in which capital is used to expand or diminish the money supply based on prevailing demand conditions. The present result of that economic increase (or decrease) is used through a mathematical algorithm which determine parameters that govern the quantity of future capital created for further expansion, thus ratcheting up growth organically. Likewise, the same leverage principle may be applied to the self-leveraging system, however, leverage is limited by use of the correcting feedback system which modulates reserve levels and lending rates within reasonable limits, around an operating point, in order to optimize growth and opportunity.

This instead of the current system that seemingly works in a similar fashion but in reality, is really not self-regulating, self-leveraging, or self-sustaining, but due to its unstable and over-leveraged nature, it requires constant crisis intervention and tuning by individuals that may have political as well as financial agendas at odds with the nation it is supposed to serve. Also, in the self-leveraging system there are many levels of competition that come into play limiting excesses and driving the system to stability and levels of efficiency not achieved by other means.

There is no theoretical limit to the non-inflationary growth rate or size of the economy that may result from this practice, however there are always unknowns and other factors that tend to emerge and come into play which limit growth. Under this system, it is within the realm of reason that annual growth rates on the order of 5% to 10% are achievable for a developed country like the US. It may also require mass participation by the populace so proper retail incentives must be carefully considered to ensure that participation.

The ***competitive self-leveraging currency method*** will perform better because the issue value is regulated by the stable nature and more or less predictability of the underlying assets which initially established the value. The issuing authority is in private hands or chartered and licensed but heavily regulated and under strict obligation and indeed mandated to control the supply, maintain interest rates, reserve, and spreads, and maintain (guarantee) its value. That effectively means that no entity, government utility, or otherwise will ever have 'free money' at their disposal. They will never be in a position to order the printing of currency for appropriations. What this describes is a ground-up (grass-roots) capital system where the 'money' to operate the nation comes from the people who will guard it jealously; not the bankers or capital monopolists. Real money is created from real wealth, not monopoly money created from paper, ink, and thin air. Other measures such as separation of commercial and retail banking, depositor's insurance, and the like can also be deployed as additional layers of protection, as risk dictates.

Self Leveraging

A self leveraging system will primarily regulate the amount of currency in circulation at any one time by a correcting feedback loop created between the productivity growth/decline of modulating[89] the money supply and the effects of 'flation' (inflation/deflation). This describes a money_supply - growth - interest_rate - 'flation' - regulating machine (see illustration below).

The value of any new issue is established and maintained by vaulting or bonding existing assets, or those produced as a result of previous capital creation cycles. The more capital in the vault, the more capital available to be loaned for expansion of the economy which in-turn, with new assets created can add more back into the existing asset base expanding it. The process goes on and on thus the loop or cycle at work. Money is created and stored by the creation of useful items as opposed to propping up the money by deceit or

---

[89] Increasing and decreasing.

force, or by backing from an unsuitable single commodity. It should be obvious that this puts a premium on the domestic production of goods and services as backing for the money. Goods that depreciate themselves out of the system must be replaced to maintain value and continued growth incentives.

It is very important to carefully choose the right underlying assets to avoid problems. The necessary types generally have long term value and are not subject to limited supply or scarcity or price fluctuations, and cannot be inflated by free spending. Assets are 'consigned' to the bank on a term contract basis and the bank will pay interest to the owner. The interest paid to the depositor will be on a depreciation schedule and commensurate with the risk class of the underlying contract, and the risk the bank incurs during the normal course of business.

Self-Leveraging System

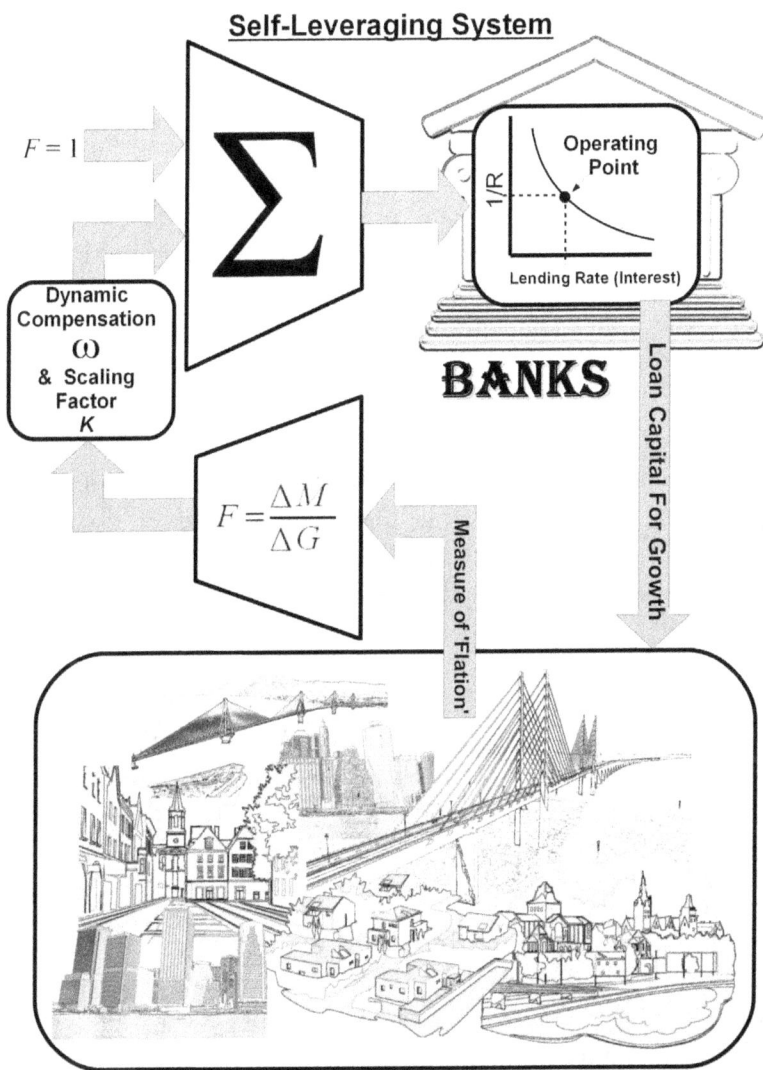

As an example; a family borrows money from the bank to purchase property. The bank with the right to foreclose, may also require the title as collateral until the loan is paid, but in addition it may also 'borrow' the borrower's equity under contract and pay interest back which may be in the form of a reduction in the mortgage rate the borrower pays or a cash payment. The borrower's equity is now an asset in the bank's vault working for the borrower because it pays a dividend instead of the status as a non productive or static asset.

This way the bank's currency issue is backed up by tangibles in the vault thus giving the bank the ability to make additional loans without inflating the issue. The balance sheet of the bank must show total loans offset by total of tangible assets within range of the loans, and not primarily paper and ink, nor the sole promise to repay as is practiced currently. Likewise with the banks cash-flow statements; it can operate and demonstrate positive cash flow; it derives its income by loan fees and the interest spread on loans it makes among the other usual financial services.

Another example: An automotive parts manufacturer produces 10,000 widgets per month. At any given time there are 7500 to 11,000 at an average of 9500 in stock at the company warehouse. For all intents and purposes this represents a static asset which can be leveraged as collateral despite that the merchandise actually flows through the business. A Tier-1 bank which specializes in the automotive industry and only serves that sector writes a contract on the value of the contents of the warehouse, the warehouse itself, and the factory and equipment used to produce the widgets and pays the manufacturer monthly interest.

Regulation and Certified Issue

Supra-state authority is given to regulate and certify the quality and soundness of each currency issue allowed to circulate. An extremely high level of compliance qualification must be achieved and maintained before a bank can issue a currency to the public. For this reason, only a small number of banks will achieve the status of registered issuer of certified currency. Each issue, although it may be referred to with a designation, shall distinguish itself for easy identification from any other by bearing the name or mark of the issuing bank.

Distribution

Certified issues will generally be distributed through networks of commercial affiliate banks and institutions.

Composite (Indexed) Issue

The need for foreign trade or even simplification of domestic distribution presents a problem with multiple competitive currencies because of the need to establish exchange rates for all of them, and for commercial and retail facilities to accept all of them.   This problem is eliminated by compositing (indexing) all Tier-1 currencies into one version that is used for domestic retail and business transactions and distributed through Tier-1 affiliate banks, or composite issue retail banks. The Tier-2 bank issuing the exchange currency must vault sufficient quantities of the competitive currencies to issue the composite, sufficient for the nation's transactions. There is no need to have more than one composite index bank, but it does not constitute a central bank.

Composite Index Bank

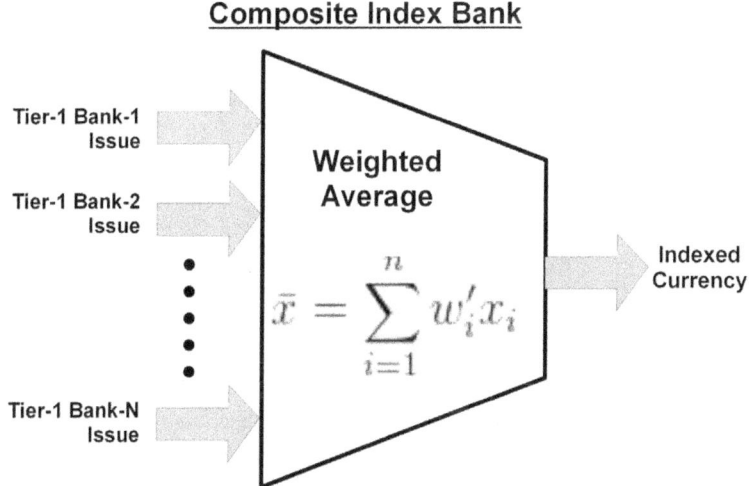

Indexed currency should never be considered or treated as a reserve currency for the world, or otherwise circulated internationally but should remain as isolated from foreign circulation as is necessary to facilitate control and stability. Foreign exchange and trade transactions should be accomplished through an alternative intermediary.

Modeling

Modeling is needed to understand the real-world dynamic behavior of the system as discussed. The ideas are theoretical and I have not had the opportunity nor resources to model it. The particular performance dynamics; the tuning parameters needed; what instabilities may be introduced or the degree of separation required for stability in a system in which there are several regulating engines operating in the same economy; all are unknown at this point. Perhaps the circumstances and events of the near future may bring that opportunity.

Dissipating Cycles

Looking to the future of the macro-economic landscape to what would grow from implementation of the model, along with regulations allowing as much unfettered growth as is rational, we could see very efficient and highly niche or specialty financing for very narrow segments of the economy. Examples are Tier-1 banks that specialize in residential and/or commercial construction; high technology financing; retail and business specific banks, automotive and transportation, etc. The nature of private enterprise with elements of competition in the monetary model will add dynamic growth to the economy, eventually filling all niche segments with diversified specialty financing. The advantage of separation and niche financing is a dissipating effect of the harmonic components of boom-bust cycles which create long downturns of correction which have a devastating effect, displacing large segments of the workforce for extended periods of time. This effect should be mitigated to some extent.

Boutique Banking

Private competitive banking should be considered just as any private corporation, able to engage and serve the public need and its own by publicly selling shares inorder to raise money for development and growth, while offering an opportunity that benefits investors willing to share the risk. The foundational principles of America have always favored small entities with the freedom to engage in enterprise and do business with others to build a successful and growing business. Why should banking, currency, and financial services be any different? It may have differing characteristics for operational acceptance into the public domain which require public sector oversight, and indeed, it absolutely can not be self-regulating but must have considerable oversight. However, that should not preclude a right to private financing and services.

This is in response to those that proclaim that money must only originate in the public domain, by government and/or further assert it must be rigidly structured by recipes and methods which were practiced over 200 years ago.

Boutique banking in which different sectors of business and commerce are serviced by their own defined needs is as necessary to a vibrant economy as any other product or service. That is the promise of the free and competitive issuance of money.

Appendix

Firing on Fort Sumpter

Abraham Lincoln gives account of how he hatched plans to bring about a war with the Confederacy.

On July 3, 1861, Lincoln spoke with Senator Orville Browning, a close friend of his for 20 years, and revealed to him that he had intended all along to provoke an incident with the South.

In an account from the diary of Senator Orville Browning, he reveals a conversation he had with Lincoln on July 3, 1861. Browning was a friend of Lincoln for 20 years, so felt assured confiding a secret to his friend. He wrote:

"He told me that the very first thing placed in his hands after his inauguration was a letter from Major Anderson announcing the impossibility of defending or relieving Sumter. That he called the Cabinet together, and consulted General Scot—that Scott concurred with Anderson, and the cabinet, with the exception of himself and PM General Blair were for evacuating the Fort, and that all the troubles and anxieties of his life had not equaled those which intervened between this time and the fall of Sumter. He himself conceived the idea, and proposed sending supplies, without an attempt to reinforce giving notice of the fact to Governor Pickins of S.C. The plan succeeded. They attacked Sumter—it fell, and thus, did more service than it otherwise could."

Also, original correspondence between Lincoln and former Naval Captain Gustavus V. Fox, Assistant Navy Secretary, further suggests that Lincoln willingly provoked the military officials in South Carolina into firing on Fort Sumter.

On May 1, 1861, after the pretext for war at Fort Sumter, Lincoln wrote to Fox, *"You and I both anticipated that the cause of the country..."* [a war on the south] *"...would be advanced by making the attempt to provision Fort Sumter, even if it should fail; and it is no small consolation now to feel that our anticipation is justified by the result."*

Several Northern newspapers recognized that Lincoln was agitating for the war he had promised in his first inaugural address on March 4, 1861, where he threatened 'invasion' and 'bloodshed.'

The Jersey City American Standard editorialized speaking about Lincoln's behavior saying, *"there is a madness and ruthlessness"* in his act, referring to him sending ships to Charleston Harbor, which in their words was, *"a pretext for letting loose the horrors of war."*

On April 13, 1861 the Providence Daily Post wrote, *"Look at the facts…, for three weeks the [Lincoln] administration newspapers have been assuring us that Fort Sumpter would be abandoned,"* however *"Mr. Lincoln saw an opportunity to inaugurate civil war without appearing in the character of an aggressor."*

From Howard Cecil Perkins, Northern Editorials on Secession, On April 16, 1861, the Buffalo Daily Courier editorialized, *"The affair at Fort Sumpter ... has been planned as a means by which the war feeling at the North should be intensified"* .

The New York Evening Day Book wrote on April 17, 1861, that the event at Fort Sumter was *"a cunningly devised scheme"* contrived *"to arouse, and, if possible, exasperate the northern people against the South."*

Rushmore G. Horton wrote in his 1868 book, *"A Youth's History of the Great Civil War in the United States, from 1861 to 1865"*

"And it was a cunning trick, precisely worthy of Mr. Seward and Mr. Lincoln, to cause the bombardment of Fort Sumter, in order to 'fire up the Northern heart,' as they called it….The war was gotten up with as much trick and skill in management as a showman uses….Our whole country was placarded all over with war posters of all colors and sizes. Drums

were beating and bands playing at every corner…the ministers of the Gospel were praying and preaching to the horrible din of the war music, and the profane eloquence of slaughter…."

"There was little chance for any man to exercise his reason, and if he attempted such a thing he was knocked down and sometimes murdered. If an editor ventured to appeal to the Constitution, mobs destroyed his office, or his paper suspended by 'the order of the Government.' The moment the war opened for the emancipation of the Negroes, the liberty of the white man was suspended. The historian of these shameful and criminal events needs no other proof that the managers of the war knew that they were perpetrating a great crime than the fact that they refused to allow any man to reason or speak in opposition to their action. The cause of truth and justice always flourishes most with all the reasoning that argument and controversy can give it. Whenever men attempt to suppress argument and free speech, we may be sure that they know their cause to be a bad one."

Fourteenth Amendment

The 13th and 14th amendments were forced upon the nation during the upheaval following Lincoln's war of aggression on the southern states who had seceded and formed a confederacy, separate, making them an independent nation. The war was viewed by them as a war of conquest, to fundamentally change the sovereign status of the people in those states which were forced back into a union they did not want. The war forced a status of subordination upon the south while the government sought to change the fundamental relationship between sovereign states and people, and the non-existent but forthcoming expanded federal republic. The problem is, those elected did not possess the power to change that relationship, war or otherwise, because there was no authority given them by any act, taking, or war that could do so. They were employees of a caretaker system; they were not a sovereign power. Therefore, not even the **Law of Conquest** could do this because they acted under the umbrella of power entrusted and leased them by the same people they ostensibly 'conquered.'

So to understand why this does not change the fundamental status of either the people, the states involved, or the federal system, consider that if someone were to sell you the city of Chicago for any sum, would you own it? Of course you would not own it because no one has the authority to sell you a city of that size. The 'seller' does not possess the power or authority to do so, regardless of declarations made or laws passed, therefore nothing has changed. The relationship of sovereign and servant remained just as it had before, as it does to this day.

With brazen Luciferian ethos, that which was in a position of subordination and entrusted with power, attempted to usurp the throne of that which brought it into existence. Both amendments were enacted and forced through under questionable circumstances of illegal representation with the force of arms used to remove opposition. The 14th amendment was 'enacted', ostensibly, to remove the sovereign status of people and states and force both into a position subordinate to a corporate creation by private interests, ostensibly rendering the people with a status of subject-citizens. Again, nothing has changed in regard to the sovereign status of Original-Americans.

This charade is contrasted in subsequent court renderings since its passage:

In the case of Blair v. Ridgely, 97 D. 218,249, S.P. the Supreme Court held *"Prior to the adoption of the federal Constitution, states possessed unlimited and unrestricted sovereignty and retained the same ever afterward. Upon entering the Union, they retained all their original power and sovereignty..."*

Since the passage of the amendments, it is believed that the sovereign status of states and people had changed even though that is not possible.

The mechanism for this is complex, but it boils down to a few passages from both 13th and 14th amendments:

The 13th Amendment states:

Section 1. *"Neither slavery nor involuntary servitude, except as a punishment for crime whereof the party shall have been duly convicted, shall exist within the United States, or any place subject to their jurisdiction."*

Section 2. *"Congress shall have the power to enforce this article by appropriate legislation."*

From the 14th Amendment:

Section 1. *"All persons born or naturalized in the United States, and subject to the jurisdiction thereof, are citizens of the United States and of the State wherein they reside. No State shall make or enforce any law which shall abridge the privileges or immunities of citizens of the United States; nor shall any State deprive any person of life, liberty, or property, without due process of law; nor deny to any person within its jurisdiction the equal protection of the laws."*

Section 5. *"The Congress shall have power to enforce, by appropriate legislation, the provisions of this article."*

Note that both section 2 of the 13th and 5 of the 14th give congress the power to enforce these. The problem is, the constitution did not authorize them to give themselves that power, therefore in reality these are beyond reach, making them null and void. Also note that section 1 of the 13th invokes *'involuntary servitude'*, which is equated with slavery which is now verboten, however, it opens the door and invokes the suggestion of *'voluntary servitude'*, which is what was created in section 1 of the 14th amendment when it says *"All persons born or naturalized in the United States, and subject to the jurisdiction thereof, are citizens of the United States and of the State wherein they reside"*, which was a new status for the person. A *"citizens of the United States"* had not existed prior to this. Again, they did not possess the power to create this status, so it is out of reach making it null and void.

Section 1 of the 14th also guarantees that this new citizen of the corporate United States is also afforded protection from a state acting to "*make or enforce any law which shall abridge the privileges or immunities of citizens of the United States*". Whereas before people enjoyed the status of a sovereign person with rights, not subject to the laws or regulation of the United States, who's jurisdiction was confined to the District of Columbia; now they are citizens of an unauthorized corporate body with "*privileges or immunities of citizens*."

As has been argued, despite these being constitutional amendments, they very much lack the authority to enact what they stipulate, so their legal status remains null and void despite decades of precedent, and numerous court rulings recognizing them.

Many will argue that the 14th amendment citizen status was only meant to apply to freed blacks and others not a part of the sovereign-body. I would agree partially, however, the vast majority of *Original Americans* are not aware of the distinction, nor their own status as DeJure sovereign individuals, which is by intent.

For more reading and study see "*THE HIDDEN 14TH AMENDMENT AGENDA*" By Michael LeMieux

http://www.newswithviews.com/LeMieux/michael108.htm

and

Bruce Ray Riggs (dirtyunclesam.com)

Administrative State
The Administrative State refers to the power vested in the unelected and unaccountable bureaucratic agencies of the US government which came about through an unconstitutional power grab, giving the federal government 'authority' to move

the nation down a path unauthorized by the people and elected government. It was the Hegelian product resulting as a response to the false-flag of the federal bureaucracy becoming too unwieldy and insufficiently responsive to effectively administrate the interest of the nation through directives given in the US constitution. In an act called the *Administrative Procedure Act of 1946 (APA),* signed by Harry Truman on June 11, 1946, the federal state assumed the power to force arbitrary rules on the nation which would not otherwise be sanctioned through the legitimate democratic process. Arbitrary agency rules are given the power of law and enforced ostensibly with the blessing of the court.

The act was motivated as an end-run around the democratic process for enacting law sanctioned by the US constitution, thus it allows agencies to arbitrarily establish and enforce what amounts to 'law' without the passage of law, to achieve an outcome as if it were based on law. Since the time it was enacted, an ocean of bureaucratic alphabet agencies have sprung up such as the EPA (Environmental Protection Agency), who has issued numerous arbitrary rules affecting property rights, industry, and commerce. The APA has also given unconstitutional authority to agencies such as the IRS (Internal Revenue Service) to make rules enforcing unlawful collection of taxes on individuals and corporations in direct violation of the 16th amendment which created the income tax. The legality of the act, and the power for the administrative state to enforce arbitrary rules outside of an act of congress, has been illegitimately recognized and upheld by federal courts. In the opinion of many scholars since its passage, the APA is illegal and illegitimate.

Some background information from Wikipedia:

The Administrative Procedure Act, enacted June 11, 1946, is the United States federal statute that governs the way in which administrative agencies of the federal government of the United States may propose and establish regulations. The

APA also sets up a process for the United States federal courts to directly review agency decisions. It is one of the most important pieces of United States administrative law. The Act became law in 1946.

The APA applies to both the federal executive departments and the independent agencies. U.S. Senator Pat McCarran called the APA *"a bill of rights for the hundreds of thousands of Americans whose affairs are controlled or regulated"* by federal government agencies. The text of the APA can be found under Title 5 of the United States Code, beginning at Section 500.

There is a similar Model State Administrative Procedure Act (Model State APA) which was drafted by the National Conference of Commissioners on Uniform State Laws for oversight of state agencies. Not all states have adopted the model law wholesale as of 2007. The federal APA does not require systematic oversight of regulations prior to adoption as suggested by the Model APA.

Historical background

Beginning in 1933, President Franklin D. Roosevelt and the Democratic Congress enacted several statutes that created new federal agencies as part of the New Deal legislative plan, designed to deliver the United States from the social and economic hardship of the Great Depression. However, following the Great Depression and World War II the Congress became concerned about the expanding powers that federal agencies possessed, resulting in the enactment of the APA to regulate and standardize federal agency procedures.

In a law journal article on the history of the APA, Professor George Shepard discusses the contentious political environment from which the APA was born. Shepard claims that Roosevelt's opponents and supporters fought over passage of the APA *"in a pitched political battle for the life of the New Deal"* itself. Shepard does note, however, that a legislative balance was struck with the APA, expressing *"the nation's decision to permit extensive government, but to avoid dictatorship and central planning."*

A 1946 U.S. House of Representatives report discusses the 10-year period of *"painstaking and detailed study and drafting"* that went into the APA. Because of rapid growth in the administrative regulation of private conduct, Roosevelt ordered several studies of administrative methods and conduct during the early part of his four-term presidency. Based on one study, Roosevelt commented that the practice of creating administrative agencies with the authority to perform both legislative and judicial work *"threatens to develop a fourth branch of government for which there is no sanction in the Constitution."*

In 1939, Roosevelt requested that Attorney General Frank Murphy form a committee to investigate practices and procedures in American administrative law and suggest improvements. That committee's report, contains detailed information about the development and procedures of the federal agencies.

The Final Report defined a federal agency as a governmental unit with *"the power to determine...private rights and obligations"* by rulemaking or adjudication. The Final Report applied that definition to the largest units of the federal government, and identified *"19 executive departments and 18 independent agencies."* If various subdivisions of the larger units were considered, the total number of federal agencies at that time increased to 51. In reviewing the history of federal agencies, the Final Report noted that almost all agencies had undergone changes in name and political function.

Of the 51 federal agencies discussed in the Final Report, 11 were created by statute prior to the Civil War. From 1865 to 1900, six new agencies were created. Most notable was the formation of the Interstate Commerce Commission, created in 1887 in response to widespread criticism of the railroad industry. The period of 1900 to 1940, however, saw the greatest expansion of federal administrative power, with 35 new agencies created by statute. Eighteen of these were created during the 1930s, from statutes enacted as part of Roosevelt's New Deal. The Final Report made several recommendations about standardizing administrative procedures, but Congress delayed action because the U.S. entered World War II.

Book, The Administrative State

Published in 1948, *The Administrative State,* written by Dwight Waldo is a dissertation written at Yale shortly after the APA was passed, in which Waldo argues that democratic states are underpinned by professional and political bureaucracies and that scientific management and efficiency is not the core idea of government bureaucracy, but rather it is service to the public. The work has contributed to the structure and theory of government bureaucracies the world over and is one of the defining works of public administration and political science written in the last 75 years. Waldo later reissued the work in a second edition with an extensively revised introduction.

History on the concept

Though the phrase *"The Administrative State"* was coined by Dwight Waldo in 1948, the concept of administrative powers and responsibilities has been the subject of debate for as long as the structure of democratic government has been implemented. Where the current debate begins is with the United States Constitution, and argues over the powers to govern under the presets of said constitution. Basically, the debate is over whether or not non-elected agencies of the government have the power to legislate as well as enforce. The argument for the power is that all federal agencies/ officials are subject to the President of the United States, who is elected accommodating the new power democratically so that it does not need to be voted on directly by the public; where the counter is that *"agencies remain inefficient, ineffective, and undemocratic;"* attempting to justify that the public's inability to vote for the policy that the agency adopts is undemocratic/constitutional (Harvard Law Review).

Dr. Michael Greve, a law professor at George Mason University School of Law, defines the current implemented administrative state of the United States as, *"a power once known as 'prerogative'—that is, the power to make binding rules without law, outside the law, or against the law, exercised by someone other than an elected legislature"* (Greve). He then goes on to say, in his opinion, that this is the opposite intention of the "founders" (Greve). Basically Greve is saying all government indenties (agencies) are power hungry and that Americans should stick to the US Constitution that set up safe guards against the despotism that agencies will ultimately strive for if left to their own whims, instead of acting in the best interest of the country. *"The presidential control model of the administrative state, perhaps most definitively expounded by now-Justice Elena Kagan, 22 suggests that top-down accountability affords agencies measure of democratic accountability and assures effective administration"* (Harvard Law Review). Basically, the Harvard Law Review is summarizing Kagen as saying that agency implemented policy/ law is subject to democracy by the citizens being able to hold the elected official at the head of the relevant chain of government responsible with the conclusion being the trickledown effect of responsibility efficient enough for Democracy, or will the government agencies become power hungry, and not act in the best interest of the people.